Title Page

Exploding the Globalist Establishment's Deceptive Myths
On Trade, Immigration, and Politics

Feedback: alsnewideas@gmail.com

Other books by Alan Sewell

https://www.amazon.com/Alan-Sewell/e/B00557PQDY

Contents

Foreword

George Orwell, known for his dystopian novel **1984**, forecast the rise of globalism in 1946:

Capitalism is disappearing, but Socialism is not replacing it. What is now arising is a new kind of planned, centralized society which will be neither capitalist nor, in any accepted sense of the word, democratic. The rulers of this new society will be the people who effectively control the means of production: that is, business executives, technicians, bureaucrats, and soldiers, lumped together...under the name of "managers."

These people will eliminate the old capitalist class, crush the working class, and so organize society that all power and economic privilege remain in their own hands.

In August 2021, the **U.K Telegraph** reported how close we are to fulfilling Orwell's prophecy:

America's internal problems are immense: its constitution is broken, its predilection for second-rate gerontocrats such as Biden unrivalled. Racked with self-doubt, its elites in the grip of a bizarre "awakening" centered around a nihilistic, ungrateful self-loathing, it no longer has values to sell, neither capitalism nor democracy nor the American dream. How can people who live in terror of "micro-aggressions" find it in themselves to defeat real evils? As to the public, it doesn't want to know about the rest of the world: how, under such circumstances, can the US empire not be in terminal decline?

People in many countries now realize, as George Orwell prophesized, that Globalists seek to concentrate the wealth and power of nations among elitists clustered in interlocking directories of big government big business, big media, and big academia that are beyond accountability to the people. In the United States, the people elected Donald Trump in 2016 to protect the nation from globalist-instigated illegal immigration and destructive trade with China. In Britain they elected Boris Johnson to lead them out of the globalist European Liberals. Russia and China have engaged in aggressions against the Globalist World Order by attacking Ukraine and invading Hong Kong, and threaten war against Taiwan. Now the Globalist Order is collapsing under the weight of failing supply chains and soaring inflation, and further raising suspicions that it is working against the interests of the people.

Why did our Globalists help China obscure the origin of COVID-19 in the Chinese Wuhan Laboratory and shield them from accountability for causing the premature deaths of over a million Americans? Why are our Globalists demanding that we drop tariffs on Chinese imports so the Chinese government / business complex can extract more jobs and wealth from us, rather than holding these entities accountable for the deaths they inflicted upon our people? Why are our Globalists so anxious to ship more American jobs and wealth to China, while telling us we need to increase our military budget by $200,000,000 billion to "deter China?" Why are we sending China $355 billion of trade deficit dollars each year to fund their military buildup, while our economy is heading into a recession that curtails our ability to fund our military? Why are we allowing Chinese spies to infiltrate our business, government, and leading universities, including Harvard's School of Chemical Biology?

And why are our Globalists so keen to open the border to immigration of indigent immigrants, many carrying infectious diseases that endanger the American citizens, while being prone to crime when they are unloaded on the streets of our cities? Why are we loading our country with indigents who drain the tax dollars of citizens, when we are groaning under $30 trillion of debt incurred in meeting our commitments to our own people?

What are Globalists trying to accomplish with this chaos they inflict on the nations they were born into? Globalists do not want their authority questioned, and will not want this book to see the light of day, but it has been well-received by the public:

- *What an encompassing, global instruction sheet for what needs to get done. Eloquent, thorough, passionate...and a great read in itself. Hope this guy writes a book, or a blog, or a Kindle single.*
- *This is the diagnosis worthy of the Nobel Prize for Economics.*
- *Alan, I agree and want to thank you, personally, as well. I thank you for your remarkable commentary supported by hard facts. You have changed my mind about some things through the excellence of your arguments, always supported by hard facts and documentation. You are an asset beyond compare to this community. Thank you so very much.*
- *Mr. Sewell has made me rethink a number of ideas I thought were set in historical concrete.*

- *This book and Alan Sewell's review are so insightful as to what needs to be done to save the economy and alas the country that for me several questions are begged. Why are the major parties and their presidential candidates so unable to deal intelligently with the free trade myth, the outsourcing problem, and the assault on the middle class? Are they intellectually delusional? Are they totally political opportunists? Why don't we have a presidential candidate with the author's or Alan Sewell's comprehension of the economic problems? Is our political system in need of an overhaul?"*

- *That's it, and it really is just common sense, Alan. There is a reckoning coming. We either need jobs for the middle class, or handouts for the middle class. It's either or. The Wall Street crowd wants to have their cake and eat it too - send jobs overseas, reap the profits, while also beating back the tide of 'socialism' and big government programs/handouts. They'll eventually lose that fight at the ballot box.*

- *Once again, thank you, Alan Sewell. You are one of the most insightful and rational Americans in existence.*

- *I always enjoy your insightful comments, Alan. Keep them coming*

- *Alan, your comment above is one reason why whenever I see your name, I know your musings will be "short, to the point, and no punches pulled."*

- *Excellent insights Mr. Sewell. I truly enjoy your posts on this forum. Your observations parallel many of my own.*

- *Your advice could not have been more eloquently phrased had Winston Churchill been your editor.*

Part I. Globalist Mendacity and Obfuscation

Globalists seek to command nations, without being accountable to their people in elections. They want to eliminate the traditions of the legacy citizens by moving working class jobs overseas and loading the country with indigent immigrants who work cheaper than citizens in jobs that can't be moved out of the country. They don't seem to care much whether immigrants work, or subsist on the welfare paid by citizens' taxes, so long as they vote for the Globalists who let them in.

Globalists create negative feedback loops for the citizens of their countries. They induce companies to move well-paying jobs to countries where labor is cheap and to import goods and services produced by cheap labor into high-income countries to sell at inflated markups. This is unsustainable because once the high-income jobs are destroyed there is no one left to purchase cheap-labor imports, so the government must prop up the economy with trillions of dollars of unpayable debt.

The more of our economy we offshore, the less tax revenue there is to fund military and civil commitments, and the more the national debt increases. The larger the debt burden grows, the less possible it becomes to service. The more we lose industrial and technology traditions in the present, the less capable we become of producing them in the future. Over time, this means slower economic growth, an increasing debt burden, and a declining standard of living as the economy narrows and well-paying jobs become scarcer. The most common phrases we hear in economic discussions are "wealth inequality" and "global slowdowns leading to the next recession." Wouldn't Globalists have eliminated all this unhappy talk if their theories had produced the prosperity they promised?

The most destructive aspect of globalism is the fissures it drives into society. It makes corporation managements think of countries as entities to be strip-mined rather than as societies of human beings who should be elevated by multinational corporations instead of threatened by them. Globalism works toward the lowest common denominator of redistributing wealth away from the working middle class in the private sector and into the elites in government, corporation management, and Wall Street money management.

Globalism encourages corporation managements to believe that putting people out of work is a first resort instead of a last. It makes it easy for them to move people's jobs overseas to countries where people work cheaper, or to import foreigners on H1-B visas to replace Americans in the United States, or if all else fails, to invite foreigners to enter the country illegally over open borders. At a time when the longevity tables are increasing, we are making it difficult for people to work past 40 due to the propensity of businesses to "cut costs" by replacing employees who work their way up to the higher incomes after years of faithful service to their employers. At the same time, the shrinking number of well-paying jobs requires young people to take on lifetimes of student loan debt to buy the college degrees of dubious value now required to give them entry to the job market.

People lose trust in business and become prone to voting Socialists into office to redistribute the wealth the wrong way via coercive government. Those opposed to socialism vote in "populist" right-of-center candidates pledged to use government to enforce the border and require companies to be fair in employing Americans before considering foreigners for open positions. It is never the best option to make government the enforcer of policies that fair-minded people of good will should be proud to undertake on their own volition

Globalists have developed a catalog of contradictory talking points to obscure the disconnect between their theories and reality. They tell us that free trade will create millions of well-paying jobs for American workers. Then when they move the well-paying jobs to cheap-labor countries, they tell us not to worry because free trade allows the unemployed to buy cheaply made imports, usually of inferior quality.

They claim that people who question their free trade theories are reincarnations of the "Luddites" who allegedly roamed the British countryside of the early 1800's burning productive factories so that people working inefficiently in their homes wouldn't lose their jobs. Then Globalists destroy American factories so they can move the work to foreign countries where cheap manual labor is employed to enable companies to *avoid* investing in productivity-enhancing machinery in the United States.

They claim that jobs are disappearing in the United States "because robots and automation have replaced all the jobs that unskilled Americans used to do." Then they open our borders to millions of unskilled foreigners who can be hired cheaply, and often illegally, to perform unskilled labor. They want the unskilled people here to provide cheap labor, so they won't have to spend money investing in robots and automation to improve the productivity of American workers.

9

They say the United States has become a high-tech economy, so we should not care if the manufacturing of automobiles, aerospace, computers, and electronics leaves the country. Then they tell us that agriculture, which dates to early Cro-Magnon days, is the linchpin of our economy that must be propped up by the importation of millions of illegal foreigners who work the land by manual labor the way their ancestors did ten thousand years ago.

Our Globalist Tradition

From the first days of our founding, Americans have understood we have a global destiny beyond our borders. In 1763 future president John Adams wrote:

I always consider the settlement of America with reverence and wonder, as the opening of a grand scene, and design in Providence, for the illumination of the ignorant and the emancipation of the slavish part of Mankind all over the earth.

We knew we could not fulfill our destiny as a continent-spanning republic without opening our doors to immigrants. We knew we could not become a great nation unless we were a welcoming nation.

We knew our prosperity depended on global trade. We were born as colonies of Great Britain's global empire. From our Eastern Seaboard, Britain and continental Europe were more accessible than our own trans-Appalachian West. The Orient loomed large even at that early day as the place where our manufactured products could be traded for silks, tea, porcelain, handcrafted furniture, and art. Even then, we saw ourselves as the future center of the world's commerce and manufacturing. We were ambitious to become the cradle of Mankind's liberty and the possessor of the industrial and commercial power to defend it.

Desire for liberty induced us to leave the British Empire, but trade was also an important factor. We wanted to trade with other countries on our terms, without having a king impose tariffs on our imports and excise taxes on our exports to enrich the British royalty at our expense. We understood that we could neither prosper nor become the cradle of liberty if we failed to develop a strong manufacturing economy. One of the first pieces of legislation that the First Congress of the United States passed was derived from Alexander Hamilton's Report on Manufacturers, which expedited our development as an industrial power:

Hamilton's Report on Manufacturers, December 5, 1791

The expediency of encouraging manufactures in the United States...appears at this time to be pretty generally admitted. The employment of machinery forms an item of great importance in the general mass of national industry...if it is the interest of the United States to open every possible avenue to emigration from abroad, it affords a weighty argument for the encouragement of manufactures...

There seems to be a moral certainty that the trade of a country which is both manufacturing and agricultural will be more lucrative and prosperous than that of a country which is, merely agricultural....

Not only the wealth, but the independence and security of a country, appear to be materially connected with the prosperity of manufactures. Every nation, with a view to those great objects, ought to endeavor to possess within itself all the essentials of national supply. These comprise the means of subsistence, habitation, clothing, and defense...

Our first armed conflicts after the Revolutionary War were fought to secure access to foreign markets. These were the Barbary (Shores of Tripoli) War of 1801-1805, the Quasi-War with France in 1798-1800, and the War of 1812 with Britain. We also took early steps to prevent the European powers from re-establishing their trade-restricting empires in the Western Hemisphere. President James Monroe declared in 1823 that any European nation attempting to establish a new colony in the Western Hemisphere would run the risk of war with the United States.

We soon began looking to Asia's markets for our exports. In 1853 Senator William Seward, who later gained fame as President Lincoln's Secretary of State, advised Americans:

"Open up a highway from New York to San Francisco. Put your domain under cultivation and your ten thousand wheels of manufacture in motion. Multiply your ships and send them forth to the East (Japan, China, and India). The nation that draws the most materials and provisions from the earth, and fabricates the most, and sells the most of production and fabrics to foreign nations, must be, and will be, the great power of the earth."

Our vital interests in maintaining free trade with China led us to war with Japan in 1941, after they conquered China and tried to turn it into an old-fashioned imperial domain. Our trading relations with Great Britain likewise made war with expansionist Germany inevitable in the two world wars.

Emerging victorious in World War II, we made free trade a foundation of peace and prosperity for the post-war world. We granted free access to our markets to our allies and our defeated enemies alike. We made our dollar, alone of world currencies, convertible to gold, so that other countries could receive our gold in exchange for their exports. We established trade-promoting agreements and organizations such as the General Agreement on Tariffs and Trade (GATT), the World Trade Organization, and the World Bank.

The effects of international trade were beneficial perhaps even beyond expectations. The demolished nations of Western Europe were quickly rebuilt. Communists, who had become prominent in France, Germany, Italy, and Greece, were made irrelevant by the return of prosperity. Incipient Communists in burned-out Japan faded away. The United States and our allies eventually convinced the Soviet Union and China to adopt capitalism. The Soviet Union disbanded. China became so prosperous with state-sponsored capitalism, that they reached approximate economy parity with the United States, albeit by using the United States as a one-way market to sell to, without buying reciprocally from us. Although Russia and China remain authoritarian states, they are much less virulent than the communist governments that preceded them.

We thus entered the 21st Century with a justifiable faith in free trade as an engine of prosperity and democracy, for ourselves and other countries. We believe that free trade is a foreign policy as well as economic interest. We believe it encourages all nations to join with us in a prosperous global trading community, as political allies, and friends with common values of human rights and democracy.

The other component of globalization is immigration. We are the haven for the world's poor and oppressed. We do not want to be like the stingy old man who has built a beautiful garden on his property and puts walls around it to keep the neighbors' kids from playing in it. We want to shine forth to the world as the lamp of liberty and opportunity. We also believe that immigration brings new blood and new life into the country. People in a prosperous country can become complacent security-seekers. We can become so affluent that we cease to take risks to grow our wealth in the way we did when we were lean and hungry immigrants looking to better ourselves.

What Went Wrong

Until recently, we used globalism to add value to the United States. We built our industries by exporting to other countries. We admitted immigrants legally.

Only recently have we allowed our corporations to use globalism as a vehicle to hand off our economy to other countries, including China, whose government is undermining us. Only recently have we allowed our Globalists to convince us to keep the border open to illegal immigration. Only recently have our elites began using Globalism to attack the institutions and traditions that made the United States the superpower cradle of liberty. Only recently have Globalists started referring to their fellow American citizens as an inferior breed of humanity who must be replaced by foreigners who work cheaper.

Even then, criticism of globalism might have remained muted if it had prospered the economy. Globalism only came under fire when it demonstrably placed our middle class on a trajectory of economic decline.

Between 1950 and 2000 our economy grew at 3.68% compounded. We were told that signing free trade with Mexico in 1994 and GATT trade with China in 2000 would increase our economic growth to at least 5%, creating a cornucopia of prosperity. Instead, the foreign trade with Mexico, China, and other low-wages countries cut our growth almost in half to 2.10% in the years between 2000 and 2020. These were years when we were piling millions of legal and illegal immigrants into the country while shipping millions of American citizens' jobs overseas.

Globalists promised that foreign trade with Mexico and China would work to our advantage as an exporting country. Vice President Al Gore's promised during the 1993 NAFTA-WITH-MEXICO debate:

"NAFTA will...greatly accelerate [our trade with Mexico]; ***we will have a larger trade surplus with Mexico than with any country in the entire world....*** *We'll create more jobs with NAFTA....an additional 400,000 jobs [already], and we can create hundreds of thousands more if we continue this trend.*

As soon as NAFTA-WITH-MEXICO was signed, our companies began replacing their American workers with cheap labor in Mexico. Our balance of trade with Mexico went from surplus to deficit, increasing every year to the present deficit of $80 billion. Over 440,000 American jobs were moved to Mexico in the automotive sector alone.

GATT-WITH-CHINA was far worse. Tens of thousands of American factories were closed, and millions of American jobs relocated to China. These factories are not there to produce products to be consumed in Mexico and China, but to use cheap Mexican and Chinese labor to produce product imported into the United States and sold at inflated markups so companies can profit more than they could by employing Americans.

We were told that immigrants' work ethic and entrepreneurial energy would boost the economy faster than we were destroying it with trade. Didn't happen. We got the worst Great Recession in 80 years, while padding the economy with tens of trillions of government debt that will either be paid with back-breaking taxes by our children or will be defaulted on with hyperinflated currency.

We were told that trade would convert Mexico and China into prosperous democracies. After numerous economic collapses and currency devaluations, Mexico has elected a socialist president, while much of the country has fallen under the control of drug trafficking warlords. Moving our manufacturing jobs to Mexico turned out not to be the panacea for Mexico or the United States that Globalists promised. It merely transferred some of Mexico's unemployment to the United States by putting our people out of work, without doing much to make Mexicans prosperous enough to purchase made-in-USA products.

At least Mexico is a neighbor. China's government is neither a neighbor nor an ally. After signing trade agreements allowing China to flood the United States with imports, China suspended its embryonic moves toward democracy, declaring their leader to be president for life. They sent hundreds of thousands of spies into our country and launched cyberattacks to steal our personal data and the intellectual capital of our businesses. They stole data from our nuclear weapons and medical labs. They bribed our politicians, academics, and business leaders to turn against the United States. They invaded Hong Kong and now threaten to invade Taiwan and sink American ships traversing international waters claimed by China.

Covid-19 originated in China, most likely from the Wuhan Virology Lab, believed to have conducted prohibited "gain of function" experiments to make Covid-19 capable of infecting human beings. Not only did China's government concoct an improbably story that Covid-19 originated in a bat cave 700 miles away from Wuhan --- supposedly when someone schlepped batwing bushmeat all those hundreds of miles into the Wuhan "wet market" --- but then they paid off our government, our businesspeople, our media, and our medical establishment to peddle their tale. Our Globalists are so much under China's thumb that they cheerfully disavowed loyalty to their own countries or to the truth. That is what Globalism creates: loyalty to disinformation fomented by the most corrupt governments on the planet instead of fealty to one's own people and to the truth.

When Globalists were no longer able to obfuscate their misrepresentations, they reversed their propaganda. They now pretend to believe that trade deficits are good, and that the industries that created the lion's share of our wealth and power are obsolete and should be offshored to other countries. According to Globalists, we need to eliminate high-value manufacturing industries that produce motor vehicles, aircraft, electronics, appliances, clothing, furniture, construction materials. They say we need to become a nation of farmers, so we can export low-value, government-subsidized surplus farm products to other countries, which do not want them, because they are trying to dump their surpluses on global markets too.

There is also the view that immigration is being used for wrongful purposes. We have been opening our borders to increased legal and illegal immigration at a time when American citizens have been shoved out of the work force in tidal waves of {downsizing, offshoring, outsourcing, re-engineering, work force reductions, involuntary early retirements}. Does it make sense to open the borders to immigration when the existing labor force --- including the most skilled engineers and professional workers ---- is being dis-employed? As recently as 2017 companies were boasting of their commitment to dis-employing America's workforce:

https://www.wsj.com/articles/the-end-of-employees-1486050443

The End of Employees

Updated Feb. 2, 2017

Never before have American companies tried so hard to employ so few people. The outsourcing wave that moved apparel-making jobs to China and call-center operations to

India is now just as likely to happen inside companies across the U.S. and in almost every industry.

Hiring an employee is a last resort…and "very few jobs make it through that obstacle course."

Globalists say that immigrants add value to the country by creating new businesses. This is true for well-selected legal immigrants who found world-beating businesses such as Google and Tesla, and uncounted numbers of well-regarded small businesses. But this is not universally true, especially for immigrants who come illegally. Many immigrant-owned businesses do not comply with wage and hour laws or pay taxes and insurance that legal businesses are required to pay. Globalism seems more aligned with the communist tradition of Karl Marx than with free enterprise capitalism:

But, generally speaking, **the Protective system** *in these days* **is conservative,** *while* **the Free Trade system works destructively. It breaks up old nationalities** *and carries antagonism of proletariat and bourgeoisie to the uttermost point. In a word,* **the Free Trade system hastens the Social Revolution. In this revolutionary sense alone,** *gentlemen, I am in* **favor** *of* **Free Trade.**

– Karl Marx.

Today's Globalists are working against Adam Smith's legacy:

No society can surely be flourishing and happy, of which the far greater part of the members are poor and miserable. It is but equity, besides, that they who feed, clothe, and lodge the whole body of the people, should have such a share of the produce of their own labour as to be themselves tolerably well fed, clothed, and lodged.

The wages of labour are the encouragement of industry, which, like every other human quality, improves in proportion to the encouragement it receives. A plentiful subsistence increases the bodily strength of the labourer, and the comfortable hope of bettering his condition, and of ending his days, perhaps, in ease and plenty, animates him to exert that strength to the utmost.

Where wages are high, accordingly, we shall always find the workmen more active, diligent, and expeditious, than where they are low.

Smith, Adam (2013-09-12). *The Wealth of Nations (Illustrated) (p. 31) Kindle Edition.*

Unless we end these negative feedbacks of globalism, the United States will become another failed socialist / authoritarian state governed the elite, while most are mired in poverty and social unrest. The economy will fail when the government goes bankrupt trying to pay the interest on hundreds of trillions of debts created to prop up a failing economy whose wealth-producing industries were handed off to other countries, especially hostile ones like China that seek to supplant us as the world's dominant superpower.

Globalism vs. Globalism

We can test the validity of the Globalists' theories by seeing how consistent they are. Poorly conceived theories are riddled with contradictory inconsistencies. Here is an example from Ian Bremmer's excellent book *Us vs. Them: The Failure of Globalism:*

https://www.amazon.com/Us-vs-Them-Failure-Globalism/dp/0525533184/

Advances in automation and artificial intelligence are remaking the workplace for the benefit of efficiency, making the companies that use them more profitable, but workers who lose their jobs and can't be retrained for new ones won't share in the gains.... As a result, large numbers of U.S. factory jobs have been lost not to Chinese or Mexican factory workers but to robots. A 2015 study conducted by Ball State University found that **automation and related factors, not trade, accounted for 88 percent of lost U.S. manufacturing jobs between 2006 and 2013.**

Then he writes:

Globalization creates new economic efficiency by moving production and supply chains to parts of the world where resources— raw materials and workers— are cheapest.... In the developed world, this process bolsters the purchasing power of everyday consumers by putting affordable products on store shelves, but it also disrupts lives by killing livelihoods **as corporations gain access to workers in poorer countries who will work for lower wages.**

So, which is it? Are all these millions of jobs being lost because of automation or because companies are moving the work to the cheapest labor countries? Of course, it is for both reasons --- that jobs are being lost both to automation **and** the removal of jobs to cheap-labor countries. However, Globalists misrepresent the proportions. They want us to believe that most jobs in manufacturing in the USA have been lost to automation. But then, in their unguarded moments of honesty, they admit that jobs are being lost to "workers in poorer countries who will work for lower wages."

The truth is that *American companies move jobs out of the USA and into cheap-labor countries because they want to avoid spending money automating their USA factories and making their American workers more productive.*

Here are some other misrepresentations and obfuscations Globalists proliferate to mask their true agendas:

We are told that "free trade will create millions of well-paying jobs for American workers who will be busy making product that we export to other countries."

Then, when American workers lose their jobs to imports from low-wage countries, we are told that "free trade is beneficial because it allows us to buy foreign-made products for less money than we can make them here."

We are told that "nobody works in manufacturing anymore because it has become a high-technology industry where all human labor has been replaced by robots and automation."

Then we are told that "manufacturing is an obsolete primitive industry that should be moved overseas to more primitive countries where unskilled labor works cheap."

We are told that American workers are the most productive in the world and deserve the opportunity to prosper by creating product to export to the world.

Then when the free trade treaties are signed, and American workers' jobs are removed to cheap-labor countries, we are told that it is because American workers are too lazy, stupid, mal-educated, and overpaid to deserve employment.

We are told that "free trade is the keystone of prosperity."

Then we sign "free trade" deals with many countries and the economy goes into a Great Recession.

We are told that to be globally competitive, we must open our markets to unfettered imports from other countries that are purposed to destroy our domestic industries, thereby making it impossible for us to export anything.

We are told that foreign markets are pots of gold waiting to be exploited by U.S. companies, and that the USA is a stagnant market of declining business opportunity.

Then we are told that the other countries' economies are so fragile that they will collapse if the USA restricts their access to our market to dump their surplus production.

We are told that we live in a high-tech economy where "robots and automation are doing all the drudge work" and that only people with college educations should expect to be employed.

Then we are told that we must open the borders to millions of unskilled foreigners to fill all those jobs of scrubbing toilets, cleaning floors, and picking turnips --- jobs that pay little and always seem to outnumber the "high-tech" jobs by at least ten to one.

We are told that manufacturing jobs will never return to the USA because they've all been automated.

Then we are told that we can't bring manufacturing jobs back from Mexico and China because American labor costs (work done by human beings, not robots) will make the products unaffordable.

We are told that we can never bring manufacturing back to the USA because "Americans will never pay $900 for an iPhone."

Then we import iPhones made in China, and we pay $900 for them.

We are told that manufacturing is a relic of the past that the USA should not be involved with anymore,

Then we are told that agriculture, which predates manufacturing by at least 10,000 years, is the key to our prosperity in a global economy --- so much so that we must open our borders to millions of illiterate foreign peons to come in here and work the land, with hoe in hand, like their great, great, great, great, great grandparents did thousands of years ago.

We are told that there is a shortage of skilled workers in the USA, and that is why American companies must locate their work overseas or bring in foreigners to do it here.

Then we find that these are the same companies that laid off most of the skilled American workers they already employed.

We are told that Americans are delusional in thinking we can build prosperity by running up unpayable debts.

Then we are told that we need to import product from other countries that don't pay taxes to our federal, state, and local governments that would limit the debt.

We are told that we must tax our people to spend $900 billion a year to defend our Asian "allies" from China and our European "allies" from Russia.

Then we are told that we don't dare put tariffs on imports on these countries that we are taxing our own people to defend from each other.

We are told that we must fastidiously adhere to the "rules based international order" decided by supra-national authority/

Then we are told that must ignore national laws on immigration. According to Globalists, citizens of a country may be held accountable to international bodies, but illegal immigrants must be held accountable to no one.

These obfuscations are proliferated by Globalists to shift the blame from people who don't want to be held accountable for their self-serving prevarications and false promises.

Globalism vs. Americans

Globalism has harmed many Americans economically, but also politically by pitting us against each other. By removing jobs from the country, globalism diminishes opportunities in the private sector and makes people prone to voting for Socialists who favor expanding government. This is what left-of-center Globalists are aiming to accomplish.

According to Globalist lore, a remarkable transformation took place in the United States between 1994 and 1998. Prior to that time, Globalists characterized Americans as intelligent, hardworking people who wanted to increase our prosperity by building world-beating products to export to other countries. "If only we had free trade!" they implored. "Then Americans could fulfill our destiny as the world's most productive and innovative providers of goods and services to the rest of the world!"

Then the "free trade" treaties were signed, and the Globalists' propaganda instantly reversed. Instead of being world-beaters, in their view Americans suddenly became has-beens. Not all Americans. Not college professors, government employees, and corporation CEO's. Just Americans whose industrial jobs could be removed to cheap-labor countries, or who could be hornswoggled out of their jobs by the importation of foreigners on H1-B visas.

According to Globalists, all those Americans whose industrial and technological skills have built the world's wealthiest economy became obsolete overnight. Americans became too lazy to do the low-skilled work done by Mexicans, too lacking in industrial skills to compete with Japanese and Chinese factories, and too ignorant to do the high-tech work that only Indians on H1-B visas could do. Globalists said we had become an island of ignorance in a world of super-intelligent foreign beings. We had to allow the rest of the world to save us from ourselves by opening our borders to tens of millions of foreigners, including those here illegally, while moving all relocatable industrial jobs overseas to countries whose citizens worked smarter than we did. In Globalist lore, no job ever left the United States in search of cheaper foreign labor, but only in search of superior foreign beings.

Globalists might have been able to keep their propaganda mills running full chisel if the economy had not fallen off a cliff in 2008, *after* we opened our economy to unfettered entry of foreign products and people. All the institutions where Globalists make *their* nests

23

--- such as big government, big finance, big academia, and big media --- fell into disrepute. However, Globalists continue to insist that the economic failures they inflicted upon the United States occurred because all Americans except themselves suddenly became too stupid "to compete in a global economy."

Globalism vs. Capitalism

Globalists say they are exporting American-style capitalism to the rest of the world, when they are really importing big government socialism into the United States.

Capitalism is the highest expression of economic freedom. It brings together the inventor, the marketer, the consumer, and the financier who together turn ideas into marketable goods and services that consumers want to buy. It creates positive feedback loops whereby all the participants in the creation of a product or service --- from business owners to managers to employees --- are incentivized to work together to provide maximum value to their customers, who are the ultimate bosses of all businesses.

The human mind operating in a capitalist economy is empowered to create infinite wealth from the common materials that nature provides. But Capitalism should be valued at least as much for its spiritual dimension as for its creation of material wealth. It encourages people to achieve excellence in their life's ambitions as inventors, scientists, businesspeople, artists, doctors, public servants, and a thousand other callings.

Capitalism embodies the defining spirit of what makes us human beings --- the idea of progress. People desire to make progress in our lives by learning new skills and putting them to work to improve their capacity to add value to themselves. We desire to leave a better world for our children. Capitalism is the catalyst of humanity's progress. Communism is the instrument of stagnation and tyranny because it denies people the opportunity to direct the progress of their lives.

People who live in unfree economies suffer not only material poverty, but poverty of the spirit. How many people born with the talent to enrich the world materially or artistically have been stifled by the constraints of unfree economies? It is no coincidence that the world's great business and technology innovators fulfill their ambitions in free economies like ours. So do a disproportionate share of the greatest artists and intellectuals. The capitalist economy provides resources to those who wish to enrich Mankind artistically and intellectually as much it does those who develop desirable material goods and services.

Capitalism shines brightest in small businesses that personify their owners' dreams of achieving excellence in the creation of products and services that the public desires to purchase. The owner whose name is on the business backs it with his or her reputation.

Many businesses are started because their founders achieved a level of expertise that makes them *too valuable* for any single company to employ. Their extraordinary expertise compels them to seek personal fulfillment by servicing many customers, spreading their expertise far and wide throughout the marketplace.

As the successful business grows, its owners hire employees to build an organization with a shared mission to prosper by increasing their customers' prosperity. The employees are incentivized to become ever more skilled in perfecting the products and services the business sells. Their economic value increases as they, under managements' direction, become ever more efficient in producing the goods and services that make their customers more efficient. The economy moves upward in a virtuous circle that increases the prosperity of all who invest and labor in it.

Abraham Lincoln described many facets of life with exquisite wisdom. He reminded us that we prosper when Labor and Capital work together in harmony:

Labor is prior to and independent of capital. Capital is only the fruit of labor and could never have existed if labor had not first existed. Labor is the superior of capital and deserves much the higher consideration…. Capital has its rights, which are as worthy of protection as any other rights. Nor is it denied that there is, and probably always will be, a relation between labor and capital producing mutual benefits.

Globalism would be praised if it improved the fortunes of Labor and Capital and thereby contributed to humanity's progress. However, many employees and small business owners see globalism as a threat to their interests, believing that when carried to extremes it subverts capitalism, labor, and democracy.

Globalism seeks to wrap big government and big business in a mutually profitable embrace that prospers well-connected corporation executives, politicians, and academics by reallocating to them the wealth that should stay in the hands of people who earn it. It seeks to remove accountability from government and business by creating unelected supranational organizations like the World Trade Association, the World Court, and the World Health Organization that are beyond the reach of the people's will. "You want to keep jobs-destroying imports and unauthorized immigrants out of your country? Sorry, but the World Trade Association and the World Court says you must let them in."

26

Big globalist multinational corporations subvert capitalism in the same way that President Grover Cleveland, a conservative Democrat, warned us in his State of the Union Address way back in 1888:

The gulf between employers and the employed is constantly widening, and classes are rapidly forming, one comprising the very rich and powerful, while in another are found the toiling poor.... the citizen is struggling far in the rear or is trampled to death beneath an iron heel.

Corporations, which should be carefully restrained creatures of the law and the servants of the people, are fast becoming the people's masters.

The existing situation stifles all patriotic love of country, and substitutes in its place selfish greed and grasping avarice.

Government, instead of being the embodiment of equality, is but an instrumentality through which especial and individual advantages are to be gained.

Communism is a hateful thing and a menace to peace and organized government; but the communism of combined wealth and capital, the outgrowth of overweening cupidity and selfishness, which insidiously undermines the justice and integrity of free institutions, is no less dangerous than the communism of oppressed poverty and toil, which, exasperated by injustice and discontent, attacks with wild disorder the citadel of rule.

I believe that globalism harms democracy and capitalism because it seeks to place big government and big multinational corporations beyond accountability to the people. It seeks to create international government by unelected supra-national bureaucrats and multinational business executives in international committees beyond the reach of the laws and authorities of national governments. A bulwark of support for Donald Trump came from small business owners --- the people who live or die by capitalism, and who do not depend on government connections and government favors for their prosperity.

Globalism: Hypothesis vs. Reality

Globalists claim that free movement of goods and people between nations will prosper the world. They want nations to dismantle their customs and immigration posts and let people and products come and go at will.

"The United States is the perfect example," they say. "We are a great country because we have free movement of goods and people between the states." True, but the operative phrase is: "we are a country." Americans live under the same Constitution, the same body of law, the same currency --- and until recently when illegal immigration infiltrated the country --- we shared a common political and social culture.

"What about the European Union?" ask the Globalists. "Haven't they prospered by uniting their countries in free trade and common movement of people between countries?" Who can say? Some of the most prosperous parts of Europe, like Switzerland, never joined it. Britain opted out of it when European Globalists tried to bequeath de facto European citizenship to the migrant peoples of the Middle East and Africa, encouraging, them to enter the E.U. over open borders.

Nor is the European Union a bastion of prosperity. Its economy is stagnant, its population declining, and its supra-national government is corrupt and unaccountable. It flames into constant economic crises in the PIGS (Portugal, Italy, Greece, and Spain) which remain as poor in the European Union, if not poorer, than they would be outside it. Its most popular rising parties want out of it. If the European Union is working so well, why is it in constant turmoil?

The E.U. is also incompetent to defend itself and relies on the USA to tax our people to fund the military that protects it from its imaginary enemies. Its main source of income is the $184 billion in trade surplus it runs with the USA. So, who can say if there has been any improvement for the people in the formerly sovereign countries that constitute it?

Nor has the USA necessarily prospered by opening our borders to unfettered trade and immigration. Our economy did not grow as anticipated with the rapid population increase from immigration and the expansion of foreign imported goods coming into the country. If it has grown at all, it is because we have added $26 trillion of unpayable debt to our federal government's ledger, which will inhibit growth in the future.

Globalists want us to believe the world will improve if people can live in any country they want to. But why should we believe this? Why would Bulgaria be any better if it is repopulated by Mexicans and Mongolians, and why would Mongolia and Mexico be improved by Bulgarians move in? This is not the way the world works. The migration is almost entirely one way. People from poor countries move to countries with higher standards of living. Mexicans move to the USA, Bulgarians move to Germany and the UK, and Mongolians would move to Japan if they could. "Free movement of people" is a one-way movement from low-wage countries to high-wage countries, thereby depressing wages in the wealthier countries.

The case for movement of goods and services by free trade makes more sense --- in part because only goods that can be sold in the USA are brought in here, whereas immigrants hop across the border whether they add value to the country or not. Economic theory teaches that each country supposedly has a comparative advantage that allows it concentrate on a few specific areas of expertise. Being able to export to world markets would theoretically allow each country to concentrate on the things it does better than anybody else, and gain economies of scale by exporting those few things around the world, while receiving in return goods and services that other countries can provide at lower cost than could be produced domestically.

In reality, most developed countries produce the same grab bag of surplus products and try to dump them in each other's laps. The USA, Canada, Mexico, Europe, Japan, South Korea, and China all produce the same surpluses of motor vehicles, aviation, architectural metals, computers, appliances, electronics, and so on. The only "comparative advantage" is that some countries --- like Mexico, Brazil, and China --- have cheap labor, and some countries --- like China --- steal other countries' technologies, copy them, and resell pirated copies below the originating countries' cost of design and production. Most countries have formal and informal barriers that do not permit the importation of foreign products. Some other countries, like Mexico, have governments that try to trade fairly with us, but whose people are too poor to buy products made in the USA and other countries.

For these reasons, the USA runs tremendous trade deficits with most countries --- $375 billion with China, $218 billion with the European Union (including around $70 billion with Germany), around $60 billion with Japan, around $108 billion with Mexico, and around $20 billion with South Korea. In every instance where we have signed a "free trade" agreement with a country, our exports have stagnated or declined, our imports have increased, and our trade deficit has soared. The U.S sold less to Canada, our oldest trading partner, in 2021 than we did in 2014. Exports to Mexico, China, Japan, and the European Union have barely budged since 2014. The only things that ever increase are our imports from these countries, and our trade deficit with them.

Most other countries take advantage of our honesty in opening our markets to their products, while only pretending to open their markets to ours:

https://www.huffingtonpost.com/ian-fletcher/how-do-other-nations-bala_b_628157.html

How Do Other Nations Balance Their Trade? Try Germany

Germany, like the U.S., is nominally a free-trading country. The difference is that while the U.S. genuinely believes in free trade, Germany quietly follows a contrary [protectionist] tradition that goes back to the 19th-century German economist Friedrich List (who was, ironically, a student of our own Alexander Hamilton). So despite Germany's nominal policy of free trade, in reality, a huge key to its trading success is a vast and half-hidden thicket of de facto non-tariff trade barriers.

It isn't possible to have free trade with Germany, or with most other countries. We believe in free trade. They don't.

In 2001 we admitted China to the World Trade Organization and committed to near-tariff-free trade of a maximum tariff of 2.5% on Chinese-made products. We were told that China would admit American exports to enter their country at the same 2.5% maximum. Eighteen years later, we import everything from seafood to construction materials to machinery to cemetery monuments from China. GM has even started importing Chinese-made Buicks into the United States. All at the 2.5% tariff.

Did China reciprocate with a 2.5% tariff on our products? No, they have tariffed our automobiles at 40% for the past eighteen years. Why didn't any American leader care about this imbalance until Trump came along? Why did we wait eighteen years to confront them, while they were tearing up our economy? China has since denied that they have promised to meet Trump's demand that they lower tariffs. And even if they do nominally reduce the tariff, how long will it take them to concoct some other scheme to keep our exports out of China?

https://www.wsj.com/articles/trump-china-to-reduce-and-remove-tariffs-on-american-cars-1543811957

Trump: China to 'Reduce and Remove' Tariffs on American Cars

'China has agreed to reduce and remove tariffs on cars coming into China from the U.S. Currently the tariff is 40%,' president says

By Trefor Moss Updated Dec. 3, 2018

SHANGHAI—China has agreed to cut tariffs on American-made cars, President Trump said on Twitter...Chinese officials didn't immediately confirm or deny Mr. Trump's assertion, with a Foreign Ministry spokesman on Monday sidestepping questions on auto tariffs.

If the country we trade with is poor, it's people can't afford to buy much from us. We are never going to export much of anything made with $25 / hour labor to Mexico and China, where the people earn $1.00 to $2.00 / hour. American companies are going to remove production out of the USA, set it up in Mexico and China, and take advantage of their $2.00 /hour labor to make product that they can sell at an inflated price list after they import it into the USA.

"But don't we benefit by buying foreign-made products cheaper than they could be produced in the USA?" Maybe, maybe not. For years we have been told that "If iPhones were made in the USA, they'd cost $1,000 and nobody could afford to buy them." iPhones are produced in China. They now cost $1,000, and Americans buy them. In other instances, we are merely trading down in quality when we buy cheap foreign-made product. Chinese dog food poisons our pets, and many foreign-made appliances are cheap because they are made with low-quality parts as well as cheap labor.

Our $810 billion yearly trade deficit harms us in several ways. First, every product imported into the USA was produced with investments in foreign physical plant, wages paid to foreign workers, purchase orders paid from foreign supplies, and taxes paid to foreign governments. Why should a company that invests in physical plant in the USA, pays wages to American workers, pays purchase orders issued to American suppliers, and pays taxes to American governments, have to compete on equal terms with companies in foreign countries that only want to strip-mine our market without contributing anything to the USA?

Furthermore, we are paying a heavy price in supporting Americans who no longer work and pay taxes because their jobs were relocated overseas and given to foreigners who build products that are imported into the United States. Americans unemployed by imports are subsidized by government welfare programs instead of paying taxes to support our government's civil and military commitments. For every can of Chinese-made dogfood and every Mexican-made washing machine brought into the United States, we can be sure that the national debt is increasing by at least that much, because Americans were not working and paying taxes to make the product sold in this country. Our descendants until the end of time are going to be paying interest on the public debt so that we can have a party now with foreign-made goods.

And notice how the Globalists keep changing their propaganda! Globalization was originally sold to the public and Congress on the promise that it would "create millions of well-paying jobs for Americans who will be put to work building products to export to other countries." Nowadays it is sold on the promise that "Globalization allows you to buy stuff cheap." And even that promise is dubious, because products with a cheap price tag are often products of inferior quality, having less value than the well-made products that they replaced. When Globalists keep changing their propaganda from one dubious point to another, then you know that their ideas are not sound.

However, globalism has many supporters including multinational companies who profit from removing American jobs overseas. Many Liberals and Conservatives cherish it on an ideological basis without understanding its real-life consequences. These people seek to hide the dire results of globalization from the American people. The following groups having personal interests in promoting globalization of trade and immigration.

1. Big business executives and stockholders sees globalism as the means to:
-   Manufacture product in cheap-labor countries like Mexico and China.
-   Import the product into the USA and sell it at inflated profit margins.
-   Practice tax avoidance by pretending that the profits originate in foreign tax shelters.

- Inflate profits in the USA by replacing American workers with lower-paid foreigners, including Illegals.
- Remove the ability of sovereign nations to police multinational corporations for money laundering, financial fraud, tax fraud, and illegal labor practices.

2. Liberals see Globalism is a trans-national Global Welfare State that atones for past U.S. "oppression of colonial people of color" by transferring American jobs and wealth to the Third World, while filling up the USA with impoverished foreigners. "Social Justice Warriors" despise the "White People's Western Culture" and want to make the USA look like a Third World country by opening the border to Third World immigrants. They see Third World immigrants as fodder to propagandize to vote for left-of-center politicians.

3. Some Conservatives see globalism as a vehicle to undermine the authority of the national government by removing Americans from employment, and thereby de-funding government by reducing the taxes it collects. Conservatives of this stripe would rather see Mexicans and Chinese building product sold in the USA than to see Americans, who might possibly belong to a union, making the vehicles and earning livelihoods for American families.

4. Establishment politicians of all political views expect to be offered lucrative positions in corporations when they retire from politics, so they do the bidding of big business.

5. Globalism creates supra-national, unelected bureaucracies unaccountable to the voters of nation states. It empowers international bureaucracies to defy the people's will by imposing leftist or corporatist agendas without their consent.

6. Many academics hold globalist views because they are primarily funded by government and corporation bureaucracies that profit from globalism. They are paid to advocate for free trade and open borders, so that is what they do. People who don't believe in free trade and open borders don't get funded with government and corporation money, so their voices are rarely heard.

These groups make up the "establishment" wings of the political parties. Because they include Conservatives and Liberals, backed by the moneyed power of multinational corporations and the intellectual influence of academics, they speak loudly,

My Experience as a Globalist

I have been an employee, consultant, and business owner who has developed business systems to manage the international trade of large and small companies in the USA, Canada, Europe, Asia, South America, and the Middle East. I understand foreign trade and its impact on our economy and people.

I worked for and consulted for companies that moved their operations overseas during the 1990's and early 2000's. I know why our American companies chose to fire their American employees, replace them with Mexicans and Chinese, and call it "globalism."

I also witnessed this enthusiastic destruction of American manufacturing, and its replacement by a shaky and shady "financial services economy." Trade data alerted me that the Great Recession was on the way. I saw Mexico, Brazil, and other Asian countries devalue their currencies to suck the jobs out of the USA. I saw American CEOs oblige them by laying off thousands of my fellow American workers in tidal waves of {downsizing, offshoring, outsourcing, re-engineering, work force reductions, involuntary early retirements} and other euphemisms for putting Americans out of work.

I thus see international trade as neither an inherent panacea nor a calamity. It can be beneficial or harmful, depending on how it is managed. In writing international trade management systems, I have seen how other developed countries manage their trade for the benefit of their people. Most other countries try to run trade surpluses to bring jobs and wealth into their countries by exporting to us while restricting our exports to them. All other developed countries impose VAT taxes, tariffs, and regulations to limit imports from the United States so that their people are kept working producing goods and services at the expense of ours. Our free trade mavens promise to put our people to work exporting to countries, then yank the rug out from under them by flooding the country with other countries' imports.

Regarding immigration, I am married into an all-immigrant family of naturalized American citizens, and have had foreign-born employers, business partners, and customers. I do not need to be told how important immigrants are to our country. But I have also seen the corrupt, illegal side of immigration, and cannot be fooled into believing that all immigration is unequivocally good.

I am a popular reviewer of books on politics, history, economics, international affairs, and business. I have debated the economics and politics of globalization and understand the views of Globalists.

I have intensively studied American history and have been paid to write for popular history magazines. I understand our political and economic history. I can place current events in context with what has happened before. I cannot be fooled by false historical analogies that seek to credit or discredit current policies by misapplying them to past events. I have read the works of Adam Smith and David Ricardo, so I know when Globalists misrepresent them to support "free trade" ideas that were anathema to their originators.

My purpose is not to condemn all aspects of globalism. I don't say that international trade is always bad, because I have earned my livelihood from international trade, and owned international companies and properties. I will only say that international trade is not a panacea for creating prosperity for any country, and especially not the USA. It makes people poorer when it is done for the wrong reasons, such as to destroy employment in countries where wages are relatively high, or when it is done with countries whose governments refuse to reciprocate trade. Trade needs to be managed to make sure that it benefits most of our people, most of the time.

Nor will I condemn immigration, because my family, and former business partners and employers, are legal immigrants. Immigrants, when let into the USA for the right reasons, bring new blood and vitality. They help legacy American citizens better appreciate our country.

I will only say that unlimited immigration across open borders, and unlimited imports from countries that do not buy reciprocally from us, are not panaceas for growing our economy and prospering our people. I believe Globalism, in the extreme way it is being foisted upon us by multinational business, government, media, and academic elites, is an existential threat to the United States.

The Globalists' Broken Promises

What, then, are the deficiencies of Globalism?

- It has narrowed the private sector economy by removing manufacturing and technology, and the knowledge and manufacturing and technology, overseas. We are becoming an unstable "casino economy" of gambling casinos, stock market roulette, and government-subsidized healthcare and education. Our economy is becoming too narrow and too government-subsidized to generate sustainable growth.

- It has diminished the middle class and made many Americans more dependent on big government social welfare; and therefore, prone to voting for Socialists who pledge to redistribute wealth instead of creating it.

- It has devalued the work of Americans. I know electrical engineers, computer science Ph.D.'s, and research physicists who were laid off by companies that imported foreigners to replace them. "My buds [in IT] who promptly took a 50% pay cut if they could find work at all…the H1B invasion and outsourcing overseas killed any hope of coming back till I retired in 2017." Globalists say we must compete in a global economy, and then they fire the Americans who know how to do it.

- It removes the pride of people who work in manufacturing making tangible products of value. Manufacturing is a skilled profession, from the assembly line workers to the professionals who manage them. It is preferable to have our people adding value to the economy both as workers and consumers than to have them put out of the labor force because manufacturing was moved to Mexico and China.

- By narrowing the economy, it makes people dependent on university educations that don't add any value to the economy. Want to work an entry level job? Then go to a university and encumber yourself with $400,000 of college debt that you'll never repay on the $12.00 / hour you're going to earn stacking boxes. And we wonder why young people are voting socialist!

- It fosters economic delusions that emerging countries like China and Mexico are markets that prosper Americans. While Mexico is in general a good neighbor, it isn't wealthy enough to be a significant market for American-made products. China doesn't want American-made products, except to buy token amounts to reverse-engineer and sell back to us. They, along with the European Union and Japan, see us as a flea market to dump their surplus productions, while setting trade barriers to keep our products out of their countries.

- It deludes American companies into transferring the profits they earn from the United States to foreign countries, instead of re-investing them in the United States where they were earned.

- It induces us to abandon our competitive strength of manufacturing well-engineered, high value products. "Why hire American engineers to make a quality product in the United States, when we can buy cheap junk from China? We can mark that junk up 60% and when it breaks, we can sell our customers replacements."

- It makes us dependent for imports of essential manufactured products from potentially hostile countries.

- Its destruction of our old economy removes the wealth needed to create a "new economy." When we give away the "old economy" we are also giving away the future economy.

- It devalues American citizenship. The United States always has money to provide free healthcare, education, food, and shelter for immigrants, and to send tens of billions of dollars in foreign aid to poor countries overseas whose governments steal it. But our own citizens are told to fend for themselves when Globalists remove their jobs to other countries.

- It weakens the concept that the United States has value as a nation. "Our American employees want a pay raise? Then ship their jobs to Mexico and China! And while you're at it, set up a holding company in a p.o. box in Ireland, so we can launder our profits through it without paying taxes to Uncle Sam."

- It undermines respect for the law. Globalists create "sanctuary cities" that shield Illegals from immigration law. They encourage companies to hire Illegals. If we do not respect immigration laws, why should we respect any laws? The encouragement of illegal immigration is turning the United States into the type of corrupt country that legal immigrants come here to escape.

Globalists promise that trade and immigration will bring prosperity to everyone, then tell people whose livelihoods are destroyed by detrimental trade and immigration that they are obsolete. The so-called "obsolete" are citizens who have worked and paid taxes in good faith all their lives. Perhaps they have fought for the country. When their jobs are shipped off to Mexico and China or are given away to migrant foreigners who work for less money, they suddenly become "Appalachians, hicks, and uneducated people who can't compete in a global economy."

People especially despise globalism when the governing elite, who protect themselves with tenured civil service, corporation, and academic jobs, tell the people whose livelihoods were destroyed by Globalists' mendacity: "It's your fault. You're lazy, mal-educated, and don't know how to work. If you can't compete with foreigners, including those who are here illegally, then that's your fault."

Globalism erodes our patriotism and our faith in free enterprise and the law. How can people love a country that multinational corporations, and the politicians they control, think of as nothing more than a cash register to be sold to the highest foreign bidder? How can our young people have faith in capitalism when they come out of college with student loans they'll struggle to repay, must compete with dozens of foreigners from unaccredited overseas universities, and are likely to be put out of work in middle age when their family responsibilities are highest?

How can we be a nation of laws when our politicians and businesspeople deliberately keep the border open to illegal immigration? How can we trust democracy when one party desires illegal immigration to beat legal residents out of their jobs, and the other party desires illegal immigration to repopulate the country with people who vote its party line?

If there is one phrase that defines the essence of globalism, it is *"The Rules Based International Order."* Globalists want to make the rules that everybody else must live by. They want to be paid lavishly with the tax dollars and public debt inflicted on the people of each nation whom they seek to oppress.

Globalists are aghast over President Trump seeking to reduce our chronic trade deficit by imposing tariffs. They are telling us that when the USA seeks to reduce our trade deficit, that it is a "threat to the international rules-based order:"

https://www.economist.com/briefing/2018/06/07/donald-trump-is-undermining-the-rules-based-international-order

Donald Trump is undermining the rules-based international order

Jun 7th, 2018

*Trade experts, policy veterans and diplomats from almost all America's allies have looked on aghast…. The most prevalent in the foreign-policy establishment and the chancelleries of Europe is despair. **The rules-based order** ushered in after the second world war, which provided both the greatest-ever increase in human wealth and global trade and a whole human lifetime without worldwide armed conflict, is being dismantled. No good will come of it.*

And this:

https://www.wsj.com/articles/donald-trump-pitches-tariff-free-trade-zone-to-g-7-allies-1528556581?mod=hp_lead_pos1

Trump Says U.S. Won't Endorse G-7 Communiqué, Threatens Auto Tariffs

June 9th, 2018

*U.S. president's unprecedented refusal to endorse the communiqué threw the final hours of the summit into disarray…. Soon after Mr. Trump left Canada, Mr. Trudeau announced that all seven countries had endorsed the communiqué, which states that leaders share a commitment to promoting a **"rules-based international order."** Under a section entitled "Investing in Growth that Works for Everyone," the statement underlines "the crucial role of a **rules-based international trading system** and continue to fight protectionism."*

The communiqué said the nations would "strive to reduce tariff barriers, nontariff barriers and subsidies."

Globalists want their rules enforced to the letter, but everybody else's rules ignored. Globalists embedded in multinational corporations believe that national immigration laws should be ignored so that millions of impoverished illegal immigrants can pour over the borders and be herded into sweatshops owned by corporate employers in low-wage industries. Globalists want **their** multinational corporations and government-sponsored enterprises shielded from compliance with national laws governing worker health and safety, environmental compliance, and prohibitions on tax evasion and money laundering. Globalists seek to inflict "cancel culture" on the freedom-loving people's of the world who have dissected their self-enriching schemes.

Globalists don't want anybody elected in the United States or any other country who will govern in the best interests of the people. They see themselves as the international rule makers, who are entitled to be paid lavishly for telling everybody else how to run their business. Their darkest fear is that the people of the United States will catch on to their scams and boot them out of positions of authority. They especially fear a populist uprising from the right or left in the United States because the USA is their biggest cash cow.

Globalists' Blinding Hypocrisy

Globalism is defined by its hypocrisy. Today (June 8, 2018) the Globalists are aflutter because President Trump has said that Russia should be reinstated into the G-8 group of leading economic powers:

https://abcnews.go.com/Politics/trumps-call-russia-join-g7-faces-swift-backlash/story?id=55750098

Trump's call for Russia to join G7 faces swift backlash

BY ALEXANDER MALLIN

Jun 8, 2018, 1:08 PM ET

President <u>Donald Trump</u>'s call Friday for <u>Russia</u> to re-enter the G7 four years after the country was kicked out from the group of countries over its annexation of Crimea has resulted in a fierce backlash from foreign policy critics on both sides of the aisle.

But look at how the Europeans, who pretend to be afraid of Russia, slink off to do business with Russia when they think nobody in the USA is watching:

https://www.reuters.com/article/us-usa-russia-sanctions-germany-idUSKBN197156

<u>WORLD NEWS</u> *JUNE 16, 2017*

Germany threatens retaliation if U.S. sanctions [against Russia!] harm its firms

Gernot Heller, Alissa de Carbonnel /BRUSSELS (Reuters) -

Germany threatened on Friday **to retaliate against the United States** *if new sanctions on Russia being proposed by the U.S. Senate end up penalizing German firms.*

Germany threatens to "retaliate" against the United States if we impose sanctions on Russia, the country that Germans say is a threat that only the United States can defend them from! Globalists are always showboating to gin up hysteria against "populist" political opponents who pledge to take away the ladles to their international gravy trains. For public consumption, they excoriate President Trump for not imposing harsh sanctions on Russia, then they whine when he does it! What blinding, self-serving hypocrisy!

From the Great Recession to the Great Elections

The political upheavals of 2016 began with the Great Recession of 2008 that destroyed the illusion that Globalism had created a world of prosperity and economic growth.

In October 2008, according to then-Federal Reserve Chairman Benjamin Bernanke, 12 of the 13 largest banks in the USA were insolvent. Business was frozen in its tracks. The stock market lost over half its value. Millions lost their jobs, then were evicted from their homes when they couldn't pay their mortgages. The Republican and Democrat establishments rallied together like a band of brothers to bail out the failed banks with taxpayer money. The economy slowly recovered, with a tailwind from the $15 trillion our government added to the national debt, that will probably never be repaid.

Both parties obfuscated their roles in instigating the Great Recession. Republicans said, as they usually do, that the economy failed because taxes and regulations were too high. Democrats said, as they usually do, that the economy failed because taxes and regulations were too low. According to them, taxes should be raised so that government would have more money to "invest" in public education and public infrastructure.

However, there were larger forces at work. Millions of Americans were being laid off from their jobs by waves of {downsizing, rightsizing, offshoring, outsourcing, re-engineering, work force reductions}. This vocabulary told the story: massive dis-employment of the labor force.

While we were removing opportunities for employment by Americans, we opened our borders to record immigration. Millions of foreigners were entering the country legally and illegally. Our population increased from 248.7 million in 1990 to 308.7 million in 2010 --- an incredible 28% increase on top of an already large population base at precisely the time when we were beating Americans out of their jobs like beating fleas out of a blanket.

We were told it was "a Goldilocks Economy." Americans who were beat out of their jobs were going to be retrained for better things. The jobs that went overseas were going to be replaced by higher-value jobs in "new technologies." The trade treaties that we signed with Mexico, China, and many other countries, were going to expand our exports. Everything was going to be fine. Until it wasn't.

While it is true that the Great Recession was a swirling tempest of many debris, its fuel was the dis-employment of so much of America's workforce all at once in the late 1980s, 1990s, and early 2000's, primarily because of globalization. Companies said that they had to fire their American employees "in order to compete in a global economy." Laying off all those people had nothing to do with cutting costs so that American products would be cheap enough to export to other countries. It had everything to do with inflating corporations' profit margins by producing at Third World labor costs and importing into the United States to sell at an inflated American price list.

1. Beginning in the late 1980s the consumption side of the economy was stunted by massive dis-employment of the American workforce. Companies gave many reasons for laying off their people --- from "redundancy" due to mergers and acquisitions, to automating jobs out of existence, to moving jobs overseas. However, the reasons all boiled down to "globalization; we have to fire our people if we're going to cut costs and compete in a global economy."

2. To fight rising unemployment, Federal Reserve Chairman Alan Greenspan lowered interest rates, believing that lower rates would boost corporate cash flows by allowing corporations to refinance their debt. The increased cash flows were supposed to encourage American companies to invest in expanding their businesses and hiring more American workers. President Bush also asked Congress to cut income taxes on capital gains and dividends to further boost business cash flow under the theory that it would be reinvested in growing the American economy.

4. Lowering interest rates and cutting taxes failed to grow the economy (in contrast to the success of these policies in reviving the economy during Reagan's years) because by 2000 many American companies were moving production overseas and hiring foreign labor to replace American workers.

5. Consumer demand slackened due to the falling incomes of those put out of work or afflicted with falling wages.

6. With consumer demand falling, investors could not profit by investing in expanding production of goods and services. So, instead of creating real wealth

by building factories that hire employees to produce goods and services, capital became disproportionately invested into real estate and leveraged real estate derivatives like collateralized debt obligations (CDOs) and credit default swaps (CDS). These derivatives were leveraged at up to 30-to-1, and only required a 3% mortgage delinquency rate to render them insolvent.

7. By the summer of 2007 the accumulation of job losses from layoffs and involuntary retirements made it impossible for large numbers of people to pay the mortgages on their homes.

8. When homeowners defaulted on their mortgages due to job losses, the leveraged CDO and CDS derivatives became defunct. When they became worthless the banks discovered that they had more liabilities on their books than assets.

9. The banks became insolvent and the stock market crashed. Business stopped dead in its tracks. The injection of several trillion dollars of printed/borrowed paper money by the government resuscitated the economy. Without that infusion many more banks and businesses might have failed, further escalating unemployment.

10. Jobs creation remained sluggish even though corporate profits were soaring as are the stocks of publicly traded companies.

Technology was hit almost as hard as manufacturing. Hundreds of thousands of America's most accomplished Computer Science Ph.D.'s and research physicists were laid off in the 1990's and 2000's when their American employers transferred their jobs to China or brought in Indians on H1-B visas. Those still working tend to be employed at economically dubious jobs like programming stock market algorithms to spoof the markets to fleece investors or are at home writing electronic slot machine games for iPhones.

Our economy has stagnated every year since we opened it to unlimited imports from China, Mexico, Japan, and the European Union. The economy has narrowed its prosperity to a few areas of finance, government-funded healthcare and education, and government itself, which are propped up with trillions of dollars of debt creation instead of wealth creation. Our true sources of wealth generation in manufacturing, technology, and research have been relocated overseas. Many of our people are in an economic tailspin of declining incomes and rising debt:

OK Boomer, Who's Going to Buy Your 21 Million Homes?

Baby boomers are getting ready to sell one quarter of America's homes over the next two decades. The problem is many of these properties are in places where younger people no longer want to live.

By Laura Kusisto

Nov. 23, 2019

Another challenge is that younger buyers also may not have the financial strength to absorb all of this new supply. New research from Harvard University's Joint Center for Housing Studies found that households in their preretirement years, age 50 to 64, are less likely to own a home than prior generations, have suffered from stagnant income growth since 2000, and are more debt-burdened, including by student loans.

We were told not to worry; that a financial services economy would replace the lost manufacturing jobs. The "poster child" for this transformation was said to be General Electric. In the 1960's GE was an industrial conglomerate employing tens of thousands of American workers. GE produced 1% of our entire economy. In the 1980's Wall Street "financial services" hucksters took over the company. They moved its industrial work overseas and fired tens of thousands of American employees. They promised to earn billions making dicey loans to dodgy customers. Instead, GE became another failed American company run into the ground by incompetent "financial services" people:

Updated Nov. 14, 2018

GE Credit Crunch Ripples Across Wall Street

A steep fall in GE's bonds to junk levels is roiling credit markets, spreading pain and gain among investors and banks

By Matt Wirz Updated Nov. 14, 2018 4:10 p.m. ET Wall Street has a GE problem.

General Electric Co. GE -3.37% raised $115 billion of debt on a reputation as one of the U.S.'s safest borrowers. Now... GE stock has lost about half its value in 2018 and ratings firms in recent weeks cut its credit rating to BBB-plus, three notches above junk.

Trillions of dollars of government debt have been issued to bail out the failed financial services economy. Despite all the grandiose promises made by Globalists, our economy seems more fragile after the implementation of their policies than before:

https://www.wsj.com/articles/markets-show-calm-after-brexit-delay-11553244944?mod=hp_lead_pos1

Stocks, Bond Yields Fall Amid Anxiety Over World Economy

By Akane Otani and Georgi Kantchev Updated March 22, 2019

Global stocks and bond yields slid Friday as weak manufacturing data deepened investors' anxiety about the health of the world economy.

…. A report Friday showed factory output in the eurozone fell in March at the fastest pace in six years, while a gauge of U.S. manufacturing activity slipped to its lowest level in nearly two years. The data sent bond yields tumbling, with yields on German 10-year debt trading in negative territory for the first time since October 2016 and yields on 10-year Treasurys at fresh lows for the year.

Meanwhile, stocks across the world retreated, with the S&P 500 losing 1.2% and benchmark indexes in France, the U.K. and Germany sliding more than 1% apiece.

"The global economy has clearly become an issue, with big headwinds there," said Tim Anderson, managing director at broker-dealer TJM Investments, pointing to mounting worries particularly in Europe and China.

We must always be alert to Free Trade Mavens trying to paper over economic debacles that their policies created, while ginning up false hysteria whenever anybody tries to rein in their destructive policies:

https://www.wsj.com/articles/global-trade-set-for-weakest-year-since-crisis-11569924455

Slowing Trade Hits Global Manufacturing

U.S. factory activity contracts for second straight month; WTO warns that slowing world trade could hit investment and jobs

By Paul Hannon and Amara Omeokwe Updated Oct. 1, 2019

The global manufacturing slowdown worsened in September, and trade flows are set to grow this year at the weakest pace since the financial crisis, as tariffs rise and economic growth cools.

Thank the trade war, which means no improvement is likely anytime soon," Ian Shepherdson, chief economist at Pantheon Macroeconomics, said in a note to clients, referring to the ISM reading, which is based on a survey of U.S. purchasing and supply executives.

Fact checking reveals that global trade was *slowing* for years before Trump was elected, and has been *growing* for the two years after he was inaugurated:

https://www.census.gov/foreign-trade/statistics/historical/gands.pdf

In 2014 US exports of goods and services were: $2.376 trillion and imports were $2.866 trillion. In 2016 US exports of goods and services *had fallen* to $2.216 trillion and imports *had fallen* to $2.719 trillion. Thus, for the two years prior to Trump's election, our exports *decreased* by $160.8 billion and imports *decreased* by $147.5 billion.

After Trump's election, trade *increased.* In 2018 US exports of goods and services *increased to* $2.501 trillion and imports *increased to* $3.129 trillion For the two years after Trump's election, our exports *increased* by $285 billion and our imports *increased* by $410 billion. I am not pleased that our imports grew 43% faster than exports for the first two years after Trump took office, but it is conclusive proof that Trump has not instigated a "trade war."

And where were the Free Trade Mavens when the economy really did collapse in 2008 at a time when we had more supposedly "free trade" with more countries than at any previous time? According to them, free trade never wrecks the economy when we fall into a real Great Recession but always triggers a "fake news recession" that never materializes.

"Where we are..."

If we could first know where we are, and whither we are tending, we could then better judge what to do, and how to do it.

We are now far into the fifth year, since a policy was initiated, with the avowed object, and confident promise, of putting an end to slavery agitation. Under the operation of that policy, that agitation has not only, not ceased, but has constantly augmented. In my opinion, it will not cease, until a crisis shall have been reached, and passed. A house divided against itself cannot stand.

I believe this government cannot endure, permanently half slave and half free. I do not expect the Union to be dissolved -- I do not expect the house to fall -- but I do expect it will cease to be divided. It will become all one thing or all the other.

- *Abraham Lincoln, June 16, 1858*

Political controversies anticipate the future. In 1858 Mr. Lincoln became alarmed by the sudden expansion of slavery that, by the revocation of the Missouri Compromise, had suddenly burst beyond its agreed-upon limits. He correctly foresaw that a danger zone had been entered that would provoke a crisis resulting in the country becoming "all one thing or the other."

Of course, globalism cannot be compared to slavery. Globalism leans more towards the utopian dream of mankind living together in harmony under a One World Government. National boundaries are to fade away. People will be free to seek their fortunes at any place on earth without having to clear through any country's customs and immigration. Goods and services will move as transparently between nations as they do between one town and the next. A benevolent government of the best and brightest in politics, multinational big business, and academia will govern in the best interests of society.

The first question that comes to mind is, "Where have we heard *that* before?" Every empire in history has promised to govern benevolently in the best interests of society, and every empire has failed to do that, and has been dissolved. That is because a "benevolent government" of the supposed best and brightest in politics, business, and academia will always govern in the best interests of *itself*. The elites and those connected to them prosper from the government's ability to tax and regulate business, and award government favors

48

to cronies, while the un-connected who work the small business, farms, factories, and offices are ignored. Even if the empire is relatively benevolent, people feel stifled and want out of it. The peoples of the United States and other parts of the British commonwealth established their independence as soon as they were strong enough to break the ties to kings and queens.

We don't have kings and queens controlling us anymore, but we do have imperialists in big government, big business, academia, and the media who want to rule the world without the people's consent, in the same way the old-time monarchs did. They seek to control the thoughts and actions of the people of the world by establishing unelected supranational bureaucracies of regulators and judges that make the law without being held accountable to people:

https://www.wsj.com/articles/italys-new-threat-to-the-euro-1527539789

The rejection of a populist coalition may stoke more populism.

May 28, 2018

Italian President Sergio Mattarella [in Italy, the president is appointed, not elected] rejected the populist right-left coalition's attempt to form a government on Sunday, explaining that it threatened Italy's participation in the euro.

It's hard to imagine a more highhanded elite dismissal of public opinion than Mr. Mattarella's diktat…. The [Italian] President has now handed the populists more evidence that the elites don't trust the Italian people…. The political result after this latest display of elitist disdain may be worse for Italy and the euro.

Globalists have been working just as tirelessly to overturn the election results of Brexit in the UK and Donald Trump in the USA -- where our homegrown Globalists tried to subvert our election even before the votes were counted, as advocated in the ***National Review***:

https://www.nationalreview.com/2016/10/replace-donald-trump-electoral-college-ballots/

October 11, 2016…the crucial fact remains that it's not too late to replace Trump. While it is too late to remove his name from the ballot, fortunately for us, the real election takes place on December 19 when the Electoral College meets. There's plenty of time to replace a candidate before then.

Globalists would like to create a world where public opinion is manipulated, and when necessary suppressed, by unelected authorities chosen from the boards of multinational corporations, government bureaucrats, government-sanctioned media, and academics. They want a world where all nations' laws are subject to review by The World Court, and where people in every country can be fined or imprisoned by a World Ministry of Social Justice for uttering any dissenting opinion that Globalists decide is "hate speech." Globalists would like to make admission to universities and employment, as well as permission to run for public office, contingent on a person parroting the Globalists' politically correct agendas.

The world that Globalists want to create is not only oppressive, but also unstable. It has resulted in slow growth, massive dis-employment of formerly prosperous people, financial collapses, currency crises, Great Recessions, and mountains of debt that can never be repaid. Globalism creates unstable economies that will lead to financial collapse, and oppressive societies controlled by unelected and unaccountable elites.

That is why globalism is being rejected in the USA, the UK, and elsewhere. Like slavery in 1858, it has burst beyond the limits that the people will tolerate.

The Gray Champion

Donald Trump was elected President in 2016, despite skepticism about his temperament. The reason can be seen in a 30-second clip, in which a working mom at the U.S. Steel plant in Granite City, Illinois thanks President Trump for bringing her job back:

https://youtu.be/Syzo-6dMoso?t=2659

It's a simple story of an American mom going back to work after two years of layoffs caused by imports of subsidized foreign steel. She's working again because President Trump imposed tariffs on imported foreign steel. The lady talks about what a job means to her and her family, and thanks President Trump for bringing hers back.

Globalism was sold on the promise of prospering people like her. We were told they would be working to produce exports to other countries. Instead, millions like her lost their livelihoods when Globalists moved their jobs to Mexico and China. Rather than admit their mendacity, Globalists blamed this woman. According to Globalist propaganda, she and millions of others had become obsolete and could not compete with foreigners who worked for less money. Globalists say we must save the United States from people like her by opening the borders to repopulate the country with foreigners who work cheaper than Americans.

The harm Globalism is inflicting on average Americans of modest means is there for all to see. Globalists transform value-creating economies that produce useful goods and services into "financialized" economies based on real estate inflation, financial shenanigans, public and private debt, and government bureaucracies and government-funded "education" and healthcare. The rise of a "populist" Republican president who would confront the Globalists has been predicted for decades. I saw it coming in 2013:

> "Mr. Trump occupies an important place in the political spectrum --- that of being a Republican Populist. He understands that if we're ever going to get our economy back on its feet the wage-earning middle class will have to prosper along with investors, who are recovering our fortunes in the stock market.

"Generational historians" William Strauss and Neil Howe employed forward-looking generational history analysis to predict the rise of a Trump-like figure their books *Generations and The Fourth Turning* published in 1993 and 1997.

https://www.amazon.com/Generations-History-Americas-Future-1584/dp/0688119123/

https://www.amazon.com/Fourth-Turning-History-Americas-Rendezvous-ebook/dp/B001RKFU4I/

The Fourth Turning is a Crisis, a decisive era of secular upheaval, when the values regime propels the replacement of the old civic order with a new one.

In retrospect, the spark might seem as ominous as a financial crash, as ordinary as a national election, or as trivial as a Tea Party.

...Before long, America's old civic order will seem ruined beyond repair. People will feel like a magnet has passed over society's disk drive, blanking out the social contract, wiping out old deals, clearing the books of vast unpayable promises to which people had once felt entitled. The economy could reach a trough that may look to be the start of a depression. With American weaknesses newly exposed, foreign dangers could erupt.

...a national election will produce a sweeping political realignment, as one faction or coalition capitalizes on a new public demand for decisive action. Republicans, Democrats, or perhaps a new party will decisively win the long partisan tug-of-war, ending the era of split government that had lasted through four decades of Awakening and Unraveling.

If the Crisis catalyst comes on schedule, around the year 2005, **then the climax will be due around 2020, the resolution around 2026.**

Strauss, William. The Fourth Turning: What the Cycles of History Tell Us About America's Next Rendezvous with Destiny (p. 276-307). Crown/Archetype. Kindle Edition.

They recalled Nathanial Hawthorne's story of the "Gray Champion" they felt would be elected around 2020 to end the oppression of the Globalist governing establishments, just as Hawthorne's original "Gray Champion" liberated New England from the tyranny of Britain's king:

https://americanliterature.com/author/nathaniel-hawthorne/short-story/the-gray-champion

The Gray Champion by Nathanial Hawthorne

"THERE WAS a time, when New-England groaned under heavier wrongs than those that brought the Revolution."

The King had ordered his army to suppress the Colonies. An old man whom no one knew stepped forth from the crowd. Alone, he commanded the King's Army to halt:

"The eye, the face, and attitude of command; the solemn, yet warlike peal of that voice, fit either to rule a host in the battle-field or be raised to God in prayer, were irresistible. At the old man's word and outstretched arm, the roll of the drum was hushed at once, and the advancing line stood still. A tremulous enthusiasm seized upon the multitude. That stately form, combining the leader and the saint.... could only belong to some old champion of the righteous cause, whom the oppressor's drum had summoned from his grave. They raised a shout of awe and exultation and looked for the deliverance of New-England."

The story foretells the return of the Gray Champion at times of extreme distress:

And when our fathers were toiling at the breast-work on Bunker's Hill, all through that night, the old warrior walked his rounds. Long, long may it be, ere he comes again! His

hour is one of darkness, and adversity, and peril. But should domestic tyranny oppress us, or the invader's step pollute our soil, still may the Gray Champion come.

Trump seemed prepared to assume that mantle:

Donald Trump's Inaugural Address, January 21, 2017

For too long, a small group in our nation's Capital has reaped the rewards of government while the people have borne the cost. Washington flourished -- but the people did not share in its wealth. Politicians prospered -- but the jobs left, and the factories closed.

The establishment protected itself, but not the citizens of our country. Their victories have not been your victories; their triumphs have not been your triumphs; and while they celebrated in our nation's capital, there was little to celebrate for struggling families all across our land....

But for too many of our citizens, a different reality exists: Mothers and children trapped in poverty in our inner cities; rusted-out factories scattered like tombstones across the landscape of our nation; an education system flush with cash, but which leaves our young and beautiful students deprived of knowledge; and the crime and gangs and drugs that have stolen too many lives and robbed our country of so much unrealized potential.

This American carnage stops right here and stops right now.

We are one nation -- and their pain is our pain. Their dreams are our dreams; and their success will be our success. We share one heart, one home, and one glorious destiny.

The oath of office I take today is an oath of allegiance to all Americans.

For many decades, we've enriched foreign industry at the expense of American industry; subsidized the armies of other countries while allowing for the very sad depletion of our military; we've defended other nation's borders while refusing to defend our own; and spent trillions of dollars overseas while America's infrastructure has fallen into disrepair and decay.

...Every decision on trade, on taxes, on immigration, on foreign affairs, will be made to benefit American workers and American families. We must protect our borders from the ravages of other countries making our products, stealing our companies, and destroying our jobs.

.... We will bring back our jobs. We will bring back our borders. We will bring back our wealth. And we will bring back our dreams.

Globalists tried to excuse their defeat by Trump in 2016 by blaming the people they put out of work for "not retraining to attain the skills required in a global economy." They still have not come to terms with why Trump and people who align with his views on reining in detrimental immigration and trade were elected. While many factors have been working to undermine the social and economic order, some blame must be allocated to the failure of globalism to live up to its promises. President Bill Clinton spoke eloquently of the promise of globalism to deliver a world of peace and prosperity when he celebrated the arrival of the new millennium in 2000:

We are fortunate to be alive at this moment in history. Never before has our nation enjoyed, at once, so much prosperity and social progress with so little internal crisis and so few external threats. My fellow Americans, we have crossed the bridge to the twenty-first century.

Alas, the "pro-growth" agenda promised by Globalists didn't pan out. On the shocking election night of 2016, a Dailykos blogger explained to dejected Democrats why Ms. Clinton lost:

People are suffering financially in ways that we haven't seen since the 1920s.... The country is still poor. The job market still s----. Bernie tapped into that anger and so did Trump. This was a referendum on poverty and what causes it.

People can see that our economy has not grown as anticipated from the globalist-mandated expansion of immigration and imported goods. The 2000s have been a period of recessionary slow growth --- massive dis-employment of Americans via {downsizing, offshoring, outsourcing, work force reductions, involuntary early retirements}; a stock market collapse in 2000; a housing bust and Great Recession with another stock market collapse in 2008, and slow growth ever since. We have added trillions of government debt and unfunded liabilities debt to our national balance sheet since 2000 and called it "growth."

People are fed up not only with the nonsense, but also with the arrogant way the Establishment presents it: "Don't worry about the American middle class losing their jobs and incomes. If these people don't know how to compete in a global economy, then they should retrain to become coders or business owners."

But how many Globalists, who make their nests in the lavishly paid bureaucracies of corporations, government, and academia, would ever "retrain" to be a coder, or take the risk to become a business owner? They would not do it. They use their connections to enrich themselves with comfortable low-risk "work" in government, government-funded positions in academia, and crony capitalist government-protected jobs in multinational corporations.

Advocates for globalism insisted that it had no harmful effects, or that if it did, it was the people's fault for not upgrading their skills "to compete in a global economy." However, political analysts who had their ears to the ground knew better. As Democrat activist Michael Moore explained months before the 2016 election, it was inevitable that Donald Trump would win:

https://michaelmoore.com/trumpwillwin/

5 Reasons Why Trump Will Win

Michael Moore

Midwest Math, or Welcome to Our Rust Belt Brexit.

Trump is going to focus much of his attention on the four blue states in the Rustbelt of the upper Great Lakes – Michigan, Ohio, Pennsylvania, and Wisconsin. Four traditionally Democratic states.... How can the race be this close...? Well maybe it's because he's said (correctly) that the Clintons' support of NAFTA helped to destroy the industrial states of the Upper Midwest. Trump is going to hammer Clinton on this and her support of TPP and other trade policies that have royally screwed the people of these four states.

And this is where the math comes in. In 2012, Mitt Romney lost by 64 electoral votes. Add up the electoral votes cast by Michigan, Ohio, Pennsylvania, and Wisconsin. It's 64. All Trump needs to win.

It happened the way Moore said it would. Trump won the three states Moore mentioned plus Iowa, Florida, Ohio, and one Congressional district in Maine, that had voted Democratic in 2012. One hundred electoral votes flipped, according to Michael Moore, because sixty million people in the thousand-mile industrial heartland between the

Delaware River in Pennsylvania and the Des Moines River in Iowa felt that their livelihoods had been destroyed by detrimental trade and illegal immigration.

In 2016, Globalists discovered that blaming American workers for the failure of Globalists' fraudulent policies does not make for effective propaganda. They are now trying to protect themselves with mendacity and obfuscation by:

- Pretending their theories are correct and seeking to obscure them with disinformation and tortured data.

- "Moving the goalposts" of scoring their theories. They told us in the 1990s that globalism would create trade surpluses and "millions of well-paying jobs for American workers." Now they tell us that globalism is good because it lets us buy cheap junk from other countries that restrict access of American products to their markets.

- Feigning sympathy for "those left behind," because after 2016 Globalists understand that the tens of millions of people harmed by their policies are voting against them.

This has worked to some degree because Trump was defeated in 2020. Globalists received help from a Globalist disease called COVID-19, which like most everything else we consume, originated in China. Globalists first parroted the Chinese and World Health Organization (largely funded by China) propaganda that the "virus can't be transmitted by humans, so it is perfectly safe to travel to China, and welcome Chinese travelers into our countries." Then, when the virus became impossible to ignore, they imposed lockdowns to confine Americans inside our homes. These same Globalist elites who'd been telling us we have no way to enforce our immigration laws "because walls don't work" were delighted to send their police out to arrest American citizens who ventured beyond the four walls of our homes.

Trump was not re-elected, but his skepticism of globalism remains. As Florida Senator Rick Scott said:

One thing that President Trump has done over the last five years is kind of reset the view of a lot of Republican politicians and help them understand the views of Republican voters. He helped reset the Republican agenda. We now are putting Americans first. We're standing up to China. We are standing up for our trade interests to make sure that we're not just giving away our prosperity.

President Trump stood up to all of establishment Washington and said, 'no.' The GOP will not win the future by trying to go back to where the Republican Party used to be.

Liberal Globalism

Our new president's family has earned much of its income from China, Russia, and other dodgy countries, so we might expect the worst effects of globalism to be amped up. Let's try to understand the motives of the various globalist tribes who will be out in full cry.

Many Liberals believe, as many Conservatives do, that globalism is the most efficient means for generating global peace and prosperity. However, they never sell globalism to the American people on that basis. They always sell it on the promise that globalism will prosper Americans, especially American middle-class industrial workers. It's only after Americans are severely harmed by the removal of their jobs overseas, or have their jobs taken by immigrants who work cheaper, that Liberals trot out the "I'd like to teach the world to sing" happy talk.

Liberal Globalism often contains an anti-American component that seeks to blame the United States for other countries' problems. Liberal Globalists say things like:

- *There needs to be a serious focus in US foreign policy to help stabilize governments teetering on collapse or we will see ever-increasing and growing exodus of people fleeing [those countries and immigrating illegally to the United States].*
- *Focusing on the border is not a solution and is far too reactive to a growing problem in our hemisphere needing a pro-active foreign policy response.*
- *Our insatiable demand for illegal drugs has totally corrupted the Americas.*
- *The only real way of dealing with 'illegal immigration' is for us to stop using illegal drugs.*

In other words, it's our fault that other countries are undesirable places to live, so we are obligated to let the world's poor into the United States. The conflation of illegal immigration with Americans' usage of illegal drugs is favored by Liberals as a method of obfuscating and deflecting attention away from securing the border. One of my Liberal friends insisted that we should not control the border until we begin executing drug sellers and drug users! He knows that executions for drug offenses will never happen, and because that will never happen, the border should never be controlled. Liberals are past masters of inventing wordy arguments that make no senses. Since most Liberals favor illegal immigration, they allocate their wordy arguments toward excusing it in order that it should continue.

When other countries take advantage of us in trade, the Liberal Globalist response is that other countries are superior to us. According to Liberals, Chinese, Mexicans, Japanese, and Europeans run a combined $800 billion trade surplus with us because they produce superior products that Americans want to buy. According to Liberals, it is never the case that these countries run trade surpluses because they refuse to buy American-made products.

Liberals use Globalism to promote their doctrine that the United States is a racist country. They want to load the country with tens millions of Latin Americans and Middle Easterners so they can indoctrinate them into believing that the United States discriminates against Latin Americans and Middle Easterners. The Liberal idea is that immigrants should vote for Liberal candidates because they are the only people in America who aren't racists. As the UK Guardian recently wrote in its United States edition:

Democrats are not going to win over enough "moderate Republicans" to defeat Trump. Nor will suburban white mothers do the trick. The only way to win in 2020 is by mobilizing (potential) new voters and (recent) non-voters. Fortunately, there are more than enough of them. Almost half of Americans do not vote. However, new voters and non-voters are disproportionately non-white and non-suburban.

Liberals advocate Globalism to repopulate the United States with "new voters" they think will be more friendly to their causes. "If we believe in free movement of goods and services across borders, we must also have free movement of people!" Liberals are so interested in bringing in tens of millions of foreigners, that they have reversed their prior propaganda about the United States being an overpopulated country that hogs too much of the worlds' resources and is killing the earth with pollution. The Liberal mania for planned parenthood and population control has been replaced with the propaganda that the United States is an underpopulated country that needs tens of more foreign-born immigrants to fill it up.

Liberals are also into "virtue signaling" to assert superiority among themselves over other people. "We are not narrow-minded American patriots, but peoples of the world." There is also a feeling among Liberals that Americans have too high a standard of living.

We should reduce it to be more like the poorer parts of the world. As Liberal Globalist Robert Reich says:

Why Can't We Be Content with Less?

The second painful adjustment for most people will be to a standard of living that's even more significantly lower than that attained by America's rich.

This is quite the opposite from how Liberals sell globalism on the false pretense a means of boosting American workers' pay. As soon as the trade treaties are signed, Liberals tell American workers they must take a pay cut because somebody in Mexico or China or Cambodia will work cheaper. But jobs that Liberals prefer, such a government employment, educators, and media pundits should remain lucrative professions.

However, Liberal Globalists have recently become alarmed when people in industrial areas vote them out of office. They have started pretending to care about America's industrial workers --- the same people they've spent the last twenty years castigating as "dumb, lazy, over-paid, mal-educated, backward-looking hicks who don't deserve to have jobs in a global economy." I don't for a moment believe that Globalists really care whether these 65 million people in the industrial heartland of the USA live or die, but they do care about their 99 electoral votes which flipped from Democrat Obama in 2012 to Republican Populist Trump in 2016. So, they are seeking to win back those electoral votes by pretending to care about the voters who live in those states. As, expected, the Liberal Globalists "care" nostrums bear a heavy dose of big-government Liberalism:

https://www.wsj.com/articles/wage-stagnation-is-everyones-problem-1534287594

Wage Stagnation Is Everyone's Problem

Low working- and middle-class incomes aren't likely to rise without new [government] subsidies.

By William A. Galston

Aug. 14, 2018

In the past two decades there has been a sharp drop in the share of national income going to working- and middle-class Americans. As the discontent among these workers begins to affect their livelihoods and the entire nation's politics, policy makers must either hope the market will somehow fix wage stagnation or enact policies to reverse it.

It may be true that trade leaves countries better off in general. But this is small comfort to those who lose out, especially because the winners rarely compensate them commensurately. The promise of job training rings hollow to workers in areas dependent on industries that have been decimated by trade. A system of wage insurance would also help workers by narrowing the gap between disappearing high-wage jobs and the lower-wage alternatives that displaced workers often adopt.

There is only one way to go. The high-earning Americans who have done so well in recent decades must pay higher taxes to support the portion of the workforce that is falling behind. This isn't charity, nor is it welfare. It's simple common sense, or self-interest rightly understood, because an economic system that fails to offer broad gains will end up with disruption.

What Should Be Done: A New Deal for the Middle Class

The most immediate way to reestablish shared prosperity is through a "reverse income tax" that supplements the wages of the middle class.

Under my plan, full-time workers earning $20,000 or less (this and all subsequent outlays are in 2009 dollars) would receive a wage supplement of $15,000.

The tax rate for full-time workers with incomes between $50,000 and $90,000—whether the source of those incomes are wages, salaries, or capital gains—would be cut to 10 percent of earnings. The taxes for people with incomes of between $90,000 and $160,000 would be 20 percent, whatever the income source.

They propose "wage insurance" to shield the Americans from the effects of having their jobs destroyed by Globalist policies:

One piece of such a reemployment system would be wage insurance. Any job loser who takes a new job that pays less than his or her former job would be eligible for 90 percent of the difference, for up to two years. After two years, many workers would have acquired enough on-the-job training to render them sufficiently productive to warrant wages nearly as high as the wages they formerly had on the job they lost.

Liberal Globalists want us to spend trillions of dollars to fix the trade problems they created! That should give pause to Conservatives who think they got a swell deal on buying a can of Chinese tuna for fifty cents, or a Mexican-made washing machine for $400. Not only did you buy low-quality products, but you empowered Liberals to run around saying that we need to raise taxes to create more government give-away programs for America's working people who lost their jobs to excessive imports and immigration. Are you proud of what you've done?

Libertarian Globalism

Libertarians think that Globalism will further their interests by undermining the ability of governments to interfere with private transactions. They are prone to saying: "If everybody maximizes their self-interest, free from excessive government restraint, then they will maximize the wellbeing of the entire society." They believe they should be able to buy and sell whatever they like from whomever they like, including foreign nations.

However, the Libertarian notion that "transactions are voluntary associations that only concern the buyer and seller" is naïve. Companies are not permitted to engage in anti-competitive practices that harm all of society, even if the buyer and seller agree to it among themselves. For example, it is illegal for a newspaper or other publication to offer an exclusive advertising contract for one of its customers, while denying similar ads to competitors. Newspapers serve a public market, not just individual customers. All entities who conduct business in public markets have rights protected by commercial laws.

Municipal laws do not allow proprietors of unlicensed flea markets to set up shop on Main Street and start peddling merchandise of dubious origin. The other merchants in town, who maintain store fronts and pay property taxes, have a say in setting the conditions under which business must be conducted in the municipality.

Besides encouraging criminal activity by selling stolen merchandise, unlicensed flea markets would put competitive pressure on the reputable business owners in town who invest in property for their storefronts and pay taxes to support the police, firefighters, libraries, and schools. Those businesses could not compete with flea markets that pay no property taxes, have no legal employees, and sell stolen merchandise. In time the legitimate businesses would close, and the town would look like a Third World shack town. People could not make a living through legitimate business ownership and employment, so they would join the mafia. Extortion rackets, kidnappings, robberies, prostitution, and selling drugs would proliferate. Gangs would terrorize the community. The USA would become just like all those Third World countries that people want to get away from.

Companies cannot legally sell merchandise below cost to bankrupt competitors and establish monopolies. Our antitrust laws do not permit these predatory practices to take place among American companies, so why should we permit Chinese companies to engage in them in our market?

Libertarians vociferously oppose restrictions on imports. They presume the right to buy anything from a foreign country, regardless of whether the foreign country buys anything from us. They think they should have a right import merchandise, without restrictions, from countries that **don't** invest in the USA, **don't** employ American workers, **don't** contract with American suppliers, **don't** pay taxes to American governments, and **don't** abide by American worker safety, environmental, and wage and hour laws --- and in the case of China and Japan steal our companies' product designs, copy them, and sell them back for us at a lower price that does not have to cover the R&D expense of the products they stole.

Libertarians often fantasize that "American businesses move production to emerging economies overseas that have less restrictive policies and better profit opportunity than investing in the USA."

https://www.wsj.com/articles/the-lefts-idea-of-generosity-11549228822

Energy-intensive manufacturing jobs, which traditionally have offered good salaries and benefits, are at risk from overseas competitors with a less hostile political environment, like China.

China is a country with a dictator for life whose government orders arbitrary arrests of foreign businesspeople, like recently arrested Canadians, tries them in a kangaroo court, and holds them in jail for years. It's a country that demands that companies that want to sell in China must produce in China with a Chinese partner to acquire their trade secrets and intellectual properties, so that China's industrial spies don't have to go to the trouble of stealing them. Then they must return cash to China by shipping surplus production to the USA and Europe.

Emerging markets rarely respect private property rights the way we respect them in the United States. Their governments are often corrupt. They impose regulations that make them silent partners in business, their currencies are unstable, their taxes are high, and their people are too poor to have the buying power that enables companies to make significant profits. Investors who buy stocks of companies in emerging markets usually lose their capital --- a story that is playing out yet again as these words are being written. The primary profit opportunity in emerging markets is to produce products with cheap labor and import them into the United States.

Most of what Libertarians say about foreign markets is based on ignorance. They complain that the United States has "the highest income taxes in the world" while not knowing that other countries impose 20% VAT taxes on every product sold in those countries, and $5 / gallon equivalent gasoline taxes. The USA is lightly taxed in comparison to other countries, and even more so now that the Tax Reform of 2017 has been passed.

Libertarians have never done business in these oppressive countries they worship as meccas of libertarian free enterprise. Common sense alone should tell them that if these countries really had free economies that generated superior wealth, then their people would not be running away from them as fast as they could and trying to infiltrate the USA.

Thus, the Libertarian idea that people should be able to unconditionally buy anything they want from anyone tax-free or tariff-free is unrealistic. It is not allowed at the local level, and there is no reason to believe it should be allowed at the national level. All business includes public interests as well as the private interests of the buyer and seller. We have every right to elect Presidents and Congresses who will protect our livelihoods from the shady foreign flea market operators of the world. Even the old-time Southern slaveholders agreed to outlaw the practice of importing more slaves from African in 1809 even though they were cheaper than the ones already here.

"You're a Luddite! (a person who cherishes the inefficiencies of the past)," retort the Free Trade Libertarians when people object to moving American industries overseas. "Don't you know that manufacturing is obsolete? If it can be done in cheap-labor countries, then that is where it should be done! Americans need to get over the loss of manufacturing and move on to other lines of work that can't be shipped overseas. Don't you know that people who used to make buggy-whips moved on to higher value jobs working in industry, and that most people used to be farmers? And now that the manufacturing jobs have gone overseas, we'll move to a services economy. People will become bankers, scientists, doctors, engineers, and spreadsheet jockeys!"

My objections to this reasoning are:

1. Free Trade Libertarians do not understand that American workers migrated away slowly, over a period of about 150 years, from the old farm and buggy-whip trades. We did not suddenly decide to pack up every farm in America and move them all to Mexico and China all at once. An economy may sort itself out according to free market principles over time, but it cannot sort itself out all at once. We had severe economic problems when we transitioned away from agricultural employment even when it was spread out over a century and a half. We are having more severe problems putting millions of industrial workers out of their jobs by removing their work overseas all at once.

2. Some Libertarians look down American blue-collar workers because they think they vote for big government Liberals and are prone to joining labor unions. Regardless of how they vote, they are our fellow ***Americans***, and deserve higher consideration than foreign peons.

3. Libertarians do not understand that it's not just industrial tradespeople who lose their jobs when factories move overseas. It's also highly skilled production planners, product design engineers, accountants, foremen, IT people, and the myriads of contractors and components suppliers required to make factories hum efficiently. Every time we move a factory overseas, we become poorer.

4. Free Trade Libertarians bring up the classic canard of horse-and-buggy-whip workers being replaced by motor vehicles when Henry Ford started up his auto factory. Note, however, that Henry Ford built his cars in **Detroit.** He did not fire all his buggy whip workers and move their jobs to Mexico because he wanted cheap labor.

5. Free Trade Libertarians want us to believe that American companies move to Mexico and China because they imagine that Mexico (which is bureaucratic and corrupt) and China (which is a military dictatorship) are oases of freedom far superior to the taxed-and-regulated USA. In truth companies move production to Mexico and China to access cheap labor, and in the case of China, Japan, and the E.U. because their governments demand that certain product categories that are sold in their countries must be made in those countries. Libertarians do not understand that even if we reduced taxes and regulations to zero, our companies would still move work overseas to replace $25 / hour American jobs with $2 /

hour foreign labor, and when other countries' governments demand that products that are sold in their countries must be produced there.

Libertarians are also naïve about believing that we can fight Chinese theft of our intellectual property (IP) by stealing American companies' technology and production processes, copying them into Chinese products, then producing them cheap and underselling us on world markets. "Let's stop the Chinese from stealing our products, so we can keep buying everything cheap from them," is the Libertarian view. Since the Chinese don't care about American courts, they will continue to steal our IP, copy it, and undersell us on world markets. That will never be stopped by anything we say, but only by what we do to keep their products out of our market. We can't stop the Chinese from stealing our IP, or pirating our companies' software, but we can keep them from using it against us.

The only product I have ever heard Libertarians and Economic Conservatives want to ban from importation are pharma products. They say that buying pharma products cheap from overseas would cause American companies to cut back on research and development, since there would be less profits to be made here. But they do not care at all about every other industry cutting back its research and development because foreign companies produce it for less, often after stealing the patented technology from an American company that spent millions on R&D to develop it and bring it to market.

Thus, I do not follow the Libertarian view that we should unconditionally admit all other countries' products into the USA tariff-free.

I do not want tariff-free trade with the E.U. and Japan, because those are crony capitalist cartels of state-run enterprises that exclude American products from their markets.

I do not want tariff-free trade with China because it is a cheap labor hole AND a cartel of state-run enterprises that are only interest in stealing American products, then underselling us on world markets, including our own.

I *do* want tariff-free trade with Canada, Australia, Singapore, and any other countries that trade fairly and have a neutral balance of trade with us. If the other countries like China, Japan, and the E.U. mend their ways and start buying reciprocally, then I would desire that the tariffs be removed. If our companies ever stop using Mexico as a base for beating Americans out of their jobs, then I would like tariff-free trade with Mexico.

I believe that trade with other countries should be based on the pragmatic principle of balanced trade whereby our exports and imports are approximately equal. I do not accept the Libertarian notion that tariff-free trade is unequivocally beneficial with all nations, and especially not with untrustworthy ones like China.

Perhaps the ultimate fallback of the Libertarian view is that they are prone to seeing the trade deficit as a vehicle to avoid paying taxes to fund our federal government, since products imported into the USA are mostly taxed at their points of production, and not when sold here. Their view is that the way to shrink the federal government is to deny it revenue. So, import as much as we can to avoid paying taxes in the USA.

My view is that even if this theory had merit, it inflicts too much collateral damage on the American people to be worthwhile. We are running near-trillion trade and federal budget deficits. If that continues, the more likely outcome is that Socialists will be elected to govern the USA, and that taxes will be raised on domestic production, consumption, and incomes, to fund the government. Trade deficits expand government by removing people from gainful employment and making them dependent on government hand-outs.

I keep warning Libertarians that big business and multinational corporations are not their friends. The people who run these companies are crony capitalists who seek favors from government. Their motive is to lobby government to impose restrictions on their competitors' businesses, while giving theirs a free pass. Big business is no friend of Conservatives. In 2016 two members of the Wall Street Journal's Editorial Board endorsed Hillary Clinton. Several others urged the Republicans to mount a sort of military coup to depose Trump and nominate a military person in his place. Now it is February 2019, and the Wall Street Journal is already talking up Senator Amy Klobuchar, a Liberal Democrat, to be president in 2020.

Big businesspeople are anti-competitive favor-seekers of big government. They are no friends of Libertarians and Conservatives.

Socialist Globalism

Libertarians need to understand that Globalism is driving people and the governments they elect toward hard-left socialism:

https://www.wsj.com/articles/europes-struggling-political-parties-promise-a-return-to-the-1970s-11561561071?mod=hp_lead_pos5

Europe's Struggling Political Parties Promise a Return to the Pre-Thatcherite Era

To fend off populists, once-dominant parties are overthrowing decades of orthodoxy, amounting to the biggest policy shift in decades

By Bojan Pancevski

June 26, 2019

BERLIN—To win voters lost to an anti-globalization backlash, Europe's mainstream parties are going back to the 1970s.

In Germany, the U.K, Denmark, France and Spain, these parties are aiming to reverse decades of pro-market policy and promising greater state control of business and the economy, more welfare benefits, bigger pensions and higher taxes for corporations and the wealthy. Some have discussed nationalizations and expropriations.

Globalization narrows the economy by destroying the industrial and trades businesses, thereby making the middle class poorer and more enthusiastic for big government socialism to tide them over the loss of opportunities to work in the private sector. Don't ever forget that Globalists consist of government-funded politicians, bureaucrats, academics, and corporation executives who depend on access to governments, and often subsidies from governments. Socialism is defined as government ownership of the economy, or at least government oversight of it, and that is precisely what Globalists are after.

Also remember that the people Globalists prefer to bring in here across open borders are the indigent and under-educated who will work cheaper than Americans. Those people are brought in here and inculcated with an entitlement attitude by Globalists who want them to vote Socialist. If we are giving these indigent immigrants everything for free, then the citizens of the country are going to demand equivalent government funding for their social welfare needs. Libertarians who think they're getting a deal on cheap labor and cheap imports may find themselves ground underfoot by Globalist-imposed socialist economies that tax most of their income and regulate them intensively. Selling out your country and your fellow citizens for what Libertarians think is cheap labor and cheap imports is a devil's bargain.

Corporate Globalism

When multinational corporation managements promote "free trade" deals they sell them to the public by claiming that they are promoting the public interest of putting Americans to work producing products in the United States that will be exported to foreign countries. That is rarely, if ever, what they intend to do. Corporations desire to make product in low-wage countries, sell it in high-wage countries, and avoid paying taxes on the profits. It is more profitable to pay Chinese or Mexicans $1.50 / hour and sell to Americans who earn $25.00 than to pay Americans $25.00 to sell to Chinese or Mexicans who earn $1.50.

When dealing with China, American companies are usually forbidden to produce in the United States and export to China. The Chinese government says: "If you want to sell in China, you must produce in China. You must generate a trade surplus for China by exporting to the United States." The United States does not make similar demands on companies that sell in the United States. American companies are therefore pressured to close their American factories, fire their American employees, move the work to China, and export product to the United States.

Over time, fewer and fewer Americans have jobs that pay $25.00. The Chinese never earn more than $1.50 / hour, because there will always be a surplus of hundreds of millions of Chinese farm laborers who come to the cities desperate for work for low wages.

Nor do American CEOs seem to care if the Chinese demand that the American company turn over its production designs for the Chinese to copy and later use to undersell the American company on world markets and even in the USA. CEOs are also gullible about over-estimating the profits they are going to make in a foreign country. They often make a lot less than they think, because the foreign government is not going to allow an American company to extract profits from their people, the way we allow foreign companies to extract profits from ours. Countries like Mexico and China devalue their currencies periodically, and the profits that were supposedly made there go up in smoke.

Free trade agreements make the destruction of American jobs a first choice rather than a last resort. Given a choice of investing in upgrading an American plant or moving the work to low-wage Mexico and China, a company will often opt to move the work overseas. If the price of energy or raw materials goes up, the company will often try to offset the cost increase by moving American's jobs to low-wage countries, rather than waiting to see if the markets will turn around and lower the prices of the raw materials. If management encounters setbacks in their business plan, they may move the work to Mexico and China and hope that cheap labor makes up for management's inability to execute its business plan.

Our "free trade agreements" therefore have the following characteristics:

1. The trade between the USA and other countries, which was often a surplus in our favor **before** the trade agreement was signed, almost always goes into deficit as soon as "free trade" is signed. Whenever a free trade or GATT trade deal is signed, companies leave the USA and start producing in foreign countries where the labor is cheap. Thus, we manufacture less product in the USA and import more from abroad.

2. Few countries honor the treaties. We have GATT trade with Germany and China. Their imports enter the USA at a maximum of 2.5% tariff. They tax our imports of our products at up 10% in Germany and 25% in China. Most nations use informal trade barriers, such as cartels that only buy from each other and never from foreigners, to keep our products from entering their countries. Some, like China, only buy token amounts of our products to reverse-engineer them, and sell them back to us at lower cost, since they did not invest the overhead in R&D to develop the product. "If you want to sell it in China, then you must make it in China, so we can steal it and sell it back to you."

3. These treaties destroy wealth by shifting $25 / hour jobs in the USA and Europe to $2 / hour jobs in Mexico and China. Trillions of dollars of wage-earning wealth is eliminated, and people's consumption is diminished when they lose their jobs. Without consumption, there can be no production. Each country piles up more inventories of unsold products that nobody at home or abroad can afford to buy. Then the world economy falls off a cliff.

4. The governments of the world try to sustain consumption artificially by piling on debt. Almost every country is piling up debt that it will never repay, especially the USA. When the interest on these unpayable principal debts becomes unpayable, the economy will collapse and return to the stone age.

5. Thus, free trade has become a vehicle for impoverishing the world. We have more Great Recessions and slower growth because of "free" trade and GATT trade than we had before them.

Multinational companies are also prone to setting up complex foreign subsidiaries to launder money through tax-free zones like Ireland and the Cayman Islands. "We don't have significant sales in Ireland or the Cayman Islands, but that's where we keep our subsidiaries that accumulate the profits. We load most of our costs on our subsidiaries in the USA, so we don't have to pay taxes here."

This tax avoidance increases the tax burden on domestic companies who are unable to engage in overseas tax avoidance, and it results in more borrowed money added to the national debt.

The things that matter to multinational corporations in free trade agreements are:

1. They can import foreign-made product into the USA without paying a tariff.
2. They can produce it in a Third World country that promises not to nationalize their factories or confiscate their offshore bank accounts.
3. They can pretend that the profits are made in overseas tax shelters, thereby enabling them to avoid paying taxes in the USA and Europe nations where the product is sold.
4. They can fire any American employees they have left in the United States and replace them with lower-paid foreigners brought into this country on H1-B visas under the pretension that "no American can do the work."
5. That no authority in any country can police the multinational corporations for money laundering, financial fraud, tax fraud, and illegal labor practices. All "free trade" treaties have a provision that sets up an "International Tribunal" appointed by multinational corporations (and bribed by them) to do the corporations' bidding.

Thus, "free trade" agreements exist for few good purposes and many bad ones.

Foreign Policy Globalism

In his Farewell Address, President Dwight Eisenhower, who led the combined forces of the USA, Britain, and Canada to victory in World War II, warned:

In the councils of government, we must guard against the acquisition of unwarranted influence, whether sought or unsought, by the military–industrial complex. The potential for the disastrous rise of misplaced power exists and will persist.

I don't believe Eisenhower meant that our military is aggressive in wanting to wage unnecessary wars. In war, our military does the fighting and dying. Our highest-ranking generals warn against military entanglements that have no strategic purpose commensurate with the cost in lives and treasure. Eisenhower was warning us against our Globalist Foreign Policy Establishment that wants us to defend every other country's borders except our own.

These days, the Globalist Foreign Policy Establishment has learned to invoke Russia's Vladimir Putin as a sort of latter-day Adolf Hitler who must be combatted in every corner of the world. "If we don't stop Putin at the Syrian border, he'll take over the world." Even though it is difficult to understand why Putin cares about a three-way war between Turkey, Syria, and the Kurds, whose insurgency spills across both countries' borders.

Foreign Policy Globalist have become apoplectic about wanting American troops to "defend Germany from Vladimir Putin" even though Germany refuses to pay the dues it promised NATO to defend itself. To hear our Globalist Foreign Policy Establishment tell it, Putin is champin' at the bit to invade Germany, even though the nearest Russian military base to Germany is the Russian exclave at Kaliningrad 450 miles away. The nearest mainland Russian armies are 850 miles and three international borders away from Germany. To get to Germany, Russia would have to fight its way through Belarus, Poland, and Lithuania, none of which post-Soviet Russia has attacked. A glance at a military map shows that Russian armies are not concentrated in the direction of Germany, but rather are dispersed along their 6,000-mile border, defending their country from intrusion by unauthorized immigrants, which our military says it cannot do to protect the United States.

Our Globalist Foreign Policy Establishment is nevertheless hooting against Trump for reallocating military funding to defend our American border, while reducing our troops deployed in Germany to "defend" from Russian armies 850 miles away. Globalists call the withdrawal of 9,500 troops from Germany --- who are being redeployed to Poland and Lithuania --- a "retreat:"

https://www.wsj.com/articles/retreat-from-germany-11591566310

Retreat from Germany

Withdrawing U.S. troops would be a win for Russia—and China.

By

The Editorial Board

June 7, 2020

There's been no official word or explanation. But the Journal reported Friday that Mr. Trump has ordered 9,500 of the 34,500 Americans stationed in Germany to leave by September. Troop levels in the country—the heart of America's presence in Europe— sometimes rise to more than 50,000. They now will be capped arbitrarily at 25,000. Some may be moved elsewhere in Europe, though infrastructure built over decades can't go with them.

Withdrawal is a gift to Vladimir Putin, who delights at divisions in NATO and has done nothing to warrant a drawdown of U.S. forces. The Russian military said Friday it is deploying a brigade with advanced equipment to the country's west. It's a reminder that Russia, despite being an economic backwater, still poses a significant military threat to Europe.

Germany is often a frustrating ally. The country spent an estimated 1.38% of gross domestic product on defense in 2019 and says it won't reach its 2% commitment until 2031. Mrs. Merkel has defied the U.S. and most of Europe in supporting the Nord Stream 2 gas pipeline, which would deepen the Continent's dependence on Russian energy.

Let's not forget that Germany is allied with Russia against the United States:

Germany threatens retaliation if U.S. sanctions [against Russia!] harm its firms

Gernot Heller, Alissa de Carbonnel /BRUSSELS (Reuters) -

Germany threatened on Friday to retaliate against the United States if new sanctions on Russia being proposed by the U.S. Senate end up penalizing German firms.

Obviously, Germany's government doesn't fear Russia if they want to do business with Russia while "retaliating" against us. So why do Foreign Policy Globalists pretend that Russia is a threat to Germany? It could be ideological inertia. We legitimately defended West Germany against the Soviet Union from 1945 to 1990, when Soviet / Russian armies were on West Germany's border, so perhaps Foreign Policy Globalists are merely intellectually lazy in thinking we should continue defending Germany from Russians 850 miles away from their border than even Germans do not believe are a threat.

There's also money. Our defense contractors and Germany's government are paying the Globalist Foreign Policy Establishment to pretend to believe that Russia threatens Germany. It's expensive to maintain American troops on foreign soil, and a lot of the funding paid for by American taxpayers goes to American and German businesses who pay our Globalist Foreign Policy consultants. Germany doesn't care about paying for their own defense because they'd rather spend their money on free college educations for all their young people, while young Americans, who are taxed to pay for America's and Germany's defense (against imaginary German enemies), come out of college loaded with lifetimes of debt burden. The European Union runs a $150 billion trade deficit with us. There's no reason why we should be spending any money defending them from imaginary enemies.

America's Globalist Foreign Policy Establishment likewise bangs the drums for hundreds of billions more money to "defend Japan from China" while demanding that we keep sending hundreds of billions of trade deficit dollars to those countries (mainly Japan, South Korea, Taiwan, and India) who are allied against us in trade. I don't mind at all being allies with these nations against military aggression from Russia and China. However, it's ludicrous for the United States to bear the lion's share of "defending" countries that are picking over the carcass of our declining economy. Let them balance the trade by buying as much from us as we buy from them, and paying a fair share for their defense, and then they will be true allies, worthy of our defending with our young people's blood if China or Russia attacks them.

The Globalist Foreign Policy Establishment pretends to care about defending every country except the United States, whose borders they want to keep open to invasion by unauthorized immigrants, including criminals and terrorists. Whether it is ideological laziness, or more payola by defense contractors and foreign governments, they are weakening us by making us waste our recourses defending against imaginary enemies on the other side of the world instead of real ones walking into our country across open borders.

Humanitarian Globalism

There is also a humanitarian aspect to globalism that motivates well-meaning people to desire our borders to be porous to foreign products and foreign peoples.

Most of us believe that to be a great nation America must also be a welcoming nation. We must not shut ourselves inside walls like an old hermit who builds walls around his beautiful garden to prevent the poor neighbors' children from playing on his property.

Keep, ancient lands, your storied pomp!" cries she [The Statue of Liberty]
With silent lips.
"Give me your tired, your poor,
Your huddled masses yearning to breathe free,
The wretched refuse of your teeming shore.
Send these, the homeless, tempest-tost to me,
I lift my lamp beside the golden door!"

Emma Lazarus wrote the poem in 1883 when the United States had arable farmland that could be given away free to qualified immigrants who agreed to settle it and farm it for a minimum of five years. Our free land was a guarantee that immigrants could be self-supporting.

Alas, our free land was all taken up by 1890, and thereafter there was no guarantee that immigrants could support themselves by living off the land. Severe economic depressions resulted from excessive immigration, beyond our ability to provide employment in urban jobs. We socialized much of the economy during the Great Depression of 1929-1941 to provide a subsistence living at government expense for millions of our own people and recent immigrants who could not find work.

Our economy can only absorb so many immigrants at any given time without degrading into unemployment, depression, and government welfare debt. The Great Recession of 2008 likewise followed a period of heavy immigration when the population swelled above our ability to employ people. Our own citizens suffered severely and ultimately elected Donald Trump to curtail excessive immigration. Humanitarian ideals thus ran up against practical constraints.

As we will see in *Part III. Immigration*, it is by no means certain that immigration adds net value to the country, at least not at this stage of history when we are fully developed with a densely populated urban economy. Immigration may be a merely redistributive process that depresses wages of American workers and re-allocates their income to business owners who hire immigrants on the cheap. There is no humanitarianism involved in taking way the wealth of a middle-class American citizen and handing to an employer who replaces the American citizen with a cheap-labor immigrant.

It is also obvious that we cannot absorb every person in the world who wants to immigrate to the United States. Yet humanitarian globalists have assisted conservative, liberal, and corporation Globalists in creating open borders and encouragement, of illegal immigration.

Shouldn't we expect countries whose people want to flee to the U.S. to put their own houses in order? Most poor countries have cultures that perpetuate poverty. Latin America will always be less well off than the USA because it is a culture that does not respect property rights to the degree ours does. When Americans discover oil or gold on their land we celebrate, because in English/American law, the minerals belong to the property owner. In Latin America, the concept of privately-owned mineral rights does not exist.

If oil or gold is discovered on land south of the Rio Grande, property owners do not report it. They do not want the government to seize their property and extract the mineral wealth, which individuals cannot own. Latin America has other customs that prevent it from attaining a U.S. standard of living. If they will not change their customs to prosper their people, then why is it our responsibility to take their people into our country? They will never change their ways if they know they can keep sending their people to the U.S. rather than make their own countries work.

Thus, we must not let ourselves be taken in by the "humanitarian" notion that we owe everybody in the world a room in our American House, or that we are obligated to depress our own people's standard of living by shipping their jobs to cheap-labor countries whose people are poor because of deficiencies in their governments, customs, and laws, that they are capable of correcting.

Green Globalism

"Green" energy is another catechism of Globalists. They are always waxing hysterical about how "rising sea levels" are going to inundate the population centers on the coasts, how the weather is going haywire because of man-made effects if it is too hot, too cold, too dry, or too wet for a day; but that if the weather is fine that day, it is just weather and not climate. They are always confusing natural effects like subsidence of land with rising sea levels, while cheerfully building their beachfront mansions on sand dunes and offshore spits that would be submerged if the sea level rose even an inch.

So, why do they champion global warming theory that they obviously do not believe? I's because it enables them to incite a government takeover of energy production and rationing, thereby removing the entrepreneurial-minded private energy producers from society. Because Green "Energy" is insufficient to power a modern economy, it must be rationed, and rationing is what left-of-center Globalist governments love. That's also why authoritarian Globalists hate nuclear energy, because it is abundant and requires no government-imposed rationing to control the people.

Part II. Globalism and Trade

NAFTA with Mexico = 440,800 lost auto jobs

The North American Free Trade Agreement known as NAFTA was the first comprehensive "free trade" treaty signed by the United States. The part of it with Canada was preceded by the USA-Canada Auto Pact of 1965 that created a tariff-free common market for motor vehicles and parts on the basis that 90% of the value of production was allocated to the USA and 10% to Canada, which was then, as now, the ratio of sales and profits between the two countries. Neither country could be used as a base to put the other country's people out of their jobs. This was a well-managed trade treaty that worked well for both countries and was noncontroversial.

NAFTA created an expanded, non-proportional "free trade" pact that included Mexico and became the template for all the promises and disappointments of our subsequent trade treaties. In the famous 1993 televised NAFTA debate Vice President Al Gore sought to persuade the public and Congress to ratify the treaty with the pledge:

http://ggallarotti.web.wesleyan.edu/govt155/goreperot.htm

"NAFTA will...greatly accelerate [our trade with Mexico]; we will have a larger trade surplus with Mexico than with any country in the entire world."

NAFTA was duly signed in 1994. That turned out to be the *last* year that the USA *ever* ran a trade surplus with Mexico. The trade went into deficit in 1995, has remained in deficit every year since then, increasing to $71 billion in 2017:

https://www.census.gov/foreign-trade/balance/c2010.html

Vice President Gore promised that NAFTA-WITH-MEXICO would expand employment in the USA: *this can be illustrated by the story of a good friend of mine that I grew up with, named Gordon Thompson ...He makes tires for a living...his job will be more secure, they'll make more tires, they'll be able to sell more tires. Mexico bought 750,000 new cars last year. The Big Three sold them only 1,000, because they have the same barriers against our cars. Those barriers will be eliminated by NAFTA. We'll sell 60,000, not 1,000, in the first year after NAFTA. Every one of those cars has four new tires and one spare. We'll create more jobs with NAFTA.*

Here is what happened to Gordon Thompson and his fellow tire-makers:

Goodyear's move to Mexico: Manufacturers must keep up

Goodyear broke ground July 28 for the first plant it will build in the Americas in 25 years, Tire Business reported. The more than 1-million-square-foot plant will be built in an industrial zone on the southern edge of the city of San Luis Potosi in central Mexico, and involves an investment of up to $550 million.... Goodyear is among many auto component makers moving into the country to supply the growing number of auto assembly plants. As such, employment in the auto supplier sector in Mexico is expected to grow from 700,000 to 1 million in the next few years.

Contrary to Mr. Gore's promises, most cars produced in Mexico are exported to the United States:

[Mexican] Auto exports to US hit record high in 2017

The biggest export destination by far was the United States, receiving more than 2.3 million Mexican-made vehicles. The AMIA said that at least four million cars are projected to be made in Mexico this year and around 3.2 million of them will be exported. However, not all news out of the sector was as positive as the export and production growth. The domestic market [Mexico] failed to keep pace, with sales declining by 4.6%. And the top three automakers — Nissan, General Motors, and Volkswagen — all recorded sales declines [in Mexico] in 2017.

Instead of allowing us to sell more autos, auto parts. and tires to Mexico, NAFTA-WITH-MEXICO enabled Mexico to become the base for exporting automobiles and auto parts, including tires, to the USA. Exports from Mexico to the United States increased, even while Mexico's domestic market for auto sales declined.

The data is compiled from three sources friendly toward NAFTA-WITH-MEXICO. The first one is the Mexican Economics Minister's interpretation of data from the Center for Automotive Research:

https://www.cargroup.org/wp-content/uploads/2017/08/Sandoval.pdf

the Second source is a pro-NAFTA article from CNN Money:

http://money.cnn.com/2017/01/26/news/companies/trump-mexican-auto-jobs/index.html

The third source is directly from the Center for Automotive Research:

http://www.cargroup.org/wp-content/uploads/2017/02/The-Growing-Role-of-Mexico-in-the-North-American-Automotive-Industry-Trends-Drivers-and-Forecasts.pdf

According to these sources:

1. 3.6 million motor vehicles are produced in Mexico by 760,000 Mexican auto workers. (These are human beings, not robots).
2. Of those 3.6 million, 2.1 million, or 58% are exported to the United States.
3. Multiplying 760,000 Mexicans working to making the 58% of automobiles that end up in the USA, **we find that 440,800 American workers' jobs have been moved to Mexico** producing cars that would have been produced in the USA if Mexico did not exist.
4. Employment of American workers in the auto industry is 939,000, less than the 951,000 it was 10 years ago. Auto sales are at record levels, but fewer Americans are employed making automobiles, because their work has been taken over by Mexicans --- human being Mexicans, not Mexican robots. And now GM has started making Buicks in China and bringing them into the USA.

And what has NAFTA-WITH-MEXICO done for (or to) American workers? Anecdotal evidence backs up the numerical analysis that **440,800 American workers' jobs have been moved to Mexico.** ask any business owner or employee in Michigan, Ohio, and Pennsylvania, what's the worst thing that's ever happened to them, they will often reply: "NAFTA. My job (or business) went to Mexico."

Nor were these destroyed jobs replaced by new automobile jobs with increased pay in the USA:

https://www.wsj.com/articles/u-s-car-making-boom-not-for-workers-1427154627

U.S. Car-Making Boom? Not for Auto-Industry Workers

U.S. auto-industry wages have declined despite rise in output due to competition from foreign parts makers

By James R. Hagerty and Jeff Bennett March 23, 2015

THREE RIVERS, Mich.—U.S. auto production is nearing all-time highs on the back of strong domestic demand and steady export increases. But American-made cars and trucks are increasingly loaded with parts imported from Mexico, China, and other nations.

The U.S. imported a record $138 billion in car parts last year, equivalent to $12,135 of content in every American light vehicle built. That is up from $89 billion, or $10,536 per vehicle, in 2008—the first of two disastrous years for the car business. In 1990, only $31.7 billion in parts were imported.

The trend casts a cloud over the celebrated comeback of one of the nation's bedrock industries. As the inflow of low-cost foreign parts accelerates, wages at the entry level are drifting away from the generous compensation packages that made car-factory jobs the prize of American manufacturing.

At an American Axle & Manufacturing Holdings Inc. car-parts factory in Three Rivers, some new hires are paid as little as about $10 an hour, roughly equivalent to what the local Wal-Mart will pay. John Childers, a 38-year-old assembly-line stocker, said he is grateful for the job but finds it tough to get by on the money he and his fiancée make at the plant.

"Lower class is what we are," he says. "Let's be honest."

Mexico was by far the biggest supplier of car parts to the U.S. last year, accounting for 34% of the imports, followed by China with 13%. Imports from China have more than doubled since 2008. Those from Mexico are up 86%.

Wal-Mart Stores Inc. recently announced plans to boost pay for U.S. workers to at least $10 an hour next year. With retail wages rising, Mr. Hobbs said, "you're going to have a hard time attracting folks into a manufacturing environment."

The above article reconciles the misrepresentations and contradictions in globalist free trade theory. First, it reveals global trade to be primarily a vehicle for destroying wealth in the USA. Wages in manufacturing have been reduced from $25 / hour to $ 9 / hour, and the blue-collar middle class has become "the lower class."

It also explains why American manufacturing companies still here claim they can't find people who want to work for them. Free trade has turned American manufacturing into a low-wage business where Americans are expected to work for Third World wages. American families can't be supported by a breadwinner earning $ 9 / hour, at least not without government welfare assistance including food stamps, housing vouchers, and the earned income tax credit that subsidizes low paid workers with money taxed away from higher earners, or increasingly, tacked on to the national debt.

It explains why the national debt has exploded to $21 trillion since all these trade deals were signed. When American workers' wage decline from $25 / hour to $9 / hour those workers become consumers of public welfare services instead of taxpayers. They no longer have pensions and healthcare that follows them into retirement. When they leave the workforce due to old age or infirmity they must be paid out of the public treasury for decades, after having paid little or nothing into it during their low-paid intermittent working lives.

It explains why the United States is beginning to look like Mexico (instead of Mexico looking like the United States) where the wealth is increasingly concentrated among fewer people, and the middle class vanishes.

"But hasn't NAFTA-WITH-MEXICO at least increased exports of some of our products to Mexico and helped some American businesses and employees?" ask the Free Trade Mavens. Yes, it has increased our exports to Mexico, but much less than expected, and perhaps less than what they would have increased if NAFTA had never been signed:

https://www.census.gov/foreign-trade/balance/c2010.html

Our trade data with Mexico started being compiled in 1985, nine years before NAFTA was ratified. In those nine years before NAFTA, our exports to Mexico were growing at 15.5% per year, our imports at 11% per year, and our trade deficit, which started at $5.5 billion in 1985 was transformed into a trade surplus of $1.3 billion in 1994. That was *before* NAFTA. In the nine years after NAFTA, our exports grew at 9% per year, our imports at 12%, and our trade surplus of $1.3 billion became a trade deficit of $40.6 billion. Exports grew more slowly, imports rose more quickly, and the trade deficit soared.

In the last five years from 2012 to 2017, our exports to Mexico grew a meager 2.2% per year, which is even slower than our tepid economies grew, our imports grew 5.3% per

87

year, and our trade deficit grew by \$9.2 billion. So much for NAFTA being a bonanza of trade. It's probably even worse than it looks, because much of the trade isn't really import / export trade. It's simply shipping a \$100 part across the border, having the Mexicans assemble it into a larger component, and calling it a \$125 import into the USA when it comes back across. Nothing was exported to Mexico. Nobody benefited except the manufacturer, who used the border as a gateway to cheap labor and was able to inflate profit margins by beating some Americans out of their jobs.

"But don't we export food to Mexico?" Yes, we export \$18 billion of low-value soybeans and corn, which are heavily subsidized by taxpayer money to pay for "crop insurance and price supports." In return we import \$23 billion of higher-value products from Mexico such as tomatoes and blueberries that undercut our American farmers. In food products, like everything else, we are importing high-value productions from Mexico and dumping our low-value, government-subsidized products in Mexico, harming farmers in both countries, while enhancing the ability of farming corporations to oppress their laborers in Mexico and inflate their profit margins in the USA.

My Congressman, a conservative member of the Freedom Caucus (a Congressional group that usually favors free trade), points out that NAFTA and its USMA revision harms Florida Farmers by letting in too many Mexican imports:

Dear Friends,

Today I voted 'no' on the shortfalls of the USMCA agreement for Florida farmers.

NAFTA was originally created to remove traditional trade barriers and facilitate economic growth amongst the U.S., Canada, and Mexico. Our great state of Florida is one of the biggest agriculture partners in the world, and our district benefits tremendously from free trade opportunities with other countries. However, international trade should not come at the expense of American farmers and workers.

I commend President Trump and his administration for renegotiating a much-needed trade deal between the U.S., Canada, and Mexico.

However, this agreement will not solve the failures of NAFTA with regards to the seasonal competition of agricultural produce that caused our fruit and vegetable farmers to lose a large share of the U.S. market to Mexican producers. Absent proper trade enforcement tools, we are maintaining the status quo that will continue to harm Florida producers.

USMCA favors Mexican producers over the hardworking Southeastern farmers. Remedies, after that fact are too late to address our farmers needs now. Without the inclusion of trade remedies in USMCA for Florida's produce farmers, I cannot, in good conscience, support this agreement.

Congressman Ted Yoho

In recent years, the NAFTA cheerleaders have been trying to disguise the failure of NAFTA-WITH-MEXICO by pretending that Mexico and Canada are the same country, and that "NAFTA has expanded trade between the USA and our other NAFTA partners." But in fact, our trade with Canada, has also grown more slowly after NAFTA than it did before NAFTA:

https://www.census.gov/foreign-trade/balance/c1220.html

We exported $282 billion to Canada in 2017, which is less than the $292.6 billion we exported five years ago in 2012. We also import about $25 billion less from Canada than we did five years ago.

As much as the Free Trade Mavens want to obfuscate the results of NAFTA, it is difficult to show measurable evidence that it has done anything to improve the economies of any of the three countries or raise the standards of living of their people. There is plenty of evidence that may even have reduced trade between the countries and enabled big business to exploit cheap labor in Mexico to make the people in all three countries poorer. If NAFTA had been signed only between the USA and Canada, countries with similar standards of living, it might have worked for our mutual benefit. Bringing Mexico into the mix was detrimental. Not Mexico's fault, because they have a sincere desire to trade fairly with us. NAFTA with Mexico failed because the historical circumstances of Mexico being only about 10% as wealthy as the United States could not be overcome by a trade treaty.

At any rate, the Free Trade Mavens' original promise that *"NAFTA will...greatly accelerate [our trade with Mexico]; we will have a larger trade surplus with Mexico than with any country in the entire world"* and will "create millions of well-paying jobs for American workers" has been shown to be one of the greatest prevarications in history.

NAFTA bad for Mexico too?

The other part of the promise that NAFTA would make Mexicans wealthy enough to buy American-made products also wasn't fulfilled. Mexico's demand for automobiles declined. If NAFTA had prospered them as much as promised, they'd be buying Cadillacs. During the recent presidential election in Mexico, the NAFTA cheerleaders tried to beat back the populist challenge by alleging that Mexico had prospered with NAFTA:

https://www.wsj.com/articles/mexicos-presidential-watershed-1530225438

Mexico's Presidential Watershed

The changes [wrought by NAFTA] have lifted Mexico from an economy dependent on oil exports to a manufacturing powerhouse with a rising middle class. From shoes and cell phones to dining out and better education at all levels, Mexicans are more prosperous than ever.

Note that when Globalists want to preserve NAFTA-WITH-MEXICO they simultaneously claim that: A) Manufacturing creates jobs and wealth for Mexicans, and B) that the loss of manufacturing jobs in the USA does not harm Americans because "robots are doing all the work."

Ross Perot, who was Mr. Gore's NAFTA debate opponent was skeptical that NAFTA would prosper Mexico:

I'm looking back at reality, and here is what I see after many years. Mexican workers' standard of living and pay, has gone down, not up. After many years of having U.S. companies in Mexico, this is the way Mexican workers live all around big new U.S. plants. Now, just think if you owned a big U.S. company and you went down to see your new plant, and you found slums all around it, your first reaction would be, 'Why did you build a plant in the middle of slums?' And your plant manager would say, 'Oh, there were no slums here when we built the plant.' And you say, 'Well, why are they here now?' They said, 'This is where the workers work.'

To maintain itself as a cheap-labor country, Mexico devalued its currency 80% after NAFTA. The people make little more now than then. Employment has risen in Mexico, but wages have fallen, the same as has happened in the United States:

Mexico remains a crime-prone country with drug cartels, extortion rackets, and kidnappings for ransom. If there has been any improvement, it is only in the fortunes of the well-connected bankers, big business owners, lawyers, and politicians and government bureaucrats who receive kickbacks from the contractors they award government contracts. It was promised that NAFTA-WITH-MEXICO would end illegal immigration from Mexico. Today we have millions, perhaps tens of millions of illegal Mexicans in our country, and up to 50,000 more are still apprehended trying to cross the border illegally each month.

Mexico has now (July 2018) elected a left-of-center populist president by the greatest landslide in decades, the opposite result of what NAFTA-WITH-MEXICO was supposed to produce.

https://www.wsj.com/articles/mexico-vote-snubs-the-political-establishment-1530560502?tesla=y&mod=article_inline&mod=article_inline

Mexico Vote Snubs the Political Establishment

López Obrador's victory marks an end to the political party system that dominated Mexico for three decades

Updated July 2, 2018

MEXICO CITY—Mexico's election was a tsunami for the country's traditional parties, which suffered unprecedented setbacks at the hands of Andrés Manuel López Obrador and the Movement for National Regeneration the leftist leader founded just four years ago.

Like Brexit and the presidential election of Donald Trump, Mexico's historic vote is the latest example of the backlash against the political establishment that has swept through Europe and the U.S. amid eroding trust in traditional political parties.

And now in December 2019, comes the usual back-peddling by Free Trade Mavens who promised miraculous results for their trade treaties, and now admit that they didn't pan out:

https://www.wsj.com/articles/trade-deal-wont-rescue-mexico-11575838200

Trade Deal Won't Rescue Mexico

López Obrador's capricious governing style is the real threat to economic growth.

By Mary Anastasia O'Grady

Dec. 8, 2019

Mexican Finance Minister Arturo Herrera...[is] wrong that passing the USMCA—or even preserving the North American Free Trade Agreement—would cure Mexico's economic anemia. A resolution of the rules for North American trade is a necessary but insufficient condition for spurring Mexican growth.

It seems that NAFTA-WITH-MEXICO merely destroyed the well-paying jobs in the USA, without bringing significant improvements to Mexican workers. Instead of elevating $1.50 Mexicans up toward the $25 / hour U.S. wage scale, it diminished the American wage scale of $25 / hour down to the Mexican wage scale of $1.50 / hour. Corporations that produce in Mexico and sell in the USA profited from the difference. Mexicans and Americans suffered.

And then came China.

The China Delusion

China fascinates Americans for many reasons, including its civilization and culture, the dynamism of its people, and its potential for economic wealth. Despite vastly different cultures, the USA and China have co-evolved during the last 250 years to become two of the world's great powers. The USA broke away from the British Empire in 1776 in part so that our "Yankee Traders" could trade with China, which even in the 1700's was viewed as a treasure house of silk, fine art, tableware, tea, and spices, and a potentially massive export market for manufactured products.

China and the USA complement each other. China looks to the USA to strengthen its mastery of science, technology, and economic development. Millions of Chinese have emigrated to America to find liberty and prosperity. Likewise, Americans have admired China's ancient culture of wisdom, patience, and beauty. The USA and China have often been on the same side of history, such as when we fought together against Japanese imperialism in World War II.

Thus, it is reasonable to expect that the USA and China should enjoy mutually beneficial economic relations. Americans should never resent China's rise to economic parity with us, nor wish anything other than prosperity and happiness of the Chinese people, that they have earned by diligent and intelligent work.

However, we must get over our delusion that China, and other Asian nations, are pots of gold to be milked of profits for U.S. corporations, while creating employment opportunities for American workers to build product to export to China. This delusion is deeply imbedded in our history. As far back as 1853, future Secretary of State Seward viewed China and as the linchpins of American prosperity and global power. He advised Americans to:

"Open up a highway from New York to San Francisco. Put your domain under cultivation and your ten thousand wheels of manufacture in motion. Multiply your ships and send them forth to the East (Japan, China, and India). The nation that draws the most materials and provisions from the earth, and fabricates the most, and sells the most of production and fabrics to foreign nations, must be, and will be, the great power of the earth."

We wanted free trade with China, but trade on our terms --- which meant manufacturing products to keep our people employed and selling them to those "teeming millions" in Asia. This did not happen because:

1. Asians, who work for a pittance then as now, don't have enough money to afford buying products made in the USA.
2. Asians are not stupid. They are never going to let other countries extract their wealth by selling them products that they can copy and then use their cheap labor advantage to sell back to the industrial powers.
3. Industrial and technology secrets cannot be kept hidden from Asians. Any product and its methods of production can be copied by intelligent and industrious people, as Asians surely are. Their cost advantage not only includes cheap labor, but also the lack of investment in R&D, since they are merely copying products that already exist instead of inventing new ones.

Thus, trade with Asia, like trade with Mexico, tends to be a one-way street of wealth and jobs out of the USA. It is never going to make sense for an American company to pay its American workers $25 / hour to sell to Asians who at best earn $1 / hour. The product that is sold in Asia will be made in Asia, and the surplus exported back to the United States.

China's government not only conspires with its companies to steal every product from the USA it can – from socket wrenches to tombstone monuments --- but also wages cyber warfare against our civilian as well as military enterprises, and routinely threatens to blow our ships out of the water that "trespass" on its preposterous claims to international waters.

https://www.wsj.com/articles/ghosts-in-the-clouds-inside-chinas-major-corporate-hack-11577729061?mod=hp_lead_pos5

Ghosts in the Clouds: Inside China's Major Corporate Hack

A Journal investigation finds the Cloud Hopper attack was much bigger than previously known

By Rob Barry and Dustin Volz

Dec. 30, 2019

The hackers seemed to be everywhere. In one of the largest-ever corporate espionage efforts, cyberattackers alleged to be working for China's intelligence services stole volumes of intellectual property, security clearance details and other records from scores of companies over the past several years.

A Wall Street Journal investigation has found that the attack was much bigger than previously known. It goes far beyond the 14 unnamed companies listed in the indictment, stretching across at least a dozen cloud providers, including CGI Group Inc., GIB -0.67% one of Canada's largest cloud companies; Tieto Oyj, a major Finnish IT services company; and International Business Machines Corp.

We are learning that China's communist government embeds spyware in the products it sells to Americans, like Huawei telecommunications and Tik Tok software. We are learning that the Chinese government has turned hundreds of American university leaders into spies for China, including the head of Harvard's Chemistry and Chemical Biology Department, who was recently arrested. Chinese citizens have been invited to work in our nuclear weapons laboratories, thereby stealing substantially all our nuclear weapons designs and selling them to China's government to potentially use against us.

Globalists see China and other Asian countries in the image we see ourselves --- as nations of free-wheeling entrepreneurs operating independently of their governments. In fact, Asian nations are regimented societies with top-down control by their governments. Their economies are based on cartels of interlocking directories of banks, manufacturers, and retailers, all under government supervision. No American-made product of any significance is going to be allowed to be sold in Asia. American-branded products like iPhones, Nike sneakers, and GM autos are sold in Asia only because they are made in Asia and provide employment to Asian workers who export the surplus back to the USA. Even so, Asian governments encourage their people to steal as much American technology as possible, and to make pirate copies of our brand names and sell them illegally around the world.

American companies who pin their hopes on China as a pot of gold waiting to be tapped, will usually be disappointed. The latest to take a hit is Apple:

https://www.wsj.com/articles/the-data-is-in-apples-sales-in-china-were-horrendous-11549966152?mod=hp_lead_pos6

The Data Is In: Apple's Shipments in China Were Horrendous

iPhone shipments were down 20% from a year earlier; local leader Huawei's were up 23%

By Dan Strumpf Feb. 12, 2019

HONG KONG—iPhone shipments in China slumped far more than overall smartphone shipments there last quarter, costing Apple Inc. AAPL -0.58% further ground against local rival Huawei Technologies Co. in the world's biggest smartphone market.

Apple's smartphone shipments in China in the last three months of 2018 were down 20% from a year earlier, according to International Data Corp., putting a finer point on Apple's shrinking sales in China late last year. Last month, Apple CEO Tim Cook blamed declining iPhone sales in China on the economic slowdown there.

Globalists are now touting China as a market for "beef and soybeans." But China rarely buys much of anything from the USA, not even beef. Back in 2003 they fooled President George W. Bush into letting them into the World Trade Organization in return for promising to "buy millions of tons of U.S. beef." They never bought so much as a single ounce for fourteen years. They only started buying token amounts when Trump told them they'd better start buying more U.S. products if they wanted to avoid tariffs:

http://www.feedstuffs.com/markets/us-beef-exports-china-increasing-after-14-year-absence

In June 2017, the U.S. began shipping beef to China after a 14-year ban that was enacted after the discovery of isolated cases of bovine spongiform...

The Chinese supposedly found once incidence of possible "mad cow" protein in one steak and banned the importation of all U.S. beef for fourteen years! How much product would the Chinese sell in the USA, if we banned the importation of an entire product line every time one defect is found in one product?

It's fine to want to export farm products to other countries. But notice the lack of proportion. We export $21 billion of farm products to China, $14 billion of which are low-value soybeans subsidized by government price supports. Our farm exports have been declining in recent years, while China is doing an "Alexander Hamilton" on us, by building up their economy by unloading $505 billion of their manufactured product on us:

In recent years, a new myth has developed that China and the rest of Asia are an untapped market for American "services." Our bankers think they are going to make a mint of money peddling the same scams in Asia that wiped out their banks and inflicted tremendous collateral damage on the rest of our economy in 2008. No Asian government is going to allow American bankers to get rich peddling "financial services" that Asian banks are competent to emulate.

Nor are Asians going to pay our software companies much in the way of royalties. Somewhere between 75% and 90% of Microsoft Windows copies running in China are pirated. Microsoft is giving away Windows in China because the Chinese won't pay for them.

Our trade deficits tell the story. China: $375.5 billion in 2017; Japan: $68.9 billion; South Korea: $23 billion; Vietnam: $38 billion; Thailand: $20 billion; Malaysia: $24 billion; Indonesia: $13 billion; India: $22 billion. Our imports from these countries are soaring, while our exports are stagnant or declining. Why would our exports to these countries increase when our companies are in a race to remove industrial operations out of the United States and replace them with $1 / hour labor in Asia?

When Free Trade Mavens can't defend their theories on their original economic promises, they fall back to making emotional arguments. Their emotional fallback regarding China is that "The United States will be 'left behind' if we do not trade with China. If we do not trade with China on their terms, they will stop doing business with us, and we will wither and die, leaving China to own the world's commerce!"

That's a preposterous argument because the Chinese are *already* well on the way to owning the world's commerce. They are peddling pirated American brand name merchandise in South America, supplying Argentina with military equipment, propping up Venezuela's failing government with loans, buying up natural resources all over Latin America and Africa (and in North America if the USA and Canada would allow it), buying up real estate in the USA and Canada, purchasing first dibs on building a new trans-ocean canal in Nicaragua, building their "silk road" to the Persian Gulf, and threatening to blow U.S. ships out of the water that "trespass" on their turf in the South China Sea.

They've used our trade deficit dollars to finance their international expansion for decades. It's the Free Trade Mavens who supported unconditional trade with China who transferred our wealth to them and made them our rival for "the commerce of the world," not anything Trump has done with tariffs.

We are making the USA poorer, and less competitive in international trade, in a reverse-alchemy process of what trade with China was supposed to accomplish for us. We do not need to resent China and the rest of Asia's rising prosperity, but we do need to make sure it does not come at our expense. They need to prosper by producing goods and services that they can sell in their own markets. We need to tariff their products until they balance the trade either by buying more from us or start producing what they sell in the USA in the USA. There's no reason why any foreign-based company should be able to import products into the USA and extract profits from our economy --- without investing in the USA, hiring American workers, or paying taxes in the USA --- when American-based producers cannot do the same in their countries.

As these words are being written China's leader Xi Jinping is in North Korea ostentatiously thumbing his nose at the U.S. by lavishing gifts on North Korea's leader who has threatened to attack the United States with nuclear weapons. The purpose of the gifts is to communicate to the world that China will not honor its promise to honor sanctions on North Korea. China is embracing North Korea and telling us to "go to hell." So why would any American view China as an honest trading partner?

Nevertheless, our Globalists are unceasing in their support of Chinese interests against American interests:

https://www.wsj.com/articles/china-wont-be-a-trade-pushover-1533079761

China Won't Be a Trade Pushover

Beijing still has plenty of tools to keep its economy growing.

By The Editorial Board

July 31, 2018

The Trump Administration shouldn't assume that Beijing will buckle under the strain of tariffs. Despite debt problems and slowing growth, Chinese leaders still have plenty of options to keep the economy expanding. The smart U.S. strategy would be to work with allies to negotiate new trade rules with China rather than engage in mutually damaging tariffs.

Globalists say we should continue to allow the Chinese to dump their surpluses in the USA while we pretend to "negotiate new trade rules" that the Chinese will just as vigorously ignore as they have ignored all the old rules. Globalists, who want us to be trade patsies for China, then warn us that we should prepare for military confrontation:

https://www.wsj.com/articles/u-s-defense-bill-seeks-to-counter-china-1533127150?mod=hp_lead_pos2

U.S. Defense Bill Aims to Counter China as Rivalry Deepens

Lawmakers get tough on Beijing, with targets including military activity in South China Sea, pursuit of U.S. technology

By Kate O'Keeffe and Siobhan Hughes

Aug. 1, 2018

Congress is preparing to enact a defense-policy bill that some lawmakers say is tougher on China than any in history, as a bipartisan movement to confront Beijing gathers steam.

On December 2, 2018, President Trump met with the Chinese leader at a G-20 summit in Buenos Aires. Trump announced that the Chinese had agreed to drop their tariffs on American products and stop stealing our intellectual property. The Chinese responded that there had been no such agreement. As is the usual case with China, they apparently made empty promises to Trump at the summit, then denied making them the next day.

The business press wrote its usual condescending articles about how Trump is an economic ignoramus because he favors reining in China's unfair trade practices with tariffs. Typical was the **Wall Street Journal's** lament:

I Am a Tariff Man'

It's a bird, it's a plane. No, it's the President of the United States.

*Markets apparently didn't see the superhero humor and promptly sold off. Perhaps they know that tariffs are taxes on commerce, and when you tax something you get less of it. Mr. T's unveiling also hit on the day after the yield curve on some Treasurys began to invert—which can mean trouble. The economy is still strong enough to survive some uncertainty, but Tariff Man shouldn't go to war with the laws of economics. **He'll lose.***

Imagine, the leading business magazine cheerleading for China to defeat the United States, because our president asked China to stop stealing our technologies and to buy reciprocally from us. I pointed out another article from that day:

China Maneuvers to Snag Top-Secret Boeing Satellite Technology

At the same time, the Free Trade Mavens insist on taxing Americans a trillion dollars a year to defend the rest of the world from "a threatening China:"

https://www.wsj.com/articles/a-trump-retreat-from-korea-11595027533?mod=opinion_lead_pos3

A Trump Retreat from Korea?

A good way to look weak on China and help Biden get to his right on national security.

By The Editorial Board

July 17, 2020

The U.S. has some 28,500 troops on the Korean peninsula. The main strategic purpose is defending against North Korea, but the deployments also protect America's security interests and reassure the region that the U.S. is committed to defending America's friends against a threatening China.

This must be a joke, because China recently invaded Hong Kong, and is threatening to invade Taiwan, sinking all American naval vessels in the vicinity in the process.

Free Trade Mavens don't care if China steals our technologies and uses them against us to destroy our jobs and wealth. They don't care if China invades our allies and threatens to sink our ships. They don't care if China loads the United States with spies. They don't care if China takes over America tomorrow. All they want is China's money now.

They are arrogant in insisting that giving away our economy to China, while loading ourselves with debt to buy Chinese-made products, is going to prosper us. All they care about is buying their baubles and gewgaws on the cheap from China and profiteering by selling them to Americans at inflated markups. Arrogant people cannot be educated. They must be replaced by new leadership, that has rational views.

Wuhan Wild Wings

In early 2020 COVID-19 spread around the world. The Chinese Government told the world that it was non-transmissible to humans because "it came from a bat wing sold in a wet market in Wuhan." Our Dr. Fauci advised our people that it was OK to book cruises and travel by plane, and recommended they not wear masks. Some of our governors, mayors, Congresspersons and Senators told their constituents in New York and San Francisco to mingle among crowds of Chinese recently arrived from Wuhan to help them celebrate the Chinese New Year in America. A year and a half later, 600,000 Americans had died prematurely from Covid, often lying on their backs in hospital beds for weeks, breathing through machines, and waiting to die.

COVID-19 most likely originated at the Wuhan Virology Institute, previously cited for lax containment standards while experimenting with viruses, possibly including prohibited "gain of function" manipulations that enable the virus to jump from bats to human beings. Given that this was known to be happening at the Wuhan Virology Lab, why would anybody believe the cover story that the virus originated as schlepped 700 miles from a "bat cave" in to a wet market that just happened to be near the Virology Lab, and sold as fried batwings.

Until 1969, the U.S. Army experimented with biological warfare at Fort Deitrick, on the outskirts of Frederick, Maryland. President Nixon ordered the facility closed and its inventory of biological warfare agents destroyed in 1969 because he judged the experiments too dangerous to be permitted to continue. What would have happened if prior to 1969 a deadly virus had originated near Fort Deitrick, and our government said it came from meat sold at the Frederick Farmers Market? Would anybody have believed that? Our media would have pointed out that the odds of the virus originating near Frederick, Maryland by coincidence were less than 5,000 to 1, given that the United States has 3.6 million square miles of land area. The odds that it would have originated from Fort Dietrick would have been near 100% given that the Army was known to be developing bioweapons there.

China has nearly the same land area of 3.6 million square miles as the United States. The odds are more than 5000 to 1 against it originating by coincidence in the Wuhan vicinity, but nearly 100% that it originated at the Wuhan Virology Laboratory, given that they conducted experiments with viruses there. So why did our medical, governmental, big business, media, and entertainment elites march in lockstep to deny that it came from the Wuhan Virology Laboratory? Do they really believe a Chinese government that rarely tells the truth about anything? Or did Chinese money corrupt them into pretending to believe something they knew was not true, and to intentionally mispresent the truth to the American public, to absolve their Chinese paymasters of blame for the catastrophe?

Given our craven response to COVID, the next question becomes what will we do about other Chinese aggressions, such as taking over Hong Kong 47 years earlier than promised, potentially invading Taiwan and claiming large areas of the high seas as Chinese sovereign territory, continuing to spy on Americans and steal the trade secrets of our companies, bribing our politicians, businesspeople, and university staffs, or possibly unleashing a more deadly virus? Judging by what we didn't do about their probable release of COVID, the answer is that the Western elites will do nothing to resist Chinese provocations, so long as their payola from the Chinese government keeps arriving on schedule.

The Global Disruption Chain

Globalists hoot buzzwords in unison. One of their favorites is "global supply chain." They think that having "a global supply chain" will cure all their bad business practices in the United States. Now, in autumn 2021, the "global supply chain" has cut off American automakers supplies of computer chips, and American auto companies can't produce the cars people want to buy:

https://www.wsj.com/articles/car-buyers-face-bleak-prospects-this-labor-day-weekend-11630661402?mod=hp_lead_pos10

Car Buyers Face Bleak Prospects This Labor Day Weekend

The holiday is historically one of the auto industry's biggest sales events, but dealers have very little inventory to sell this year

The availability of vehicles—new and used—has been dented by a global computer-chip shortage that has hampered U.S. auto production through the spring and summer.

Sept. 3, 2021 5:30 am ET

The U.S. auto industry is heading into one of its biggest selling weekends of the year with dealership lots stripped bare of inventory and some buyers having to drive great distances to secure a new ride.

For a second year in a row, car shoppers are facing bleak prospects in trying to buy a car this Labor Day weekend. The period has historically been a time of blowout deals and big sales events for car companies and dealerships trying to clear out old vehicle stock to make way for the new model year.

Some dealers are so short on vehicles that they are cutting their advertising budgets for the month and closing Friday and Saturday.

Around this time last year, the U.S. car business was still trying to recover from the pandemic-related factory shutdowns in the spring, disruptions that at the time led to slim pickings on dealership lots over the holiday weekend.

Since then, the availability of vehicles—new and used—has deteriorated, dented by a global computer-chip shortage that slammed the auto industry earlier this year and has hampered U.S. auto production through the spring and summer.

"Customers are walking in and saying, 'Hey, I really want this vehicle.' Well, yeah, so do we," said Scott Smith, president of Smith Automotive Group, which operates dealerships in the Atlanta area. "It's been tough to meet all of the demand."

This week, both General Motors Co. GM -0.59% and Ford Motor Co. F -0.89% said they are extending production cuts at several North American factories—including highly profitable pickup truck plants—into September because of a lack of semiconductors, used in everything from air bags and engines to media displays.

Globalists thought they were being clever in outsourcing American jobs to their global supply chain. Now it's a become a global disruption chain that's kicking them in the shins.

Trans-Pacific Partnership, R.I.P

It seems incredible after our experience of NAFTA-WITH-MEXICO and GATT-WITH-CHINA that any American would believe that entering so-called "free trade" agreements with a dozen Asian countries that already drain the USA with massive trade deficits would improve our economy. It has been demonstrated that "free trade" agreements with low-wage countries accelerate the loss of jobs and wealth from the United States. People in low-wage countries can't afford to purchase American-made products and would not be allowed by their governments to purchase them even if they could afford them.

The rallying cry of the Free Trade Mavens for the Trans-Pacific Partnership became "Let's get together with a bunch of little parasitic Asian fish to gang up on the big parasite, which is China." Did they really believe that the parasitic little fish would detach from Uncle Sam and go latch on to China to suck its economic blood? Did they think China's government would allow it? All the trade parasites, large and small, were bound to go where the economic "blood" was flowing, which is in the United States.

Although China would not formally have been included in the pact, there was even a "back door" that made China a de facto member. Here is how the Japanese explained it:

http://thediplomat.com/2015/10/what-the-tpp-means-for-japan/

What the TPP means for Japan

*Second, the [**Japanese**] auto industry will benefit from a phase-in in the reduction of tariffs on their exports. Also, they will be allowed to buy more parts for their products from Asia, including, significantly, from countries not in the TPP. The "rule of origin"*http://ajw.asahi.com/article/behind_news/politics/AJ201510050005 *requires only 45 percent of the vehicle to be made in the TPP zone; in the North America Free Trade Agreement (NAFTA), the equivalent figure is 62.5 percent.*

*Being able to buy cheaper parts from countries such as China, and then sell vehicles with reduced tariffs to markets such as the U.S. is good for the **Japanese** auto industry.*

The Japanese said the treaty was good for them because the "45% content rule" would allow them to source 55% of their production in low-wage China and import it into the USA tariff free. Japan and China would have been the winners; The USA, as always, the loser. The USA, which currently runs a cumulative $520 billion trade deficit with China, Japan, and Mexico, would have seen the deficit expand toward $1 trillion with those three countries alone.

"But wouldn't China and Japan, and have purchased more from the USA?" ask the globalists?" The answer, as we have already seen, is that free trade agreements accelerate the removal of our industries offshore, and therefore decrease our exports.

Since the Free Trade Mavens couldn't sell the TPP to the American people with economic propaganda, they told the gullible that it would "help the United States stand up to China." Yeah, right. The Japanese wanted the treaty so they could produce 55% of the value of their products in China's cheap labor pits, pretend it was Japanese-made product and dump it in the USA, thereby transferring even more jobs and wealth out of the USA and into Japan and China.

"Those TPP countries will do their own deal without us," chimed the Free Trade Mavens on cue. "We will be isolated from Asia!" What a pant load. Those Asian countries never wanted to dump their surplus production in each other's laps. They wanted to dump their surpluses on the only country in the world dumb enough to take them, which was Uncle Sam, the Global Sugar Daddy. Fortunately, Trump was elected to kill TPP deader than a doornail, and that he surely did.

The Horsemen of the Free Trade Apocalypse

Free Trade Mavens no longer fool as many people as they used to. They are now reaching deep into the past to conjure up ancient ghosts. Not to honor them, but to misrepresent their ideas. The Horsemen of the Free Trade Apocalypse are Adam Smith, Karl Marx David Ricardo, and two Depression-era Senators named Reed Smoot and Willis Hawley.

Adam Smith

Free Trade Mavens usually begin discussions of their theories by talking about Adam Smith, the 17th century customs official, who wrote that nations should prosper by producing the goods and services they are most efficient at, while importing goods and services they don't produce well or at all. However, Adam Smith never advocated for trade based on cheap labor. He opposed substituting high wages in one country with the low wages of another country's peons:

No society can surely be flourishing and happy, of which the far greater part of the members are poor and miserable. It is but equity, besides, that they who feed, clothe, and lodge the whole body of the people, should have such a share of the produce of their own labour as to be themselves tolerably well fed, clothed, and lodged.

Smith, Adam (2013-09-12). The Wealth of Nations (Illustrated) (p. 30). Kindle Edition

The progressive state is, in reality, the cheerful and the hearty state to all the different orders of the society; the stationary is dull; the declining melancholy. The liberal reward of labour, as it encourages the propagation, so it increases the industry of the common people.

The wages of labour are the encouragement of industry, which, like every other human quality, improves in proportion to the encouragement it receives. A plentiful subsistence increases the bodily strength of the labourer, and the comfortable hope of bettering his condition, and of ending his days, perhaps, in ease and plenty, animates him to exert that strength to the utmost.

Where wages are high, accordingly, we shall always find the workmen more active, diligent, and expeditious, than where they are low;

Smith, Adam (2013-09-12). The Wealth of Nations (Illustrated) (p. 31) Kindle Edition.

Karl Marx

The 19th Century personality who most favored free trade was Karl Marx:

*But, generally speaking, **the Protective system** in these days **is conservative,** while **the Free Trade system works destructively.** It breaks up old nationalities and carries antagonism of proletariat and bourgeoisie to the uttermost point. In a word, **the Free Trade system hastens the Social Revolution. In this revolutionary sense alone,** gentlemen, **I am in favor of Free Trade.***

Marx believed in free trade only because he believed it would impoverish workers, making them desperate for communist revolution.

Adam Smith and Karl Marx understood that there is a social as well as an economic aspect to work. When we put millions of our countrymen out of work to buy something made by other countries' peons, the people who are suffering are going to seek to even the score. They may respond by electing socialist governments that raise taxes and fund government make-work and welfare programs that provide them with subsistence. If their circumstances become desperate so that they cannot find any means to feed their families, they will be prone to becoming full-blown communist revolutionaries who seize private property the way Marx wanted and then redistribute it equally.

David Ricardo

Next in order of appearance comes David Ricardo (From Spencer P. Morrison's blog, and book *The Land of (Rancid) Milk and Honey)*:

https://nationaleconomicseditorial.com/2016/12/13/problems-with-comparative-advantage/

Everyone and their dog has heard of Adam Smith, John Maynard Keynes, and Milton Friedman.... But unless you are a lonely economist, you probably have never heard of David Ricardo (d. 1823) .... That's a shame. Ricardo might be the most important of the bunch. His big idea, the theory of comparative advantage, underpins modern economic globalization, if not international free trade itself.

Globalization is the house Ricardo built.

109

*One tiny problem, though: comparative advantage doesn't always work. In fact, its misapplication is largely to blame for the **decline of Victorian Britain** in the 19th century, and **America's decline** since the 1970s.*

Ricardo became notorious for wrecking the economies of Portugal and Britain. He advised Portugal's government to stop investing in the Industrial Revolution, and to concentrate instead on the ancient arts of growing wine and wool, then selling it to Britain in return for manufactured products. He advised Britain's government to buy its steel from Germany instead of investing money in building steel mills in Britain. Doesn't he sound just like a modern-day Globalist?

Acting upon his advice, Portugal stopped its industrial development in its tracks. They were a nation of wine makers and goat herders when Ricardo advised them to stop investing in industry, and they remain a nation of wine makers and goat herders today. They have not amounted to much since David Ricardo came to town. Same thing happened to Britain. Acting on Ricardo's advice, they stopped making steel and started buying from Germany, which along with the USA became the world's premier steel making country. Luckily, the British remained allied with the USA and had a friend when the Germans ran them out of Europe with their steel-armored panzer armies.

The USA became the strongest economy because we never let David Ricardo pollute our country with bad ideas. We listened to Alexander Hamilton and William Seward who emphasized expanding our industries, while Ricardo trashed the economies of Britain and Portugal by telling them to get rid of their industries. Ricardo failed to understand that once an industry moves out of a country, it is gone for all time. It never comes back. You lose not only the present value of the industry but all future value. Portugal gave up its industry. Two hundred years of progress passed it by. It will remain a poor and backward country forever because the Portuguese turned their back on progress, thanks to David Ricardo.

This is what the Free Trade Mavens want for the USA: to make us give up our industry to Mexico and China, then return us to those ancient days when Indians walked the land, hoeing taters and picking turnips. If there are not enough Native American Indians to do that work, they will bring them in from Mexico and Central America.

Smoot and Hawley

Bringing up the rear of the Free Trade Apocalypse come the Free Trade Mavens' favorite demons --- Senator Reed Smoot and Congressman Willis Hawley who authored their namesake tariff, signed into law by President Herbert Hoover on June 17, 1930. According to Free Trade Maven lore, the Smoot Hawley Tariff of 1930 caused, or at least significantly contributed to the Great Depression, which began a year earlier in 1929. Were Smoot and Hawley the first time-travelers? To this day, the Free Trade Mavens insist that tariffs imposed on any country's products will instantly lead to another Great Depression.

However, the economy failed in 1929, as in 2008, for reasons having nothing to do with tariffs. The economy failed because banks engaged in reckless stock market and real estate speculations that imploded and rendered them involvement, and because wages stagnated (due in part to excessive immigration), and consumers could no longer afford to consume the productions of the factories that employed them:

https://en.wikipedia.org/wiki/Smoot%E2%80%93Hawley_Tariff_Act

Most economists hold the opinion that the [Smoot Hawley] tariff act did not greatly worsen the great depression:

Douglas A. Irwin writes: "most economists, both liberal and conservative, doubt that Smoot Hawley played much of a role in the subsequent contraction. Milton Friedman also held the opinion that the Smoot-Hawley tariff of 1930 did not cause the Great Depression."[16].

According to Paul Krugman, "Protectionism was a result of the Depression, not a cause. Rising tariffs didn't even play a large role in the initial trade contraction...Where protectionism really mattered was in preventing a recovery in trade when production recovered".[17]

William Bernstein writes "most economic historians now believe that only a minuscule part of that huge loss of both world GDP and the United States' GDP can be ascribed to the tariff wars "because trade was only nine percent of global output, not enough to account for the seventeen percent drop in GDP following the Crash. He thinks the damage done could not possibly have exceeded 2 percent of world GDP and tariff "didn't even significantly deepen the Great Depression."

If the Free Trade Mavens are really convinced that the Smoot Hawley tariffs caused the Great Depression of 1929-1940, then ask them why the economy also failed in the Great Recession of 2008 --- *after* we signed all those free trade deals that eliminated tariffs?

Furthermore, our foreign trade in 1930 was the reverse of what it is today. We manufactured most of what we consumed at and sold the surplus to other countries. We ran a trade surplus with almost every country, instead of importing most of what we use and creating trade deficits. It makes no sense for a country that runs a chronic trade surplus to tariff other countries' productions. It makes all the sense in the world for a country that is bleeding jobs and money to most other countries to protect its economy from being bled dry. The Smoot Hawley Tariff of 1930 has no more relevance to our current trade situation than the Treaty of Versailles.

Free Trade Mavens also have a hard time explaining why the economy performed well between 1945 and 1995 when we had an abundance of tariffs, and performed especially well during Ronald Reagan's administration when tariffs were imposed on hundreds of items:

https://mises.org/library/ronald-reagan-protectionist

Ronald Reagan: Protectionist

When he imposed a 100% tariff on selected Japanese electronic products for allegedly "dumping" computer memory chips, he said he did it "to enforce the principles of free and fair trade." And Treasury Secretary James A. Baker has boasted about the protectionist record: Reagan "has granted more import relief to U.S. industry than any of his predecessors in more than half a century."

The [Reagan] administration has thus far:

- *Forced Japan to accept restraints on auto exports.*
- *Tightened considerably the quotas on imported sugar.*
- *Negotiated to increase the restrictiveness of...trade in textiles and apparel.*
- *Required 18 countries, to accept "voluntary restraint agreements" that reduce their steel imports to the United States.*
- *Imposed a 45% duty on Japanese motorcycles for the benefit of Harley Davidson.*
- *Raised tariffs on Canadian lumber and cedar shingles.*
- *Forced the Japanese into an agreement to control the price of computer memory chips.*
- *Removed third-world countries on several occasions from the duty-free import program.*
- *Pressed Japan to force its automakers to buy more American-made parts.*

- *Demanded that Taiwan, West Germany, Japan, and Switzerland restrain their exports of machine tools.*
- *Accused the Japanese of dumping roller bearings.*
- *Accused the Japanese of dumping forklift trucks and color picture tubes.*
- *Extended quotas on imported clothes pins.*

I am not advocating putting tariffs on every product from every country. A few countries like Canada, Australia, the UK, and some in South America trade fairly with us. They do not run trade deficits and should not be tariffed. We should not tariff products such as coffee and bananas and jewels that we do not produce in the USA.

But we should tariff products from countries that run persistent trade surpluses with us in high value manufactured products. After all, the Free Trade Mavens promised us that free trade would create trade surpluses and "millions of well-paying jobs for Americans who will build product to export to other countries."

That's what they promised. It's not our fault that they were wrong.

Is Industry Really Obsolete?

Free Trade Mavens want us to believe that industrial jobs are obsolete and fit only for desperate people in Third World countries. Americans should only want to work in the comfort of easy chairs in air-conditioned offices. Let the Chinese and Mexicans bend metal and assemble parts.

People would certainly prefer to work comfy jobs that don't have a lot of stress. However, those are the types of high overhead jobs that companies are most prone to eliminating in waves of "cost-cutting." The high-pay, do-nothing jobs only really exist among government employees and pampered corporation executives and tenured academics. Most jobs that in the private sector are boring and stressful. Most people work jobs they don't like doing, because that is the only way they can get paid. If jobs were recreational, employees would pay employers to do them.

Industrial jobs pay well because they require a mind for skilled labor to make a quality product that has tangible value. Yes, I am aware that industrial labor unions used to make a mockery of the words "pride and quality," and were always on strike for higher pay for less work. I am aware that labor unions did their share to poison the manufacturing work ethic in the United States. Yes, I agree that they have had their deserved comeuppance by the removal of their work to countries where people still take pride in their work.

However, one must not beat a puppy for the rest of its life just because it makes a mess on the carpet one time. Perhaps our industrial people have learned their lesson that their jobs are relocatable and that they must be competitive on the job. Even if one does not like labor unions, they are only 6% of the private sector labor force. Even Michigan, once a bastion of UAW unionism, is now a "right-to-work" state, meaning that labor unions cannot force workers to join them.

Beyond all that, manufacturing broadens our economy to include value-added work, and not just the zero-sum game of finance and government-funded bureaucracies. Industrial jobs pay well and offer upward mobility to those who want it. Besides assembly line labor, there are foremen, inventory control clerks, production managers, sales managers, cost accountants, computer programmers, and so on. When industrial jobs leave the country, they take the professional jobs higher up the value chain with them. Industrial jobs spawn jobs for other companies that service factories and the industrial equipment within.

Industry expands the demand for finance, healthcare education, retail, and entertainment. Anyone who doubts this can take note that since we removed most of the industry from the United States in the late 1990's, we have produced nothing except unemployment, public and private sector debt, a Great Recession, and slow growth that lingers to this day. The future of the post-manufacturing economy looks bleak because it is.

Trade Deficits don't Matter?

Free Trade Mavens have reversed course 180 degrees on their trade propaganda. They now spend much of their time obfuscating the trade deficit and pretending to believe it doesn't matter. Let's recall Vice President Al Gore's 1993 promise that: *"NAFTA will...greatly accelerate [our trade with Mexico]; we will have a larger trade surplus with Mexico than with any country in the entire world."*

That's what they promised when they sold their cockamamie theory to the public and Congress. They said they wanted the other countries to have trade deficits with *us!* Now that we have become greatest trade deficit country of all time, they have changed their propaganda to: "The trade deficit doesn't matter because all the money we send overseas must eventually come back to the USA."

Let's look at how the trade deficit dollars leave the USA when we buy goods and services from sources in foreign companies. These companies could be foreign-owned, or they could be American-owned subsidiaries. Most of what we buy overseas is the same stuff we produce domestically --- motor vehicles and auto parts, machinery, electronics, computers, aircraft, semiconductors, furniture, and textiles. We even import most of the same food we grow here including tomatoes, blueberries, and citrus. The common denominator is that we run trade deficits with most of these products, including much of our food that is imported, even though we can produce enough food in the USA to feed ourselves twenty times over.

The trade deficit is taken out of the paychecks of American workers, and out of the profits of American businesses that produce in the USA. American workers do not earn wages producing products that are imported, and companies that import products do not pay taxes to the USA. They merely profit from selling the products to us, without paying anything for the privilege of profiting in our market. In that regard, imports are a loss for American workers, a loss of profits for American companies that produce in the USA, and a loss of tax revenue to our federal, state, and local governments.

That would not matter if the trade were balanced such that American companies were selling the same amount of goods and services overseas as foreign companies are selling here. Were that the case, American companies would be putting Americans to work exporting product to sell overseas, like the Free Trade Mavens promised. However, that did not happen. The trade deficit has grown to $810 billion --- 46% of which is allocated to China, 20% to the European Union, and approximately 8% each to Germany, Mexico, and Japan.

So how does the $810 billion per year that was removed from American workers return to the U.S? The Free Trade Mavens have recently learned to insist that "it comes back to the U.S. in *services*!" Yet, I have never heard any Free Trade Maven talk intelligently about what these "services" are.

Diligent research reveals that our largest "exports of services" are tourism and education, when foreigners tour the U.S. or educate their children here. The rest of it comes back as purchases of U.S. debt and assets. Other countries, especially China buy our government's debt, American real estate, and American stocks and bonds. Our "exports of services" is thus primarily a transfer of wealth away from American middle-class wage-earning workers and toward foreigners who can afford to travel to the USA, educate their kids here, buy our government debt, our stocks and bonds, and our real estate.

Now, it is true that foreigners travelling to the USA and educating their children here is mutually beneficial. It's great to see Chinese, Japanese, and European tourists spending money in the USA and sending their children to be educated here to learn American values. However, tourism and education only offset 22% of the merchandise trade deficit. And the fact remains that foreigners touring the USA and educating their kids using trade dollars that were taken away from American wage-earning families. Do we really want Chinese millionaires sending their kids to American universities that an American can't afford because their mothers and fathers lost their jobs to Chinese imports? Why can't we have the best of both worlds --- balanced trade in merchandise produced by middle class labor, *and* a surplus in services by foreigners who want to spend their money touring the USA and educating their children here?

As you might expect, the Free Trade Mavens have exaggerated the value and sustainability of "services" we "sell" to other countries:

https://www.wsj.com/articles/u-s-dominance-in-global-services-economy-weakens-11575283275?commentId=7b816480-bc28-4124-8089-f2b6428fe580#comments_sector

U.S. Dominance in Global Services Economy Weakens

Some softness in demand reflects cyclical factors, such as slowing foreign economies, but other forces are weighing on exports and prompting Americans to buy more foreign services

By Paul Kiernan

Dec. 2, 2019

WASHINGTON—Over the past half-century, the U.S. has evolved from an industrial superpower into the undisputed champion of the global services economy…. Growth has since stalled, however. Exports of services barely rose in the first nine months of 2019, while imports increased 5.5%. The services surplus, at $178.5 billion through September, was down 10% from a year earlier, on pace for its steepest annual decline since 2003.

Services are down because fewer foreigners are coming to the United States in hopes of becoming permanent illegal residents by overstaying their visas. In the meantime, Americans are buying more foreign services, because like everything else from overseas, they are cheap. We may soon be running as severe a trade deficit in "services" as we are in merchandize.

The rest of the trade deficit dollars are returned to the USA in less beneficial ways, by foreigners purchasing our government debt, and our real estate, and stocks and bonds. When foreigners buy our government debt, we are levying future taxes on our children and grandchildren, without their consent, to pay back the principal and the interest on what we have borrowed to fund our consumption of foreign-made products. Foreign purchases of American real estate inflate the value of our real estate in high-demand cities, making it more difficult for Americans to find affordable housing:

https://www.wsj.com/articles/chinese-real-estate-investors-retreat-from-u-s-as-political-pressure-mounts-1532437934?mod=hp_lead_pos4

Updated July 24, 2018

Chinese real-estate investors, facing pressure from Beijing, are reversing a years-long buying spree in the U.S. where they often paid record prices for marquee properties like New York's Waldorf Astoria hotel.

Isn't that swell: we are beating America's middle class families out of their jobs and handing off their paychecks and pensions to Chinese who buy our "marquee properties" and rent them back to us! This has become a noticeable problem in Canadian, Australian, and New Zealand cities where Chinese use American trade deficit dollars to buy the prime properties and rent them back to the locals at extortionate rates:

https://www.wsj.com/articles/western-cities-want-to-slow-flood-of-chinese-home-buying-nothing-works-1528294587

Western Cities Want to Slow Flood of Chinese Home Buying. Nothing Works.

Governments from Vancouver to Sydney to Toronto are using taxes and other restrictions to tackle real-estate bubbles

Sydney's home state of New South Wales doubled its foreign-buyers tax to 8% in July 2017, but that didn't arrest demand.... Chinese property buying is an "unstoppable juggernaut..."

After the first Vancouver 15% tax failed to put a lid on foreign buyers...province officials raised the foreign-buyers tax to 20% and expanded coverage well beyond Vancouver. Officials also imposed a new levy—0.5% of the property value and climbing to 2% next year—on homeowners who don't pay income tax in Canada.

One desirable target has been the harbor city of Auckland, New Zealand, home to just over a million people. Last year, a political backlash erupted over complaints that the city had grown too expensive. New Zealand homeownership rates are at their lowest since 1951, national data show; a quarter of residents under 40 own their home compared with half that age group in 1991.

The money to buy this inflated real estate was taken from the pockets of families who are struggling to keep humble roofs over their families' heads. It is a replay of the 2008 crash when Americans of modest means were put out of work, while Wall Street banks and money funds wrecked themselves, and the entire nation, with reckless speculations on inflated real estate. Now the Chinese want to throw gasoline on the raging fires of real estate speculation. But I wonder if all trade deficit dollars really return to the United States. Dollars are a de facto currency in many countries, so I suspect that many remain overseas and add to the wealth of currency in circulation in other countries and subtract it from ours.

119

Also bear in mind that trade deficit dollars are not taxed. Instead of spending $1 trillion in the U.S. and having the value of production (labor and profits) taxed at perhaps 25% by federal, state, and local governments, imported products are not taxed by the United States on the value of production added abroad. With the trade deficit now rising to $1 trillion, that leaves a tax deficit of $250 billion that must be made up by increasing taxes on Americans, issuing more debt, or expanding the money supply.

The trade deficit also involves more than money. There is the irreversible loss of manufacturing expertise that is on the way to making the USA a weak country like Portugal. We no longer know how to make the products we require for our comfort and necessity. Every day the trade deficit continues, we become more entangled with other countries that are potentially hostile.

This poses a national security risk, which Alexander Hamilton mentioned in his Report on Manufacturers. A country cannot be strong without manufacturing. During World War II we replaced our early losses of equipment destroyed by the Japanese at Pearl Harbor, the Philippines, and the naval battles at Guadalcanal; and destroyed by the Germans in North Africa and the Battle of the Atlantic. We converted the entire USA into a factory producing tens of thousands of tanks and other motor vehicles, aircraft, warships, transports, and all manner of weapons, including the atomic bomb. We fought a two-front war against the Germans and Japanese with a population of 131 million. Would we be able to fight a rival power like Russia or China (or both in combination) if, God forbid, the early battles went against us? Without manufacturing capacity, we lack the ability to replace our losses, and would be ground down in a war of attrition.

And there is the social cost of unemployment that Adam Smith warned us about. When Americans are unemployed by the trade deficit, they lose their dignity and their spirit. Having no means to support their families, they turn to substance abuse and suicide. Their children's future may be constrained by their parents' inability to educate them. Families whose breadwinners are unemployed before their time become laden with social pathologies. The entire nation weakens, and its politics becomes radicalized as "those left behind" seek redress of their grievances through extremist candidates who advocate redistribution of wealth. Karl Marx loved free trade because he thought it spawned revolution. Adam Smith was opposed to jobs-destroying free trade because he wanted to preserve his society by enabling all its people to have employment at wages that supported their themselves and their families in reasonable comfort.

Now let's parse the Free Trade Mavens' (FTM's) propaganda that seeks to obscure the deleterious effects of trade deficits:

FTM Propaganda point #1: "You have been running a trade deficit with your local supermarkets for your entire life, are you going to accuse them of unfair trade?"

A Chinese person, perhaps an agent of their government, posited the above well-worn cliche when I mentioned the trade deficit with China. My response:

No, because:

1. *I do not have to mortgage my paid off house to buy groceries or write interest-bearing IOUs to the grocer.*
2. *My grocer is not burglarizing my house to steal my personal and business information.*
3. *My grocer is not going behind my back to sabotage my business with other trading partners, for example counterfeiting my trademarked products and selling knockoffs on the sly to my customers.*
4. *My grocer does not steal the vegetables out of my garden and sell them back to me, as Chinese companies steal American companies' products and sell them back to the Americans.*
5. *My grocer does not go back on his word, such as promising to give Hong Kong 50 years of autonomy and invading them 3 years later. I don't do business with people who have no integrity.*
6. *My grocer does not insult me every time I go into his store.*
7. *My grocer does not bioengineer a disease and put it in my food.*

FTM propaganda point #2: "There is no trade deficit, because we export 'services' to balance it out."

If you ask an FTM to explain what these 'services' are, they can't do it, because they have no idea what they are. In fact, it is true that 'services' cancel out about a quarter of the merchandise trade deficit. However, that number is diminishing as foreigners learn to

121

export 'services' to us, the same way they ran our merchandise trade from surplus to deficit. Most 'services' we sell to foreigners are hospitality for foreign tourists and tuition for foreign students. A 'service' is also rendered when an American-owned hotel in a foreign country rents a room to a foreigner, or when an American company receives a royalty on a patent used in a foreign country. But since some countries, like China, ignore our patents, that revenue stream is diminishing.

The holy grail of services is banking. Our banks would love to be able to set up shop in other countries and run the same scams on them that wrecked our economy in 2008. Bankers are always out in full cry touting globalism. They don't understand that few other countries are ever going to let them set up shop in their homelands, because few governments trust them.

FTM propaganda point #3: "The trade deficit exists because we consume more than we produce."

The implication is that Americans are irresponsible spendthrifts who are to blame for the trade deficit. This would be like having your car stolen, and the police come out and say: "It's your fault that the car was stolen. If you'd saved your money in a bank instead of spending it on a car, nobody would have stolen it."

The truth is that we have a trade deficit because:

A) Our companies moved production overseas, and that is where Americans must buy the products we use, and

B) other countries discourage the importation of American-made product into their market.

FTM propaganda point #4: "We run a trade deficit because the United States dollar is the world's reserve currency."

If you ask the FTM's to define what they mean by "reserve currency" they never answer the question directly, because they don't know what a reserve currency is.

A reserve currency is government-issued paper currency that is redeemable in some valuable commodity like gold. In 1944, near the end of World War II, our government pledged to redeem one ounce of gold for each $35 of our dollars. Our dollar was "good as gold." Any foreign government could exchange $35 for an ounce of gold, so the $US maintained a constant fixed value relative to gold. Our dollar became the standard for settling trade balances.

Over time, our gold reserves depleted as our foreign trade balance worsened, and as our presidents and Congresses asked our Federal Reserve to print vast quantities of paper dollars to fund the social welfare programs and the Vietnam War. When our dollars could no longer be redeemed in gold, President Nixon revoked the gold standard in August 1971. The dollar devalued by 96%, stoking stagflation. Since then, our dollar has been a floating currency like all others. It has no special status in trade. It is used to settle the lion's share of trade balances only because the USA is the country where the lion's share of other countries' trade surpluses are dumped.

Thus, it's fairer to say that the increase in imports into the USA is what broke the dollar's back as a reserve currency, and not that being a reserve currency promotes imports. The $US is no more a "reserve currency" than any other country's money. The FTM's keep hooting about "reserve currency" because they don't understand it and don't think anyone else will either. They are trotting out the "reserve currency" nonsense to cover up all their lies about how free trade would make us "an export nation that creates jobs for American workers."

A typical conservation with an Free Trade Maven about the dollar being a reserve currency:

FTM: The dollar is the global reserve currency.

Response: The dollar is an informal "reserve currency" (not a designated one) because we're the country that buys all other countries' surplus productions, while they protect their markets from imports of American-made products.

If the dollar breaks, it will be the trade deficit and the federal budget what did it. The more trade deficits we run, the more dollars are accumulated overseas, and the more the Fed has to print here to make up the difference. The bigger the budget deficit, the more bonds the Fed has to sell to time-warp dollars of the future into dollars of the present.

So far, we've managed both deficits. Then again, the banks told us they were managing their balance sheets prudently in 2008. Until one day we found out they weren't, the day the whole [ ] economy came crashing down like a house of wet cards in a hurricane.

Will it happen again? Maybe it will if the Fed tries to dump a trillion dollars of bonds on the market, and have to offer them at 30% interest to attract buyers.

That might happen even without the Fed selling any of the Treasurys on its balance sheet. All that is needed is the wider bond market rebelling against negative real interest rates. It has taken them longer than I expected, but surely with CPI running at 5-10% in January of next year, and bonds still yielding next to nothing, bond holders will finally realized that they are being robbed. I really wish someone will ask Paul Tudor Jones about his thoughts two and half months after that interview.

FTM: We run trade deficits because the dollar is the reserve currency.

Response: The dollar was a reserve currency prior to August 1971 when we ran trade surpluses. It was a reserve currency because it was redeemable in gold by our government at the fixed rate of $35 for one ounce of gold. It was a reserve currency because the reserve was gold. President Nixon took us off the gold standard in 1971, when the first trade deficits depleted the gold inventory. At that moment the dollar stopped being a reserve currency, and promptly devalued 96% relative to gold, thereby creating massive inflation in the USA, when we had to pay for imported foreign product, especially most of our oil, with devalued dollars.

The dollar isn't anything now except a currency of convenience, because we print trillions of dollars to buy products we import from overseas. We print those dollars by issuing government debt to (maybe) be repaid in the future. Other countries have dollars because they sell to us, not because the dollar is a reserve currency, which it hasn't been in 40 years.

FTM: [crickets].

FTM propaganda point #5: "Other countries offset their trade surpluses with us by investing in the USA. Trade deficits give us an investment surplus, which is good!"

So, where is this "investment surplus?" Our economy fell off a cliff in 2008, during the time when the trade deficit was escalating. We bailed out our failed private sector economy with $10 trillion of public debt, which we still carry on our ledger. The principal will never be repaid, and the interest will be a permanent drain on our future economy until the end of time. If we had all these "investment surpluses" because of trade deficits, then why did the economy roll over and die? Why weren't people investing in creating new businesses and jobs? Why did we have to add $10 trillion of public debt to cover for all the private sector "investment" dollars that went up in smoke?

FTM propaganda point #6 "We have a global supply chain that can't be disrupted."

The truth is that it's a global **labor** chain. It's a one-way flow of product from countries where labor is cheap to countries where prices are high. Pay the Chinese $1 / hour to assemble iPhones, then sell them in the USA for $650.

FTM propaganda point #7: "At least we're buying stuff cheap from Mexico and China."

This is the ultimate fall back of FTM propaganda. It is quite a change from their "Foreign trade will create millions of well-paying jobs for American workers who will build product to export to other countries," isn't it? When people keep changing their propaganda, it is usually because their theories are unsound. We are not importing product cheap from other countries. We are importing cheaply made products, in many cases inferior to what we used to produce here.

Aside from that, I do not want to live in a country with Third World living standards, where people eat out of garbage cans, sell their children into prostitution, and walk barefoot through streets that double as open sewers. We worked hard in the USA for hundreds of years to attain a high standard of living for our people. Industrial production was a major factor in increasing our standard of living. We do not need to go back to the Stone Age just because people in other primitive countries live like that.

There's also a matter of perspective. If you only look at imports of manufactured items as products, you may be prone to saying it doesn't matter whether they're produced locally or abroad. If you look at manufacturing as an infrastructure that employs people, creates investment in the USA, and is a source of national wealth, then it does make a difference.

We protect our agriculture like it is the most important aspect of our economy because we care about food as a national security and economic issue. We know there is more to agriculture than just what comes out of the ground. If we offshored our agriculture to other countries, we would lose the knowledge of modern agriculture, and the knowledge of industries that revolve around agriculture, including genetics, veterinary medicine, and the manufacture of farm equipment. Shouldn't we feel it's important to maintain our industrial economy, as Germany, Japan, and China take pains to do as a matter of national policy?

Now let's do a bit of extrapolation. Let's say that pre-Trump trends continue and more of our industry moves overseas. How are we going to pay for our trade deficits then? We're not going to sell the Chinese enough turnips, taters, and beans to pay for imports of motor vehicles, electronics, and computers. So, what do we do then? Sell them more government debt? How are we going to pay the interest? Sell them our real estate? How are we going to pay the rent when we become their landlords? Sell them our companies' stock? Then they will become our employers.

This is a link to the government's statistics on our balance of trade in goods and services:

https://www.census.gov/foreign-trade/statistics/historical/gands.pdf

My view is that the trade deficit (combined goods and services) grew 12% in 2018, while the economy grew only 2.5%, and more than 100% of that "economic growth" was an increase in the national debt by nearly a trillion dollars. We're growing the private sector economy slowly, if at all; and are merely substituting imports and government debt for products we used to make here.

Trade deficits are a sign of dependency, not prosperity. But people are hard-headed and refuse to accept realities that they don't agree with until they have no choice. Nobody wanted to believe we had an unsound economy in 2008 until it fell apart all at once. Trade deficits are a sign of an unsound globalist economy that needs to be shored up before it falls off a cliff again.

Is Cheaper Better?

Globalists have reversed their propaganda about free trade creating "millions of well-paying jobs for American workers." They've become flea market operators who peddle cheap foreign merchandise, much of it pirated from us. They claim that importing product from cheap-labor countries lowers its cost to American consumers.

But companies are in business to maximize profits, not to offer low prices. They charge whatever the market will bear. When an American company fires its American workers and moves their jobs to Mexico and China, why would it lower the prices it charges to American consumers? The workers were replaced with foreigners to cut costs and increase profits, not to give American consumers a deal.

Quality suffers at companies that make a fetish of pretending to sell foreign-made products on the cheap. American-made products used to be quality products. Now our companies are substituting plastic parts for high-strength steel in their outdoor equipment and cheap circuit boards for mechanical parts in their indoor appliances. Many appliances they import from Mexico and China are cheap junk with short operational lives.

Buy a cheap riding lawnmower or a washing machine from a "big box" store and odds are it is going to fall apart due to shoddy manufacturing and inferior components. You think you're getting a bargain on an imported $1,000 riding lawn mower or a $399 washing machine. You're more likely to find yourself owning a hunk of hunk that breaks down and isn't worth the cost of repairing.

The low-quality mania by so many American companies has persuaded American consumers to pay more for European-branded products. An outdoor equipment maker said that Husqvarna products imported from Sweden cost 60% more than equivalent American-branded products because people are learning that Mexican-made and Chinese-made products sold under American brand names are junk.

I learned from appliance shopping that to protect their profit margins, some American appliance makers have formed a manufacturers' cartel in Mexico. They all use the same Mexican-made, low-quality components in each other's machines to keep their costs the same and discourage any company from underselling the others. They are peddling these cheaply made, inferior products in the USA because our manufacturers have gone to Mexico and set up a price fixing cartel!

Manufacturers love selling low-quality, cheaply made products at inflated prices because the products wear out faster and must be replaced more often. What manufacturer *wouldn't* prefer to sell $400 washing machines that have to be replaced every three years than sell a $1,000 machine that lasts 15 years? Our manufacturers also enjoy having docile workers in Mexico or China who work under lax health and safety laws. If workers are killed or injured by accidents or by inhaling toxic chemicals, or are harassed inappropriately by management, the consequences are much less severe than in in the United States.

And even if foreign-made products were cheaper, Americans would rather be employed and receive paychecks that allow them to purchase some goods and services, even if relatively expensive, than to be unemployed and unable to purchase any products, even if they are relatively cheap.

Bringing Back the Jobs

It's worthwhile to repeat the feeling of Americans on election night 2016:

https://www.dailykos.com/stories/2016/11/8/1593014/-Election-night-2016-Finally-Liveblog-12

People are suffering financially in ways that we haven't seen since the 1920s. We are close to losing in this election because democrats who have enough money to be comfy don't see it. Don't know it and refuse to believe it. The country is still poor. The job market still s——. Bernie tapped into that anger and so did Trump. This was a referendum on poverty and what causes it.

And look how they feel now after going back to work, some for the first time in years: https://youtu.be/Syzo-6dMoso?t=2659

Those re-employed workers are telling us that jobs are more than just dollars and cents. They are people's livelihoods, and the foundation of their families and their communities. When we destroy an American's job just because a foreigner will work cheaper, we have betrayed our people, and discredited the capitalist system as being anything good for the middle class. It is fine to hire Mexicans and Chinese to produce product that is sold in Mexico and China, but not to beat Americans out of our jobs by importing it into the USA. Free Trade Mavens are angry that Trump's tariffs are bringing back jobs to the USA:

https://www.thenews-messenger.com/story/money/companies/locally-in-business/2018/01/23/new-import-tariffs-bring-200-jobs-clyde-whirlpool/1056903001/

Import tariff brings 200 jobs to Clyde [Ohio] Whirlpool

Jan. 23, 2018

CLYDE - More jobs are coming to the Clyde division of Whirlpool after President Donald Trump upheld a 50 percent tariff on imports of large residential washing machines.

The announcement means 200 new jobs at the Clyde plant, company officials said, adding that the tariff levels the playing field for U.S. factories competing against competitors saturating the market with inexpensive machines built outside the United States.

"This is a victory for American workers and consumers alike. By enforcing our existing trade laws, President Trump has ensured American workers will compete on a level playing field."

https://www.southstrandnews.com/news/a-new-era-celebration-marks-reopening-of-georgetown-steel-mill/article_6db8bee2-7899-11e8-8e22-f3f80f448489.html

A new era: Celebration marks reopening of Georgetown steel mill

By David Purtell Jun 25, 2018 "Reopening a closed down steel plant is a very special feeling," Gupta said. "When you see something coming back to life, it has a special place in itself."

https://www.nbc4i.com/news/politics/republic-steel-planning-to-reopen-ohio-plant-after-pres-trump-announced-tariffs/1096449097

Republic Steel planning to reopen Ohio plant after Pres. Trump announced tariffs

This could result in Republic bringing back 1,000+ jobs to its Lorain, OH facility.

https://www.constructiondive.com/news/texas-port-moves-16b-steel-factory-forward/522321

Texas port moves $1.6B steel factory forward

https://www.prnewswire.com/news-releases/nucor-to-build-rebar-micro-mill-in-florida-300612204.html

Nucor to Build Rebar Micro Mill in Florida

CHARLOTTE, N.C., March 12, 2018 /PRNewswire/ -- Nucor Corporation (NYSE: NUE) announced today that it will build a rebar micro mill in Frostproof, Florida, which is located in Polk County. This is a $240 million investment and is the second rebar micro mill Nucor is constructing. In November 2017, Nucor announced a rebar micro mill project in Sedalia, Missouri.

https://www.kbbonline.com/news/business/lg-electronics-breaks-ground-u-s-home-appliance-factory/

LG Electronics Breaks Ground on U.S. Home Appliance Factory

August 24, 2017

LG Electronics today broke ground on its new one-million-sq.-ft. home appliance manufacturing facility near Clarksville, Tenn. The project, in the heart of Montgomery County, is expected to bring at least 600 full-time jobs to the area and will accelerate the delivery of LG's innovative, premium home appliances to better meet U.S. consumer demand.

https://news.samsung.com/us/samsung-south-carolina-home-appliance-manufacturing-plant-investment-newberry/

Samsung to Expand U.S. Operations, Open $380 Million Home Appliance Manufacturing Plant in South Carolina

Samsung Newsroom 06.28.17

Newberry County facility will create 954 local jobs and support advanced R&D and production of premium home appliance products

https://www.wsj.com/articles/fiat-chrysler-to-open-new-assembly-factory-in-detroit-1544127162?mod=hp_lead_pos5

Fiat Chrysler to Open New Assembly Factory in Detroit

Auto maker plans to make a sport-utility vehicle at the new factory

By Christina Rogers and Adrienne Roberts Updated Dec. 6, 2018 3:47 p.m. ET

Fiat Chrysler Automobiles FCAU -2.97% NV plans to open a new factory in Detroit, according to people briefed on the plan, the first new U.S. assembly plant to be opened by a major domestic car maker in at least a decade.

The Italian-American auto maker plans to make a sport-utility vehicle at the new factory, the people said.

Moving the Goalposts

Free Trade Mavens are doing what people usually do when their theories are nullified by observed reality, which is to "move the goal posts" by introducing new ways to measure the results. They have been proven wrong on all their points, specifically:

1. Free Trade with countries that don't buy from the United States create jobs in the United States.
2. That the American jobs that were destroyed by detrimental trade were really destroyed by "robots and automation."
3. That once jobs are destroyed by trade it is impossible to get them back by improving trade deals where possible and imposing tariffs on countries that insist on maintaining a belligerent trading attitude against us.

Their newest theory is to claim that tariffs "raise prices on consumers." Free Trade Mavens who don't know anything at all about the steel business, are certain that tariffs on imported steel have raised prices and therefore prices in all products made with imported steel. In truth, the price of steel rises and falls by as much as 60% per year for reasons having nothing at all to do with tariffs:

http://steelbenchmarker.com/files/history.pdf

Note the volatility of prices going back for years before the tariffs. Most of what drives steel prices is anticipation about the future of the economy, the same thing factors that drive stock prices. Steel prices collapsed in 2015, along with the stock market, when it seemed the economy was headed toward recession. They began increasing in 2016 and 2017 when the economy improved after Trump's election. As of this writing in July 2018, steel prices are lower than they were in April 2011. It is much more likely that an improving economy is boosting steel prices, not anything having to do with tariffs. In summer 2019, steel prices are 20% *lower* than they were before Trump's tariffs.

Free Trade Mavens are simultaneously claiming that tariffs reduce companies' profit margins. So, which is it? Are consumers paying more for steel, or are steel importers reducing their profits to maintain the same prices they charged before tariffs? It could be some of both. Or perhaps it is neither. Perhaps American companies are holding prices steady now that tariffs have reduced imports and the volume of domestic production is increasing. They are producing more steel, thus maintaining their profits, regardless of tariffs.

Thus, it is possible that tariffs on certain products like steel are providing the best of all worlds:

- More production in the USA
- More jobs in the USA
- More investment in the USA
- More taxes paid in the USA
- More corporation profits from expanded production in the USA
- Less volatility in steel prices since more of it is produced continuously in the United States and less is imported form volatile overseas producers.

The Free Trade Mavens' Tortured Data

Free Trade Mavens are like sports announcers for an underperforming baseball team. The announcers' job is to keep fans watching, even when their team is losing three games out of every four. The announcers therefore seek to obscure their team's poor performance by trotting out goofy statistics:

- "Yet another record day, folks. This is the first time one of our pitchers has ever beaned seven batters in a row!
- Our batters are doing great, too! They don't have any hits, but one of them got on base on error, and another when the pitcher balked.
- And concession sales are going gangbusters! We sold over a thousand hot dogs and three beer-keg equivalents today."

Free Trade Mavens are past masters of obscuring the bad results of their trade agendas with misleading statistics. They start out by doing what every proponent of a dubious positions does, which is citing statistics without context. For example:

Please, check the link below and see for yourself, that our [American] tariffs are higher than the ones of Canada, Germany, France, and other European countries.

https://www.indexmundi.com/facts/indicators/TM.TAX.MRCH.SM.AR.ZS/rankin gs

According to these "statistics," the USA supposedly imposes tariffs of around 3.5% on other countries' imports, while their tariffs on our products are supposedly a few fractions of a percent lower. Now let's examine the details about how other countries' tariffs and informal trade barriers restrict our exports:

https://www.quora.com/Many-Trump-supporters-point-to-the-EUs-existing-tariffs-on-American-goods-as-justification-for-Trumps-tariffs-Does-the-EU-have-any-such-tariffs-and-if-so-what-justification-do-they-claim-for-retaliatory-tariffs

Example: EU has a 29% tax (10% tariff and a 19% import VAT) on all American made cars. Their claim that they charge an average of 3% is statistically true but a lie, because that average is not in actual trade dollars, but across all product categories (definitions,) many of which the USA does not export into EU. The 3% average gives American car imports as exactly the statistical weight as non-existent American Penguin imports. They have very high tariff's that target American products that compete with their domestic producers. Their tariff on American potato: 0%. Their tariff on American headphones: 42%.

There are also informal trade barriers. You cannot sell American Wine in France for fear of getting your shop burned down. The core EU airlines refuse to buy Boeing airplanes. To understand these trade barriers, go to EU and you'll find that only American products available are ones that do not compete against EU products.

A favorite tactic of Free Trade Mavens is to pretend that "tariffs hurt the very working people they are supposed to help." Here is a "study" written by two "economists" paid by a steel consumers' consortium. The study is still relevant because the authors dusted it off and reused it as opposition to President Trump's proposed tariffs on steel in 2018. The study delivered what it was paid to deliver, an "estimate" that 200,000 jobs were lost in the steel consuming industries because the tariff.

http://www.tradepartnership.com/pdf_files/2002jobstudy.pdf

However, if you look at their actual employment data (blue line on Chart 1) on page 13, you'll see that jobs in "steel consuming industries" INCREASED from 12,000,000 in February 2002 when the tariff was imposed, to 12,600,000 in May 2002 --- an increase of 600,000 jobs *after* the tariffs were imposed! Why, then, did the authors claim that 200,000 jobs were "lost?" Because they were paid to invent that number. They claimed that there should have been 800,000 jobs created instead of 600,000, so 200,000 jobs were "lost." Reading the "fine print" reveals that the authors backpedal their dubious conclusions:

How many of these job losses [there weren't any] are attributable to high steel prices [supposedly due to tariffs]? ***This is not an easy question to answer.***

Free Trade Mavens will always invent numbers that purport to show that tariffs cause job losses, even when the evidence shows the opposite. They ignore the evidence, and seek to obscure it, because they are paid by globalist corporations that hate tariffs that complicate their mission to put Americans out of work and replace them with cheap labor in other countries.

When information is supplied that places the Free Trade Mavens' statistics in proper context, they must work harder to mask the damage their trade treaties have caused. That's when they start "torturing" their data. Here's a statistic from the St. Louis Federal Reserve that purports to believe that, despite moving much of our manufacturing capacity overseas, it is all still here:

https://www.stlouisfed.org/on-the-economy/2017/april/us-manufacturing-really-declining

Is U.S. Manufacturing Really Declining?

Tuesday, April 11, 2017

A popular narrative over the past decade has been U.S. manufacturing's precipitous decline. But has manufacturing really become an afterthought in the U.S. economy?

At first glance, the numbers seem to paint a bleak picture for the health of the manufacturing sector. After holding fairly steady through the 1990s, the number of manufacturing jobs in the U.S. dropped from over 17 million in 2000 to just over 12 million in 2015.

The employment share of manufacturing has been declining even longer than that. About 32 percent of workers held manufacturing jobs in 1953, but that share was down to just 8.7 percent in 2015. Also, manufacturing's share of nominal gross domestic product (GDP) has dropped from 28.1 percent in 1953 to just 12 percent in 2015, as seen in the next figure.

...[but] in real terms, growth in manufacturing has kept up with growth in the rest of the economy over the past 70 years.

This sounds like tortured data --- how can manufacturing's "share of the nominal gross domestic product fall from 28.1 percent to 12 percent and still have "kept up with the growth in the rest of the economy?" Another graph of manufacturing output from the same St. Louis Federal Reserve contradicts the tortured data:

https://fred.stlouisfed.org/series/OUTMS

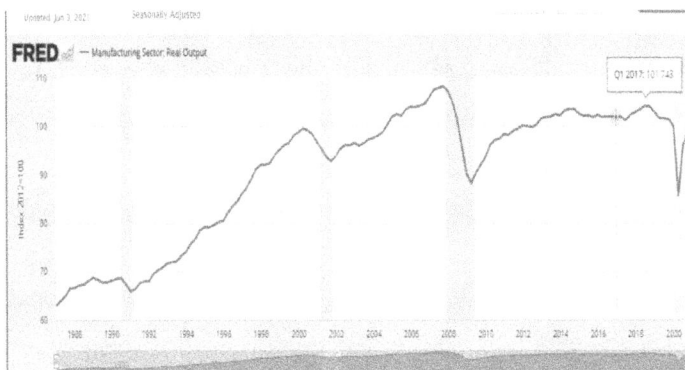

Note that:

- in the 13 years between 1987 and 2000, our manufacturing output grew 3.6% per year, from 70 to 110.

- In the 20 years after 2000, when the effects of "free" trade became felt, it has grown at only .05% (one half of one percent) from 110 to 119.

- Manufacturing output has not grown at all since the end of 2007. The quantities of what we produce in the USA, such as motor vehicles, are falling:

https://www.statista.com/statistics/198488/us-and-global-motor-vehicle-production-since-1999/

In 1999 the USA produced 13.0 million vehicles. In 2017 we produced 11.1 million, a decline of 1.9 million, even while our population has grown by 37 million in the interim. So where are the missing 1.9 million motor vehicles? They have gone to Mexico, which exports 2.1 million motor vehicles to the USA. They are also leaving for the European Union, which runs a $151 billion trade surplus with us, Japan which runs a $68 billion surplus, and China which runs a $375 billion surplus. China's surplus will grow even larger, because GM is now building Buicks in China and importing them into the United States, resulting in an additional $782,000,000 trade deficit with China in Buicks alone!

More imports of electronics, aircraft, appliances, electronics, and even food means that lower quantities are produced in the USA. Free Trade Mavens are finding it harder to torture their data, so they have become "data time travelers" to find a reference point that bolsters their opinion that manufacturing in the United States has not declined, despite all

137

evidence that it has. They are now using "the late 1980's" as their reference point. They are saying, "U.S. manufacturing had doubled since the late 1980's." Against, referring back to the Federal Reserve Chart:

https://fred.stlouisfed.org/series/OUTMS

We find that manufacturing has not "doubled" since 1988 but has risen a cumulative 67% in those 30 years. That is 1.5% a year, substantially all of which happened before 2000, when we opened our borders to free trade. We can count on our Free Maven "data time travelers" to go ever further backward in time to root out their comparison points. Before long they will be saying "We now manufacture more than we did in 1776."

The Free Trade Mavens' tortured data would be declared a crime against humanity if data could talk.

Who are the Luddites?

Free Trade advocates like to associate tariffs with ancient things like buggy whips, poor dirt farmers, and old fuddy-duddies with names like "Smoot" and "Hawley." Advocates of tariffs are likened to the followers of the fictional "Ned Ludd," an imaginary character who supposedly roamed the British countryside in the wee hours of the early 1800's, wrecking factories in order to protect the manual labor of home-spinners and blacksmiths operating out of shacks and barns.

Free trade with low-wage countries is the true haven of modern-day Luddites, because it enables companies to avoid spending money on automation to improve their productivity in the USA. Automation only happens when wages rise to the point where companies can get a payback on their investment in new machinery Companies ship jobs out of the United States and into low wage countries to avoid having to spend money automating their American factories. What's a company going to do, given a choice of:

A) Spending $25,000,000 to modernize an American factory so 1,000 American workers earning $25 / hour (wages, benefits, employer-taxes) can be more productive.

B) Firing the 1,000 American workers at $25 / hour, hiring 10,000 Mexicans or Chinese at $1.50 / hour, and pocketing the $25,000,000 as executive bonuses and extra dividends for the investors.

The favorite canard of anti-tariff propagandists is "buggy whips" --- the sticks with leather thongs used to beat slow horses pulling old wagons before Henry Ford put the wagons and the horses out to pasture. The implication is that people who favor tariffs want to protect obsolete jobs that have no place in the modern world. "You want to protect the buggy whip industry with tariffs! Ha! Ha! at you!"

This is a false analogy. Our buggy whip workers never needed any tariff protection. We never put our buggy whip makers out of work by shipping their jobs to Mexico and China, then using Mexicans and Chinese to make buggy whips that were imported into the United States, as American companies do today.

Secondly, our buggy whip makers were able to transition to work making automobiles because the automobile industry developed in the United States. When Henry Ford started building his cars in the USA, the workers were already here. If today's free trade people had been around in 1900, they would have sent the buggy whip industry to Mexico and China, and that is where Henry Ford would have had to go to find workers. The motor vehicle industry would have developed overseas.

Free trade advocates do not understand that new industries usually develop from old ones. People built wagons and buggy whips first, then put motors in the wagons to turn them into cars. The same workers did both jobs, but they were all Americans, building the product in the USA.

The next ancient occupation Free Trade Mavens like to talk about is agriculture. "You have to understand there was a time when farming employed 80% of Americans. Now it only employs 3%. The same will happen with industry. Don't you know that industry is destined to wither away now that robots and automation are doing all the work? So why do you want to protect obsolete industries with tariffs?"

Free trade advocates have a curious view of agriculture. On one hand they like it, because they think it is highly automated, and therefore can portray it as being more "modern" than a factory. On the other hand, they demand open borders so that millions of peons from Mexico and Central America can enter United States and work the farms. "If we don't have open borders, we won't have food." So how can agriculture be "automated" and still require millions of peons to work the fields?

I suppose Free Trade Mavens worship agriculture because farms can't be removed out of the country the way factories can. If Free Trade Mavens could figure out a way to ship our dirt overseas and re-establish corporation-owned farms in Mexico and China, they would be just as much against agriculture as they are against industry.

But to hear the free trade advocates tell it, agriculture is our most important product --- as central to our lives as the patches of maize that the Indians grew around their villages thousands of years ago. Free Trade Mavens talk about agriculture as if they were born with a pair of overalls and a hayseed in their mouths. They pretend to be Mr. Greenjeans' best friends.

A couple of questions come to mind:

140

1. Why do Free Trade Mavens want to ship our industrial jobs to Mexico and China, if robots and automation are doing all the work? Do robots in Mexico and China work cheaper than robots in America? The answer is that it is not robots and automation the free traders are seeking, but cheap human labor.

2. Why do Free Trade Mavens insist that "only low wage jobs are moved overseas?" When an industry moves overseas, it is not just the production workers that lose their jobs It's also highly skilled production planners, product design engineers, accountants, foremen, IT people, and the myriads of contractors and components suppliers required to make factories produce efficiently.

3. Why do Free Trade Mavens like to compare employment in industry to employment in agriculture? Our farm workers migrated away from the land slowly, over a period of about 150 years. We did not suddenly decide to pack up every farm in America and move them all to Mexico and China all at once. Even now we subsidize agriculture with tens of billions of tax dollars and the importation of foreign peons to work the fields.

4. Why do Free Trade Mavens want to shoo all the high-value, high-wage industry to Mexico and China, while letting low-wage labor from Mexico and Guatemala into the United States to ensure that low-value turnips and taters keep being yanked from the bowels of American dirt?

5. Why do Free Trade Mavens insist that advocates for tariffs are "Luddites who want to protect dying industries" when it is the Free Trade Mavens who want to prevent robots and automation in the United States by replacing American workers with cheap overseas manual labor?

"Attack of the Robot People"

Free Trade Mavens will never admit that the 2.1 million cars being imported into the USA from Mexico (not to mention all other countries that run trade surpluses with the USA) cost Americans their jobs. The FTM's pretend to believe that nowadays manufacturing is done entirely by robots instead of by human being workers. According to the "Robot People" millions of robots are humming along, doing all the factory work that used to employ the Joe and Jane Lugnuts of middle America.

Visible evidence, such as factory parking lots filled with the cars of human being workers, suggests otherwise. As do reports of people going back to work after President Trump took steps to encourage manufacturing to return to the United States, including imposing tariffs on steel and aluminum:

https://www.courier-journal.com/story/news/politics/2018/06/01/braidy-industries-breaks-ground-aluminum-mill-eastern-kentucky/646290002/

Braidy Industries breaks ground on Bevin-backed, $1.5B aluminum mill

Louisville Courier Journal Published June 1, 2018

Ashland, Kentucky, looks forward to Braidy Industries building an aluminum plant nearby that may boost the economy.

Braidy Industries broke ground Friday on a future, $1.5 billion aluminum rolling mill, sending a hopeful message to Eastern Kentuckians that it will help lead a long-awaited economic revival and keep its promise to create hundreds of high-paying jobs. "

It's an exciting moment for this area," said 68-year-old Tom Hilgendorf, of Ashland.

Business closures and mass layoffs have become commonplace in Eastern Kentucky, but Braidy expects its project to generate at least 1,000 construction jobs. The mill ... will employ about 600 people.

Whenever you refute Globalists' theories by observation, they will accuse you of citing "anecdotal" evidence (common sense) to refute their carefully crafted propaganda. So, let's use the Globalists own studies to refute their propaganda. Let's look at the employment data in the USA and Mexico, presented in studies written by Globalists, to determine whether:

1. Every human being job that is lost in the USA is taken by a robot.
2. No human being job created in Mexico has ever cost an American his or her job.

Let's recap the auto production and employment data as it relates to the U.S:

We produced 1.9 fewer motor vehicles in the USA in 2017 than we did in 1999. The rest of the world now produces 41 million more than in 1999. 3.6 million motor vehicles are produced in Mexico by 760,000 Mexican auto workers. Of those 3.6 million, 2.1 million, or 58% are exported to the United States. 440,800 American workers were replaced by Mexicans. They were not replaced by robots. And that's just with jobs lost to Mexico alone.

We run a $71 billion trade deficit with Mexico. We run a $810 billion trade deficit with all countries, about half of which originates from China. Prorating the 440,800 jobs lost due to the $71 billion trade deficit with Mexico over the $810 billion total deficit, we can estimate that employment in the USA is about 5,028,000 less than it would be if the trade were balanced. Because it is primarily industry product that is imported into the United States, these job losses have been concentrated in the industrial states of Pennsylvania, Ohio, Michigan, Indiana, Illinois, Wisconsin, eastern Iowa, and northern Kentucky. This is a region of about sixty-five million people, or 20% of our population.

Giving away 20% of our country to foreigners is a high price to pay, especially since we are getting nothing but expanding trade deficit and budget deficit debt in return. For the people who have been put out of work by the removal of their jobs overseas, the loss has been total --- homes lost, families busted, children not educated, and our fellow citizens lost to depression, despair, and suicide.

It's no wonder that the Free Trade Mavens want to blame robots, instead of themselves, for inflicting on much misery on our country.

Have "robots and automation" caused job losses? Yes, but not as directly as the Globalists want us to believe. Prior to the mid-1980s, companies did not usually lay people off when they increased productivity by automation. They had the option of expanding their employees' job responsibilities. For example, training payroll clerks to become worker safety monitors when computers eliminated manual data entry of timecards. But when "globalization" became the buzzword, the layoffs started. The Great Recession followed.

Automation only happens when wages rise to the point where companies can get a payback on their investment in new machinery Companies ship jobs out of the United States and into low wage countries to avoid having to spend money automating their American factories. What's a CEO going to do, given a choice of:

C) Spending $25,000,000 to modernize an American factory so 1,000 American workers earning $25 / hour (wages, benefits, employer-taxes) can be more productive.

D) Firing the 1,000 American workers at $25 / hour, hiring 10,000 Mexicans at $2 / hour, and pocketing the $25,000,000 as an executive bonus.

Free Trade Mavens refused to abandon their propaganda about how "No job has ever left the USA because Chinese and Mexicans work cheaper than Americans. Jobs only go to China and Mexico because Chinese and Mexican companies have superior technology and smarter workers." They will never admit the truth:

https://mashable.com/2017/04/25/iphone-factory-dejian-zeng-apple-china/#Y6JjNkvRCmqW

Dejian Zeng may have built your phone. Or at least worked on it, anyway.

The second-year masters of public administration student at NYU Wagner spent six weeks last year working in a Chinese factory manufacturing iPhones for Cupertino-based Apple. Six days a week he screwed approximately 1,800 screws into 1,800 iPhones. Every day. Over and over again.

So much for the Free Trade Mavens' tall tales about "robots and automation are doing all the work." American companies move work to Mexico and China to avoid having to automate their operations in the USA..On rare occasions, when Free Trade Mavens, forget their robot propaganda, they write tolerably accurate articles like this:

https://www.wsj.com/articles/bringing-iphone-assembly-to-u-s-would-be-a-hollow-victory-for-trump-1537368671?mod=searchresults&page=1&pos=1

Bringing iPhone Assembly to U.S. Would Be a Hollow Victory for Trump

The president's tariffs on Chinese imports could hurt Apple without addressing the real challenge of China.

The factory workers who assemble iPhones in China contribute just 1% of the finished product's value. Apple's shareholders and employees, who are predominantly American, capture 42%.

Suppose Apple decided that all the phones it sells in the U.S. would be assembled here. Mr. Dedrick estimates each phone requires two hours of assembly. For 60 million phones, that means 120 million hours of work, or roughly 60,000 jobs.

Assuming Apple could find 60,000 workers, it would have to hire many away from other employers given how low unemployment currently is. The benefit of the wages they earn would be offset by the higher prices other Americans pay for their phones.

How much would that add to the price of a phone? Mr. Dedrick says about $30; Mr. Shih thinks it would be more because of the cost of shipping individual components to the U.S. Still, such an increase would hardly kill sales of iPhones, now priced at $449 to $1,099. The bigger cost of U.S. assembly, says Mr. Dedrick, would be the inability to quickly add hundreds of thousands of workers when new phones are launched, which is only possible in Asia. Apple can charge premium prices in part because it introduces superior features before its competitors do.

So here we see what happens when Free Trade Mavens admit that 60,000 jobs would be created building iPhones in the USA, and that the $30.00 increased cost per phone would be insignificant given the $499 to $1,099 cost. However, the Free Trade Mavens never turn off their propaganda engines. According to the author, it is now "too late" for the USA to bring back the jobs:

This is where the real stakes in the current trade row lie. It's too late for the U.S. to bring back all of the supply chain. The time to act would have been in the early 1980s, before Western manufacturers began outsourcing the assembly of personal computers and many components to east Asia.

And where were the Free Trade Mavens in the 1980s? Why of course they were busy in those days telling us that Asia would be the export market for **our** supply chain! The

145

best policy with Free Trade Mavens is to never believe a word they say, because they've been wrong 100% of the time.

Save them Turnips, Taters, Beans, and Tree Nuts!

Free Trade Mavens have spent the last thirty years hurrahing the removal of thousands of American factories and millions of well-paying American industrial jobs to Mexico and China. They have shown complete indifference to the distress they have inflicted on millions of American families in the industrial belt between the Delaware River in Pennsylvania and the Des Moines River in eastern Iowa. They are prone to mocking these people as "too mal-educated and lazy to deserve jobs in the global economy." So much for the promises the Free Trade Mavens made to create "millions of well-paying jobs for Americas industrial workers" when they were peddling their trade deals to the public and Congress. Now they have developed two contradictory lines of propaganda to excuse their broken promises:

A) manufacturing is a low-technology business no longer worth of being done in the USA, and

B) manufacturing has become so high-tech that it only employs robots, so human beings should no longer expect to work in it.

"It is futile to protect our industries," hoot the Free Trade Mavens in unison. "If the economics [of cheap overseas labor and disruption of our market by other countries dumping their industrial surpluses in the USA] require it to leave the country, then that is how it has to be."

But the one business the Free Trade Mavens are keen to protect is agriculture. It's as if every Free Trade Maven has suddenly donned the suspenders of Mr. Greenjeans and stuck a hayseed in their mouths. They insist that the U.S. will become the economic powerhouse of the world by exporting farm product like soybeans, grain, turnips, potatoes, and "tree nuts." They are out in full cry, alleging that President Trump's imposition of tariffs to protect American remaining industrial jobs from going overseas, and his tightening of the immigration controls on the border to keep out Illegals, will ruin the livelihoods of farmers:

https://www.wsj.com/articles/trade-fight-threatens-farm-belt-businesses-1530529201?mod=hp_lead_pos1

Trade Fight Threatens Farm Belt Businesses

147

Many farmers, who depend on shipments overseas for one-fifth of the goods they produce, say they are anxious

Updated July 2, 2018

The U.S. Farm Belt helped deliver Donald Trump to the White House, drawn to his promises to revive rural America and deregulate industry. Now, the president's global trade offensive is threatening the livelihoods of many farmers.

Mounting trade disputes, spurred by U.S. threats to withdraw from the North American Free Trade Agreement and tariffs on billions of dollars' worth of goods from key trading partners, have cut U.S. agricultural exports and sent commodity prices tumbling. Many farmers, who depend on shipments overseas for one-fifth of the goods they produce, say they are anxious, especially because they are already expecting bumper harvests or grappling with a dairy glut.

Note that farmers are having trouble selling their productions at a profit because of the *bumper harvests or grappling with a dairy glut.* They are over-producing far more products that the American market wants. Because of overproduction, farming is a tough business even in the best of times:

https://www.wsj.com/articles/two-brothers-tied-to-the-land-face-wrath-of-americas-farm-bust-1513615986

Updated Dec. 18, 2017

Growing food has become a troubled business in the U.S. because of mounting international competition and mercurial demand for crops and livestock. Grain prices are near multiyear lows, sparking the deepest farm slump since the 1980s, and Russia, Brazil and other countries are elbowing out American operations. More farms are becoming mammoth operations to maximize narrowing profit margins. Yet many...that are highly leveraged with rented land, can struggle when markets drop, or a bad season hits.

The farmers' problems with overproduction have been amplified by Free Trade Mavens puffing them up with the idea that they should produce way more crops and meats than the U.S. market needs because Mexico and China will buy their surplus. This is the same fantasy the Free Trade Mavens peddled when they told us that trade with Mexico and China would increase our exports of manufactured products. The reality turned out to be that Mexico and China have purchased little of our industrial or agricultural products, and instead dump their surpluses on the USA.

Part of the problem is also that we import more food from low-wage countries like Mexico than we export. As I mentioned above, my congressman is concerned about the detrimental impact of imports of farm products from Mexico:

USMCA favors Mexican producers over the hardworking Southeastern farmers. Remedies, after that fact are too late to address our farmers needs now. Without the inclusion of trade remedies in USMCA for Florida's produce farmers, I cannot, in good conscience, support this agreement.

Congressman Ted Yoho

Rather than admit that their promise to export ag products to foreign countries were fantastic misrepresentations, the Free Trade Mavens are blaming the buildup of agricultural inventories on other countries' responses to President Trump's industrial tariffs:

https://www.wsj.com/articles/meat-piles-up-as-production-grows-and-exports-slow-1532268000?mod=hp_lead_pos4

2.5 Billion Pounds of Meat Piles Up in U.S. as Production Grows, Exports Slow

Profits, prices are threatened as record amounts of red meat and poultry fill U.S. warehouses

By Jacob Bunge July 22, 2018 10:00 a.m. ET

Meat is piling up in U.S. cold-storage warehouses, fueled by a surge in supplies and trade disputes that are eroding demand.

Note, however, that this is the same problem that was mentioned in 2012, when tariffs were not in effect:

https://www.drovers.com/article/cme-high-frozen-meat-inventory-revealed-cold-storage-report

CME: High frozen meat inventory revealed in cold storage report
May 22, 2012

USDA'S monthly Cold Storage report was released Tuesday and it contained little good news for the meat and poultry businesses and was particularly ugly for the pork sector. The total inventory of pork, at 659.532 million pounds is the second largest on record.

Economics 101 suggests that farmers should decrease production until supply comes back in balance with demand and prices rises enough to cover the cost of their production. However, it turns out that despite the rah-rahing about free markets, farming is a government-subsidized socialistic business. Farms, especially the big ones owned by corporations, are massively subsidized by billions of dollars of taxpayer money to ensure that farmers are paid regardless of whether anybody wants to buy what they produce. Farming is called a "strategic" industry that must be shielded from the risks that other businesses face. Globalists and Free Trade Mavens claim that growing turnips, taters, soybeans, and 'tree nuts' is essential for the nation's survival, while manufacturing motor vehicles, aircraft, machinery, and computers is not.

According to Free Trade Mavens, agriculture is so vital for the national security that it must not only be subsidized with public money, but with imported peon labor from Mexico and Central America. Instead of importing those two-cent turnips and taters from Mexico, where they are already grown by peon labor, we must import the peon labor into the United States to grow them here! We must grow them here, so we'll have products to export to China. We are taxing our people and importing Mexicans and Central American peons, whose off-the-job welfare must be paid for by the taxpayers, so we can sell turnips, taters, and soybeans to the Chinese below their cost of production!

We protect our lowest value, government-subsidized turnips, taters, and beans, so we can export them below cost of production. China and other countries protect their highest value exports of manufactured goods so they can sell them to us. Our Free Trade Maven model of a strong economy is Mr. Greenjeans paying Mexicans to harvest his two-cent turnips, then collecting a government "crop insurance" check at the end of the year to eke out a profit on a money-losing crop. The Chinese model of a strong economy is new manufacturing cities employing millions of production workers and engineers to produce the high-value, technologically advanced products that we have shunned, and sucking jobs and wealth out of the United States in massive trade deficits.

There is nothing wrong with wanting our farmers to prosper, and to generate cash for themselves and for the country by exporting their produce to other countries. But it is dishonest for Free Trade Mavens to pretend that we only export food and never import it. The truth is that many countries produce huge surpluses of the ag products we produce --- from apples to wheat --- and try to dump them in each other's laps below the cost of production, just as we do. Yet the Free Trade Mavens never cease to champion the next "pot of gold" that they think is going to be made by dumping some surplus, low value product on China:

https://www.wsj.com/articles/SB118903703171618696

Looking for Gold in Them Thar Trees

Investors Rush Into Almonds, But Will They Stick Around As Prices Slip, Costs Rise?

But many of the people jumping into almonds are doing so even as prices for the nut have been sliding. In 2005, farmers received $2.80 to $4 per pound of almonds. Now, about a third of the way through the almond harvest, farmers are getting $1.50 to $1.80 per pound.

Once an American farmer finds a crop that earns a decent profit, farmers in every other country are going to start producing it and trying to dump it on us. A surplus that exceeds demand is created, and the product can no longer be grown profitably. Few farmers are ever able to earn profits that cover their costs of production, so governments everywhere waste their people's money subsidizing agriculture and trying to dump their surpluses on other countries.

I accept the argument that food is an item of national security, and that perhaps it should be subsidized to ensure that we can always feed ourselves rather than depend on imported food. But is that not also true of all other products? Do we really want to be in a position of importing our steel, motor vehicles, aircraft, computers, electronics, and other appliances from other countries? If turnips and taters are precious, then so are automobiles and computers.

Free Trade Mavens want us to believe that other countries will retaliate mightily against our farmers --- whom they never cared about before Trump was elected president --- if we impose tariffs on imports of high-value manufactured goods. In truth, farm products are commodities that can be bought anywhere. The only reason to buy them from us is because our government subsidizes them more heavily than other countries.

Even neighboring Mexico doesn't want our farm products, at least not nearly as much as the NAFTA cheerleaders told us they did. As in every other product category, Mexico sells more farm produce to us than we sell to them.

https://ustr.gov/countries-regions/americas/mexico

U.S. total exports of agricultural products to Mexico totaled $19 billion in 2017,

U.S. total imports of agricultural products from Mexico totaled $25 billion in 2017,

Our farm exports to Mexico were the same $19 billion in 2017 as they were in 2010. They grew not a single dollar in all those years. So much for the Free Trade Maven theory of farm exports being a bonanza that is going to save us from the destruction of our industrial economy.

So why is America, the great farming power of the world, in a trade deficit of $6 billion with Mexico in farm products? It's for the usual reason that most other product categories are in trade deficits with Mexico, which is because Mexico pays its farm workers next to nothing:

http://graphics.latimes.com/product-of-mexico-behind-the-scenes/

Behind the series: Product of Mexico

"... the living conditions [of] the people who are picking it, growing it, planting it, watering it? Are like, the worst I've ever seen."

Read the series:

Part 1: Farm exports to the U.S. from Mexico have tripled to $7.6 billion in the last decade, enriching agribusinesses, distributors, and retailers. But for thousands of farm laborers south of the border, the boom is a story of exploitation and extreme hardship.

Part 2: A raid exposes brutal conditions at Bioparques, one of Mexico's biggest tomato exporters, which was a Wal-Mart supplier. But the effort to hold the grower accountable is looking more like a tale of impunity.

http://graphics.latimes.com/product-of-mexico-labor/

Scorpions and bedbugs. Constant hunger. No pay for months. Finally, a bold escape leads to a government raid, exposing deplorable conditions. But justice proves elusive.

Second of four stories

Part 3: *The company store is supposed to be a lifeline for migrant farm laborers. But inflated prices drive people deep into debt. Many go home penniless, obliged to work off their debts at the next harvest.*

Part 4: *About 100,000 children under 14 pick crops for pay at small- and mid-size farms across Mexico, where child labor is illegal. Some of the produce they harvest reaches American consumers, helping to power an export boom.*

The Times found:

Many farm laborers are essentially trapped for months at a time in rat-infested camps, often without beds and sometimes without functioning toilets or a reliable water supply.

Some camp bosses illegally withhold wages to prevent workers from leaving during peak harvest periods.

Laborers often go deep in debt paying inflated prices for necessities at company stores. Some are reduced to scavenging for food when their credit is cut off. It's common for laborers to head home penniless at the end of a harvest.

Those who seek to escape their debts and miserable living conditions have to contend with guards, barbed-wire fences and sometimes threats of violence from camp supervisors.

Major U.S. companies have done little to enforce social responsibility guidelines that call for basic worker protections such as clean housing and fair pay practices.

Why do America's Free Trade Mavens worship agriculture, a low-value commodity business, while despising industry, which produces many times more value per unit of labor?

It's because the Free Trade Mavens have not figured out a way to export dirt.

If they could sell American farmers' dirt for a profit, they'd want to export every farm out of the USA and import all our food. Since there's no international market for dirt, they want to import foreign labor into the USA to produce food products that can't earn a profit even with cheap labor unless they're subsidized by the government.

If you're beginning to sense that "free trade" is not really an ideology so much as a ruse to beat people out of their jobs in the USA and exploit sweatshop labor in other countries, then you're on the right track. Free Trade Mavens never believe in trading on the economically sound principles of comparative advantage. If they believed that, we'd be producing high-valued manufactured product in the USA and importing cheap food from other countries.

Instead, the Free Trade Mavens have convinced us to do the opposite: to destroy our high-value industries so we can import manufactured product from cheap-labor countries, while subsidizing our low-value farm products with public money so our farmers can keep producing surpluses of low-value products that can't be sold for enough to cover the cost of production. The Free Trade Mavens have misled farmers into fantasizing that they are going to be able to bail themselves out of the intractable problems of overproduction by unloading their surpluses on China. Farmers should remember the pack of lies the Free Trade Mavens told industrial workers about free trade creating millions of high paying jobs in industry.

Free Trade Mavens have even started destroying the cherry industry, a mainstay of my summer home area in Northwest Michigan:

https://www.wsj.com/articles/cherry-capital-of-the-u-s-faces-threat-from-turkish-imports-11564410934

Cherry Capital of the U.S. Faces Threat From Turkish Imports

In Michigan, some growers chop down trees or leave crop on the ground as prices tumble

By Shayndi Raice | Photographs by Keith King for The Wall Street Journal

July 29, 2019

WILLIAMSBURG, Mich.—Dorance Amos pulls handfuls of tart red cherries out of large tanks filled with cold water, looking for blemishes. "These will grade well," he says.

The apparent bounty hides a grim reality: He hasn't made a profit in three years.

Mr. Amos is one of many Michigan tart-cherry farmers struggling amid a flood of low-price dried cherries from Turkey. The industry petitioned the U.S. government to impose duties on the imports, claiming Turkish importers underprice the fruit and the Turkish government unfairly subsidizes the industry. The U.S. government said in June that there was enough evidence to proceed with an investigation.

"If we don't have luck with the tariffs, I don't know how any of us can survive," Mr. Amos said

Free Trade Mavens propagandized these farmers into believing that the world was beating down the door to get their cherries, and that they'd all become millionaires unloading them on other countries, if only Trump would drop tariffs on imports of Chinese manufactured products.

Now these farmers are facing the brutal reality that the world does not only not need their surplus products but wants to dump their surpluses in our laps and run our farmers out of business. So now Michigan farmers are chopping down their cherry trees, rendered worthless by imports, and using them for firewood.

According to legend, George Washington chopped down one cherry tree. Globalists have chopped down millions.

Free Trade Mavens remain passionate about their turnips, taters, beans, and tree nuts. According to them, the defining theme of American history is The Mr. Greenjeans Address:

"Four score and many years ago, Mr. Greenjeans brought forth upon this continent, a new nation, conceived in farming, and dedicated to the proposition that all turnips, taters, beans, and 'tree nuts' are created equal.

"Now we are engaged in a great trade war, testing whether those turnips, taters, beans, and 'tree nuts' can long endure. We have subsidized them with hundreds of billions of tax dollars and public debt to pay for 'crop insurance and price supports,' and with the labor of millions of foreign peons who work these hallowed turnip and tater patches for less money than Americans.

"Since we can't eat all them turnips, tapers, beans, and 'tree nuts' by ourselves, let us pawn them off on China and similar countries. It is altogether fitting and proper that we should do this.

"Let us now rededicate ourselves to the great task remaining before us --- that farming of turnips, taters, beans, and 'tree nuts' will not perish from God's Green Earth in the land of the tree and the home of the grape."

Dissecting Free Trade Maven Propaganda

Globalists are amazingly nimble in changing their propaganda to try to stay ahead of the truth that is chasing them. They claim that trade with dodgy countries will "create millions of jobs for hard-working Americans. Then when millions of Americans lose their jobs, they celebrate the "creative destruction" of high unemployment. They claim that "tariffs are taxes on consumption paid by the working poor" and then complain that "tariffs are taxes on importers" when companies that buy from China and resell to the American public at 60% markups must reduce their markups to pay the tariffs. Free Trade Mavens will say anything to protect their inflated markups of selling cheap-labor foreign products into the American market. Let's dissect some Free Trade Maven opinion pieces to discern common propaganda themes:

https://www.wsj.com/articles/how-tariffs-hit-u-s-exports-not-just-imports-1531128600?mod=hp_lead_pos2

U.S. Exporters Will Be a Surprise Loser from Tariff Fight

By Greg Ip Updated July 9, 2018

Though completely counterintuitive, theory and evidence show that taxes on imports act just like a tax on exports.

Though it's early, the Trump administration's recent round of tariffs is already rippling out to exporters: **Soybean farmers face plunging prices as China raises tariffs**...*Like Harley-Davidson, many manufacturers who export from the U.S. may have to shift that activity abroad.*

Note the propaganda points common to Free Trade Maven propaganda

Free Trade Maven Propaganda Motif #1: U.S. Exporters Will Be a Surprise Loser from Tariff Fight

This assumes that the public will be "surprised" by the effect of tariffs imposed on countries that cause the USA severe trade deficits. The implication is that the public is too stupid and misinformed to understand the implications of tariffs. This idea is usually spun with the notion that "Trump States will be most impacted."

In truth, the "Trump States" that swung the election are Pennsylvania, Ohio, Michigan, Indiana, Wisconsin, and Iowa --- states where people are prone to saying, "Trade with China and Mexico is the worst thing that ever happened to us."

As for the farm states, prices for soybeans and other bulk crops have been declining for decades as farmers produce more than the market wants to purchase. They are not falling because of Chinese retaliatory tariffs. China never has and never will purchase much American ag products, because these products are in surplus in many countries. China does not want to send money to the United States. They are trying to eliminate us as a competitor in world markets, not elevate us. They will buy their ag products from other countries that have the same surpluses we do, to align those countries against the United States. Farm prices are falling because farmers have borrowed money to expand their production in expectation that China is a pot of gold waiting there to make them rich by buying all their surplus bulk commodities that can't be sold for enough to cover their costs of production, let alone cover the interest on their loans to buy more land.

Farmers have joined industrial workers in becoming victims of the "China is a pot of gold" propaganda proliferated by Globalists.

FTM Propaganda Motif #2: An ode to the soybean:

In Free Trade Maven lore, the soybean is one of Mankind's most important discoveries. It was first cultivated in China 3,000 years ago, and from there spread to the rest of the world. It is nowadays produced in many countries, including China, but the USA is the largest producer. The U.S. exports about $20 billion of soybeans, about $10 billion to China. According to FTM lore, if we constrain China's ability to dump $500 billion of manufactured products in our laps, China will "retaliate" by boycotting those $10 billion of soybeans, which constitute .05% of our economy, and probably would not be exported at all if not subsidized by $2 billion of taxpayer dollars.

As we have seen in the "Save them turnips..." chapter, soybean farmers faced "plunging prices" long before tariffs, due to overproduction here and abroad. It's a low-value product that can't be sold for enough to cover the cost of production here or anywhere else.

FTM Propaganda Motif #3: Like Harley-Davidson, many manufacturers who export from the U.S. may have to shift that activity abroad.

They've been shifting activity abroad for decades. Harley Davidson can't produce motorcycles in the USA and sell them countries like Thailand and Brazil where people have low disposable incomes. They must produce in Thailand and Brazil what they sell in Thailand and Brazil. That's fine. The tariffs are here to prevent their producing in Thailand and Brazil and dumping the surplus that the other countries don't want on the USA.

Free Trade Maven Propaganda Motif #4: Exaggerating the effects of tariffs.

Whenever a business falters, the Free Trade Mavens are out in full cry alleging that tariffs are to blame. Farm prices have been falling for years due to over-production. This obvious fact did not deter Free Trade Mavens from insisting that farm prices have only ever fallen because China has cancelled its orders after Trump put tariffs on their four-to-one trade imbalance with us.

FTM Propaganda Motif #5: The bogus historical analogy.

Free Trade Mavens are past masters of ginning up historical analogies that turn out to be outrageously bogus. Here's the ultimate Free Trade Maven Propaganda Extravaganza comparing tariffs on soybeans to slavery and the start of the Civil War:

https://www.wsj.com/articles/so-much-trade-losing-1530916720

So much Trade Losing:

The tariff shooting begins with China, and where's the deal-making?

By The Editorial Board July 6, 2018

The shooting has begun in the U.S.-China trade war, and let's hope it's not Fort Sumter. *The South figured the Civil War would last a few weeks, but things happened. That's the nature of trade wars as well, and while no one is likely to win this confrontation, both sides could certainly lose.*

Early Friday the U.S. followed through on President Trump's threats by imposing tariffs of 25% on $34 billion of Chinese imports, and Beijing retaliated on an equal value of

U.S. goods. *Those amounts are too small to tank either economy, but trade talks have stalled, meaning more tariffs could come as soon as next month.*

The damage is already serious for American soybean farmers whose biggest customer is China.

Note the ubiquitous Free Trade Maven element of hysteria, in this case that imposing tariffs on Chinese imports is the new "Fort Sumter" that triggered the Civil War and killed over 600,000 Americans. It spawned a typical Free Trade Maven talking points:

Isn't what we're doing pretty much like starting a world war? If so, we're making the same mistakes Germany did. We're fighting on multiple fronts, against countries near and far away. Countries have tried to appease us, but we've gone further with our demands.

I reminded the commenter that Germany was a military aggressor in WWII, and a trade aggressor today:

If Germany is your basis of comparison, then it is far more accurate to say that they are the Trade Nazis:

https://www.huffingtonpost.com/ian-fletcher/how-do-other-nations-bala_b_628157.html

How Do Other Nations Balance Their Trade? Try Germany

Germany, like the U.S., is nominally a free-trading country. The difference is that while the U.S. genuinely believes in free trade, Germany quietly follows a contrary [protectionist] tradition that goes back to the 19th-century German economist Friedrich List.... So despite Germany's nominal policy of free trade, in reality, a huge key to its trading success is a vast and half-hidden thicket of de facto non-tariff trade barriers.

We run a 2x trade deficit with Germany to the tune of $63 billion. Plus, we spend billions more protecting them from Russia. And now they're cursing us for putting sanctions on Russia that they asked for! And the Free Trade Mavens call us the aggressor!

Another commenter said: *If Americans can't compete in manufactured goods with the Chinese, we might want to take a look at some of the reasons why. Do you think unions make Americans more competitive?*

Here is the popular FTM notion that Americans are to blame for the trade deficit because we are {stupid, mal-educated, lazy, and belong to labor unions}. My response is that if we're stupid, mal-educated, and lazy, why do other countries want to dump their junk all over us? Why do we have money to buy the products they can't peddle in their home markets?

As to labor unions, they certainly earned their share of disrepute in the 1960's and 1970's when they were always on strike to win eight hours of inflated pay for five hours of shoddy work. However, labor unions have been reduced to 6% of the private sector labor force. Michigan, home of the UAW, is now a "right-to-work" (no compulsory unionization) state. Private sector union workers' pay, adjusted for inflation, is well below what it was 50 years ago. Labor unions certainly got too big for their britches, but even an annoying dog doesn't deserve to be beaten to death after it has quit barking.

When Free Trade Maven propaganda is dissected it usually resolves to these common components:

1. Pretend that there will be numerous deleterious effects of imposing tariffs, that "Trump Voters" are too stupid to understand until they get whacked in the face.

2. Worship some low-value product like the soybean and assert that the USA will wither and die if trade predator countries decline to buy it.

3. Assert that we run enormous trade deficits with other countries because of some supposed defect in the American character --- such that we are lazy, mal-educated, overpaid, save too little, or belong to labor unions.

4. Pretend that tariffs are the reason for every business problem that's ever been encountered.

5. Pull up some bizarre historical event that the Free Trade Mavens do not understand and warp it into a false analogy of free trade vs. tariffs. Assert that putting a tariff on China and other trade predator countries that keep our products out of their markets is akin to starting Armageddon.

6. Pretend that the USA is the "aggressor nation" when we ask other countries to reciprocate trade with us.

Microcosm #1: Nailing it

Let's dissect a microcosm of Free Trade Propaganda, this time involving nails. The propaganda is that American companies can't make nails because of Trump's tariffs on foreign steel:

https://www.wsj.com/articles/nailed-by-steel-tariffs-1536531985

Nailed by Steel Tariffs

Trump protectionism is driving a Missouri company to the brink.

By The Editorial Board Sept. 9, 2018

When President Trump promised to make America great again, the employees at Mid Continent Nail in Missouri probably didn't expect he would put them out of work. But the steel tariffs imposed in June have the company hanging by a thread.

Mid Continent is the largest nail manufacturer in the U.S. and has been in Missouri for more than 25 years. It had 500 employees at its Popular Bluff plant and was the second largest employer in the small town before the Trump tariffs hit.

The trouble for Mid Continent is that foreign producers making nails abroad use low-price steel and export their production to the U.S. They can offer better prices than their U.S. rival because, as Chris Pratt, operations general manager for the plant, explained in a Journal op-ed last month, the tariffs pushed costs up "overnight" and made the company uncompetitive. "Orders dropped 70% in two weeks, and our workforce shrank from 500 employees to 370," he wrote.

Question #1: Did customers "orders drop 70% in two weeks" because of rising steel prices caused by tariffs? We might note first that steel prices have risen 150% since 2015 due to an improving economy, which has nothing at all to do with tariffs:

http://steelbenchmarker.com/files/history.pdf

Steel tariffs at most are 25% of that increase. So, why doesn't he complain about the other 125% due to other factors?

Secondly, there is no mention of the fact that at the time this article was written, the housing market is "headed for its worst slowdown in years:"

The U.S. Housing Market Looks Headed for Its Worst Slowdown in Years

Updated on July 26, 2018

The U.S. housing market -- particularly in cutthroat areas like Seattle, Silicon Valley and Austin, Texas -- appears to be headed for the broadest slowdown in years. Buyers are getting squeezed by rising mortgage rates and by prices climbing about twice as fast as incomes, and there's only so far they can stretch. "This could be the very beginning of a turning point," said Robert Shiller, a Nobel Prize-winning economist who is famed for warning of the dot-com and housing bubbles, in an interview.

When the housing market slows, the demand for nails plummets. That's the true reason his customers cancelled their orders. But the Free Trade Mavens will never admit that orders are cancelled for any other reason than tariffs.

Finally, there is no disclosure of the fact that Mid Continent Nail in Missouri is a wholly owned subsidiary of a Mexican steel company.

Mid Continent Steel & Wire roots date back to 1952 when our parent company founder, Don Cesar M. Gutierrez started a small wire shop in Monterrey, Mexico. He started small as all entrepreneurs do, supplying handmade chain link fence using second hand wire he purchased from the U.S. This was merely the beginning of the journey of our parent company, Deacero. The origins of the name reflect the rich history of our subsidiary Mid Continent Nail Corp with a presence in Missouri for over 25 years, which joined the Deacero family in 2012.

The Mexican Steel Company is annoyed that they must pay a tariff to send their steel across the border to their American nail company subsidiary. The tariff is harming the profits of the steel company in Mexico, not the American nail company.

So here we have a typical hidden agenda that the Free Trade Mavens rarely disclose. They are pretending that business problems at an American nail company are caused by Trump's tariffs, when the tariffs are on affecting the Mexican parent company. The American subsidiary can buy its steel from any company in the United States and not pay the tariff. Here again, the Free Trade Mavens rarely, if ever, "tell the truth, the whole truth, and nothing but the truth" when their propaganda engine is running full tilt.

Microcosm #2: Crying in my Beer

A recent staple of Free Trade propagandists has been that tariffs are crippling the beer industry:

> https://www.wsj.com/articles/how-tariffs-lead-to-more-tariffs-11574636899
>
> **How Tariffs Lead to More Tariffs**
>
> **Steel makers asked for protection. A keg maker did next. Now brewers?**
>
> *Nov. 24, 2019*
>
> *There's a nursery rhyme about an old lady who swallowed a fly—then swallowed a spider to catch the fly, then swallowed a bird to catch the spider, and on it goes, all the way up to a horse. Protectionist trade policies can be like that.*
>
> *At the behest of steel makers who griped about foreign competition, President Trump last year imposed a 25% tariff on imported steel. At that time, we reported on the collateral damage to American Keg Co., which says it's the only U.S. maker of stainless-steel beer kegs. With metal prices rising, American Keg divulged it had laid off a third [10] of its 30 workers. "We're very concerned," the CEO said, "that this could put us out of business."*
>
> *Direct and indirect jobs in the beer business are down 40,000 since 2016, trade groups said this spring. The Beer Institute's CEO has called Mr. Trump's aluminum tariffs "an anchor on a vibrant industry." The logical conclusion is to fizz up breweries by levying tariffs on foreign beer: Corona, Heineken, Sapporo, you name it. Our teetotalling President won't mind.*
>
> *This is how Donald's Trump protectionism, like Barack Obama's overregulation, gradually leaches economic growth with compounding political intervention.*

Compare this anti-tariff propaganda in the article to what the "beer study' cited in the article actually says:

> *The industry report noted that while overall beer sales are down about 2.4 percent from 2016, there are some areas of growth, with brewing jobs up 8 percent. It attributed the increase to "tremendous growth in micro and brewpub employment as well as growth in higher margin products from all brewers."*

The number of distributor jobs alone in the industry has also increased by more than 19 percent over the past decade,

The total number of brewing facilities has grown by 1,191 in two years – most being very small brewers or brewpubs.

There continues to be a shift away from less expensive products to more expensive local and "craft" beers....

Consumers purchase smaller volumes of these higher priced beers than they do of less expensive domestic light lagers and pilsners, suggesting that fewer employees are required to serve beer in a given bar or tavern.

It turns out that the beer industry is booming. People are buying higher quality beer in glass bottles, instead of swilling cheap brew from aluminum kegs. The layoffs of 10 people in the beer keg company have nothing at all to do with tariffs. The business press, which never cared about 10 *million* people being laid off when their jobs were moved to Mexico and China, is trying to make out like the layoffs of 10 people at the aluminum keg company will sink our entire economy.

Microcosm #3: The Tariff that stole Christmas

December 2019 is another holiday season in full swing. While most people are mailing cards and shopping for presents, the Free Trade Mavens are out in full cry, complaining that tariffs on imported Christmas trees made in China will ruin the holiday for business:

https://www.wsj.com/articles/tariff-threat-dims-holiday-cheer-for-christmas-tree-company-11576146600

Tariff Threat Dims Holiday Cheer for Christmas Tree Company

Seller of artificial trees expects hit to growth even if President Trump's new levies on Chinese imports are delayed

By Alex Leary | Photographs by Hannah Yoon for The Wall Street Journal

Dec. 12, 2019

President Trump's threatened new tariffs on Christmas decorations from China won't take effect until next year—but that's no comfort to Mac Harman, who has to do his 2020 holiday shopping now.

Mr. Harman said the lighted Christmas trees sold under his Balsam Hill brand are made only in China. The privately held company expects $170 million in sales this year, up from $160 million in 2018, he said. Since tariffs will force him to take either lower profit margins or fewer sales, Mr. Harman's company is holding off plans to add 50 people to its U.S. workforce of 130.He says that because his sales rose 6% from $160 million to $170 million, he was going to increase his workforce by 38% from 130 to 180 to handle the increase of 6%, but now he's not going to hire anybody because of 15% tariffs on Chinese-made Christmas trees? Is this really the way people do business? Increase your staff by 38% because sales increased 6%, and then cancel the whole deal because tariffs on Chinese Christmas Trees might rise to 15%? Do businesspeople not have other options between those extremes, such as filling the 15% by asking the Chinese to cut their wholesale prices by 5%, while raising the retail price by 5%, and taking a hit on profit by 5%; or of buying trees from one of the thousands of Christmas Tree farms in the USA or Canada? Does the imposition of tariffs destroy everything, including Christmas? According to the Free Trade Mavens, they do.

Microcosm #4: Till the Cows Come Home

Trade agreements are sold as panaceas that will solve all economic problems. Since farmers and agricultural interests control the votes of about 40 senators from "farm states," the promises made about agriculture are always outlandish. Every free trade treaty ever enacted has been sold to Congress and the public on the promise of "increasing farm exports."

This is an unlikely promise because most countries already have farm surpluses. They are not going to allow the United States to dump our surpluses on them. However, the promise of a cornucopia of farm exports is made to pass trade treaties, including beneficial ones like USMCA:

https://www.wsj.com/articles/got-trade-dairy-farmers-stand-to-gain-from-the-usmca-11576276775?mod=opinion_lead_pos7

Got Trade? Dairy Farmers Stand to Gain from the USMCA

The newly signed deal is sweet relief to farmers in rural districts like mine in North Carolina.

By [Congressman] Ted Budd

Dec. 13, 2019

U.S. milk prices are in the fourth year of a slump due to chronic oversupply. Canada has historically restricted how much U.S. milk it imports, putting U.S. dairy farmers at a disadvantage.

The U.S. Department of Agriculture reports that 2,731 dairy farms across the U.S. closed last year due to a combination of low profit margins and a gradual decline in milk consumption.

Under this new deal, U.S. dairy farmers will be able to sell three times as much to Canadian markets as they could before.

"Without these agreements," Mr. Dobson says, "you're going to see a disappearance of the industry."

168

The propaganda is that without the USMCA agreements, the American dairy industry will "disappear." This is an outrageously ridiculous assertion on the face of it. Canada, whose market is only 11% of ours, and which already has its own dairy surpluses, is somehow going to bail out our industry that is many times larger?

In truth, the USMA agreement is to increase access to Canada's market for American dairy framers from 3% to 3.6%. That's a six-tenths of one percent increase for a market 11% as ours. Thus, American farmers are going to see an increase of their potential market by .11 * .006 = 1.00066 (two-thirds of one-tenth of one percent) which is too small to measure.

Canada severely restricts American access to its dairy market because its secession-prone Province of Quebec is its dairy heartland. There is no way that Canada's government is going to give the Quebec Secessionists another reason to leave Canada by subjecting Canada's dairy industry to competition from U.S. dairy products. The six-tenths of one percent increase is window-dressing to make it appear as if Canada is making a concession of substance when they're not.

USMCA should be ratified as a modest improvement over NAFTA. However, the grandiose promises for agricultural exports will never pan out. Their most likely effect will be to persuade American dairy farmers that Canada is an untapped pot of gold, and that they should expand their production of surplus dairy products, that can't be sold for enough to cover the cost of production. They will dig themselves deeper in debt because Canada isn't going to buy their surplus production.

This is how Free Trade Mavens over-promise and under-deliver. Even a beneficial treaty like USMA is going to harm our farm economy because it cannot possibly deliver what the Free Trade Mavens have over-promised.

Myths of "The New Economy"

Globalists constantly talk up the idea that we are living in a "new economy" that will replace the American jobs they are sending out of the country. There is some truth in that. New industries do develop from time to time. However, most new jobs are created by evolution within existing industries --- the very ones that Globalists are trying so hard to remove from the country. Talk of a "New Economy" usually means that the current economy is about to fall apart. It happened ninety years ago, just before the onset of the Great Depression:

"There never was a time in which one could fairly count on a long period of sustained prosperity in this country," wrote an economist in 1928. "no one can examine the panorama of business and finance in America during the past half-dozen years without realizing that we are living in a **new era.***"*

Nation's Business published an article in 1929 tilted "This Amazing Decade" which stated, "The period just ended has leaped forward by arithmetical progression; 2, 4, 6, 8, 10. The high gear of our industrial machine will bring changes in the next decade by geometrical progression: 2, 4, 8, 16, 32. It is glorious to contemplate."

A few years later the economy was in ruins and 25% of the workforce was roaming the streets, unemployed and hungry. Fears of communist or fascist revolution rattled people's nerves. It required a massive expansion of government spending and regulation under Franklin Roosevelt's New Deal to put the millions of unemployed back to work. Some of it went too far, and was later rolled back, but the fact is that the private economy had to be bailed out by the government printing hundreds of millions of dollars of paper money. The same thing happened all over again in 2008.

The 1920's are a useful frame of reference. They are the earliest a present-day person could theoretically time-travel back to and still make sense of the world. Go back any further, and you'd be lost in a world of horses, outhouses, and ignorance of most aspects of medicine.

In the 1920s we developed a recognizable economy based on production of motor vehicles, electricity and electric appliances, telephones and radios for rapid communication, paved highways, the emergence of aviation, the financing of business and technology by public stock offerings, and so on, Speculations about manned space flight to other planets and atomic energy became staples of science fiction.

If somebody had said back in 1928 that "All the jobs in motor vehicle manufacturing, are obsolete and should be removed out of the country because other countries can make them cheaper," we would have thought that person insane. If we had followed that advice, we'd have not been able to enter WWII, and Hitler and the Japanese would rule the world. Even if that calamity had been forestalled, our ability to produce motor vehicles would have been forestalled for all time. Instead of having tens of millions of Americans employed at good wages and good pensions, we would have had tens of millions scraping out meager livings in the turnip, tater, and corn patches. We would have sent trillions of dollars out of the country to buy motor vehicles produced abroad. We'd have become a has-been nation like Portugal, that degenerated for two hundred years after David Ricardo told them to give their industry to Britain.

Today's Globalists want to destroy not just our motor vehicle manufacturing, but all industry, including production of aircraft, smartphones, computers, furniture, clothing, and all electronic devices and appliances. The one and only business they worship is agriculture, which originated in Neanderthal times, because they haven't figured an economical way to ship dirt overseas.

Globalists keep talking up all these "new industries" that they think people are going to work in. However, the very companies that will supposedly invent all these new industries --- like IBM, AT&T, Lucent, and Hewlett Packard --- have also been dumping hundreds of thousands of Americans out of employment and replacing them with foreigners who earn less money.

https://www.vox.com/2018/4/20/17261798/ibm-layoffs-retirements-older-workers-age-discrimination-claims

How IBM quietly pushed out 20,000 aging workers

Despite older employees consistently having stronger performance reviews.

By Ranjani Chakraborty Apr 20, 2018

Last month, **_ProPublica reported_** *that over the past five years, IBM has targeted its older American employees for layoffs. The numbers are staggering: Since 2013, it's estimated that IBM eliminated more than 20,000 employees ages 40 and older in the US.*

https://features.propublica.org/ibm/ibm-age-discrimination-american-workers/

As the world's dominant technology firm, payrolls at International Business Machines Corp. swelled to nearly a quarter-million U.S. white-collar worker in the 1980s. Its profits helped underwrite a broad agenda of racial equality, equal pay for women and an unbeatable offer of great wages and something close to lifetime employment, all in return for unswerving loyalty.

But when high tech suddenly started shifting and companies went global, IBM faced the changing landscape with a distinction most of its fiercest competitors didn't have: a large number of experienced and aging U.S. employees.

The company reacted with a strategy that, in the words of one confidential planning document, would "correct seniority mix." It slashed IBM's U.S. workforce by as much as three-quarters from its 1980s peak, replacing a substantial share with younger, less-experienced and lower-paid workers and sending many positions overseas. ProPublica estimates that in the past five years alone, IBM has eliminated more than 20,000 American employees ages 40 and over, about 60 percent of its estimated total U.S. job cuts during those years.

Newer companies like Apple, Microsoft, Salesforce, and Facebook have come along to pick up some of the slack, but these companies do not hire the workers who lost their jobs at other tech companies, and they are just as prone to dumping their employees at the first hint of a sales slowdown or management miscue.

Financial services and wealth management are supposed to be growing areas of the economy, but the banks and stockbrokers keep culling their herds in the cube farms, just like every other company. Healthcare is doing great, but it is subsidized by government debt via Medicaid, Medicare, and Obamacare, because few people earn enough money to pay their hospital bills and insurance premiums out of their own pockets. This industry is headed for a crash as soon as the government's ability to continue issuing debt is curtailed by default.

New industries will surely develop, but not nearly so fast as the Globalists imagine, and not nearly fast enough to replace the jobs the Globalists are destroying today. Globalists have recently revised their propaganda, as they frequently do, to insist that all those imaginary "new economy" jobs exist but can't be filled because "there is a skills gap," i.e. Americans don't have skills to fill all these glorious new jobs. This is just another tactic to make it look like Americans are responsible for the failures of Globalists' theories.

If it were true that "Americans don't have skills for the new economy," then whose fault would that be? Millions of computer scientists, including Ph.D.'s were booted out of their jobs by IBM, Lucent, Hewlett Packard, Microsoft, and other technology companies during the last 30 years. These people had stellar work histories and performance reviews. Why did their corporate employers boot them out the door when they had many years left to work before normal retirement? Information technology is a profession like any other. We do not say that architects, civil engineers, financial planners, bankers, construction contractors, dentists, doctors, airline pilots, and other professionals suddenly become obsolete at age 50. So why is computer science the only profession where people become obsolete at age 50?

Despite all the hype, computer technology changes no more rapidly than any other business changes. The applications packages like Oracle, SAP, Microsoft have been around since the 1980s. Today's "cloud computing" is simply a gussied-up version of the Service Bureau model of the 1960's when people dialed in to access computers owned by others. Our IT people were not put out of work because their skills were obsolete. They were put out of work because our companies did not value their work, and it was easy to replace them with foreigners on H1-B visas who worked for half the pay.

There's recently been a boom of the "coding" myth that vast numbers of people should be trained "to write code." This myth is mainly perpetrated by for-profit coding schools and echoed by Globalists who are always looking for ways to polish their rusted-out theories. "It's too bad your factory jobs went to Mexico or China, but you can learn to code."

The reality is that fewer people write computer code now than were writing it decades ago. It's a low-level, primitive, non-productive activity. These days, people purchase off-the-shelf software instead of writing it from scratch. And with the return of the "cloud computing" / service bureau model, there will be a lot less coding in the future than now.

And when companies do hire "coders" they almost never hire Americans. The foreign "coders" here on H1-B visas are cheaper.

However, this myth of "everybody who lose their job can learn to code" is persistent. On December 30, 2019 Democrat presidential contender and former Vice President Joseph Biden said:

Foxnews.com/media/joe-biden-coal-miners-learn-program-code

Joe Biden says coal miners should 'learn to program'

By David Montanaro | Fox News

Democratic presidential candidate Joe Biden's suggestion that coal miners should "learn to program" as the United States transitions away from fossil fuels shows "disdain" for the profession, a representative of West Virginia miners said Wednesday on "Fox & Friends."

Chris Hamilton, co-chair of the West Virginia Coal Forum, hit back at the former vice president for essentially saying coal miners should learn to code or focus on preparing for a revamped green economy.

"Anybody who can go down 300-3,000 feet in a mine sure as hell can learn how to program as well," said Biden at a campaign event Monday in New Hampshire. "But we don't think of it that way. Anybody who can throw coal into furnace can learn how to program for God's sake."

Why would anybody, let alone a leading politician, say anything that ignorant? Because they are Globalists who don't know anything about the real world and who don't care. "You don't like us Globalists destroying your jobs? Then learn to code. And if you can't code, then die."

Another twist on this "New Economy" propaganda is that new technology jobs are overflowing, but only in a few spots like San Francisco and Seattle and Boston. All those millions of people who lost their industrial jobs because the Globalists moved them to Mexico and China should just pack up and move to San Francisco and Seattle. But in fact, those places are already overcrowded. Amazon is building a second headquarters to get away from Seattle, while San Francisco has become a Third World city of wealth and poverty, that people are trying to get away from:

174

Bay Area exodus? Nearly 50 percent of Californians say they want to move out soon, poll finds

A whopping 46 percent of California Bay Area residents fed up with the region's high cost of living and soaring home prices are planning to pack their bags and move out in the next few years, a poll has found.

The poll, conducted by the Bay Area Council, which describes itself as a business-sponsored, public policy advocacy organization, also found that homelessness and heavy traffic are among the things that most irk residents who live there.

On the downside of it is all the people who need to be here to provide all the services are being priced out," Wunderman said to KTVU. "We're seeing teachers, government workers, firefighters, police officers actually not able to live in the communities."

This is characteristic of a Third World economy where jobs and wealth is packed into such small parts of the country (usually the national and provincial capitals were tax revenues support governing bureaucracies) that it isn't possible for many people to benefit from it. The industrial economy that the Globalists destroyed was spread all over the USA, not just in a few isolated places.

Another Globalist ploy is to assert that Americans who have lost their jobs to foreign trade remain unemployed because they have failed to take responsibility for retraining themselves for "better jobs in new industries." But, as author Amy Goldstein points out, in **Janesville [Wisconsin]: an American Story:**

...when people desperate for a job try to retrain, as the Job Center has been encouraging, they don't always succeed.....Retraining laid-off factory workers is not easy. Even at a little college like Blackhawk, which has been trying like hell.

...the Job Center's retraining gospel was worth believing. Certainly, the gospel has been spread wide. Last year....543 other out-of-a-job factory workers in Rock County— and about 100,000 nationwide at a cost to U.S. taxpayers of $ 575 million— got the kind of Trade Adjustment training subsidies.

...Nationally, nearly half the trainees who got this help last year, and about one third this year in which he is graduating, will not quickly find a job. Two months ago, Mike [a laid off factory worker] began to apply for jobs. Dozens of jobs. He figured that his résumé might get noticed, with his near-perfect grades and his decade on the union side of human resources work, including five years as the shop chairman of an eight-hundred-person factory. He would get noticed, he figured, because of the contracts that he negotiated, the grievances he handled, the employee contract language he interpreted, the Kronos workforce management system that he already knows how to use.

Mike is surprised that all he has gotten are rejection letters when he has heard anything at all. Company after company telling him that they are looking for someone with a bachelor's degree and three to five years' experience in human resources management.

Goldstein, Amy. Janesville: An American Story (Kindle Locations 2360-2362). Simon & Schuster. Kindle Edition.

People have been getting laid off in waves of {downsizing, offshoring, outsourcing, work force reductions, and involuntary retirements} since the mid-1980s. Even as far back as1994 Wallace Peterson warned of the coming collapse in their book **Silent Depression:**

If you feel you are making and spending more money than you did ten or twenty years ago, but are losing ground, if it appears that your children will do less well than you have done, if your job is less secure than it used to be, you are not alone. Millions of other Americans are equally perplexed.

*Well, the truth is that the since the early 1970s --- since 1973, to be specific --- the American economy has not performed well. The corporate buzz word of the late 1980s and early 1990's has been "downsizing," as top management in the nation's corporate giants slashed payrolls in a frenzied effort to cut costs and boost productivity in the **face of increasingly tough global competition.***

Of course, the "global competition" is companies being allowed to substitute cheap foreign workers for Americans. They are still at it today:

https://www.wsj.com/articles/the-end-of-employees-1486050443

The End of Employees

Updated Feb. 2, 2017

Never before have American companies tried so hard to employ so few people. The outsourcing wave that moved apparel-making jobs to China and call-center operations to India is now just as likely to happen inside companies across the U.S. and in almost every industry.

The contractor model is so prevalent that Google parent Alphabet Inc., ranked by Fortune magazine as the best place to work for seven of the past 10 years, has roughly equal numbers of outsourced workers and full-time employees, according to people familiar with the matter.

The shift is radically altering what it means to be a company and a worker. More flexibility for companies to shrink the size of their employee base, pay and benefits means less job security for workers.

No one knows how many Americans work as contractors, because they don't fit neatly into the job categories tracked by government agencies. Rough estimates by economists range from 3% to 14% of the nation's workforce, or as many as 20 million people.

Steven Berkenfeld, an investment banker who has spent his career evaluating corporate strategies, says companies of all shapes and sizes are increasingly thinking like this: "Can I automate it? If not, can I outsource it? If not, can I give it to an independent contractor or freelancer?"

Hiring an employee is a last resort, Mr. Berkenfeld adds, and "very few jobs make it through that obstacle course."

Now it's two years later, on March 1, 2019, and the business propaganda has changed its tune to "we can't find enough workers. Even barbers are earning $180,000 a year:"

https://www.wsj.com/articles/inside-the-hottest-job-market-in-half-a-century-11551436201

Inside the Hottest Job Market in Half a Century

A look at who's getting ahead, who could be left behind and how long the boom can last

177

This sort of "anybody who wants to work can get a job paying $180,000 a year" propaganda is written to promote the idea that we need more illegal immigration so that companies can continue laying off their higher-paid American employees.

Even In places where jobs are plentiful, housing prices have risen faster than wages, which remain modest, due to the Globalist mania for shipping jobs out of the country and letting in immigrants, including Illegals, to fill the rest. Here is a recent lament from a young lawyer who lives in Seattle:

http://highline.huffingtonpost.com/articles/en/poor-millennials/

"All of us are one life event away from losing everything," says Ashley Lauber, a bankruptcy lawyer in Seattle and an Old Millennial like me. For most of her clients under 35, she says, the slide toward bankruptcy starts with a car accident or a medical bill. "You can't afford your deductible, so you go to Moneytree and take out a loan for a few hundred bucks. Then you miss your payments and the collectors start calling you at work, telling your boss you can't pay. Then he gets sick of it and he fires you and it all gets worse." For a lot of her millennial clients, Lauber says, the difference between escaping debt and going bankrupt comes down to the only safety net they have—their parents.

"So what?" we may ask. "Life isn't supposed to be a bowl of cherries. Our ancestors crossed the oceans, prairies, and mountains, to pioneer our country. Why are these Millennials, who spend $5 for coffee at Starbucks, whining all the time?"

It's a fair question, and nobody denies that there is a lot of whining by people who are spoiled by the easy life in the USA. But some of the "whining" is justified. Incomes should allow people to afford houses as they did in our parents' generation. The country is supposed to become wealthier, and life easier, as time moves forward. We are not supposed to have to chop wood to make our own log cabins.

And what risks do Globalists ever take? Does the CEO of the multinational corporation who demands tens of millions of dollars in up-front money to accept the job take any risk? He / she is paid many lifetimes of average pay even if his / her performance is abysmal. Does the government-paid bureaucrat or academic ever take any risk of being unemployed by the globalist policies he/she advocates for? Does the politician who furthers the interests of globalist corporations take any risk of poverty when he/she "retires from politics?" Of course not. The former politician who does the bidding of his/her corporate masters while in office is guaranteed fantastic wealth working as employees or lobbyists for those corporations after "retiring from politics."

The risks of globalism are to be born only by the "little people" who have no means to protect themselves from it.

Part III. Balancing the Trade

As we have seen, Globalists oppose tariffs on predatory trading because they think manufactured products are isolated from the rest of the economy. "Manufactured products are commodities like water that we can buy anywhere, so who cares if we buy them from a foreign producer, including adversary countries like China whose governments don't permit their people to buy American-made products?

Globalists don't care about the infrastructure that goes into making the manufactured products we use --- the trillions of dollars of capital investment, the thousands of engineers who design the products, and the millions of people who are employed making them. "Let the steel manufacturing industry go to China," say the Free Trade Mavens. "Let the manufacturing of computers, appliances, motor vehicles, dog food, cat food, people food, clothes, furniture, bassinets, and tombstones go to China.

Globalists imagine that there is a great "New Economy" somewhere out there that will replace all the tens of millions of jobs we are bleeding out of our economy --- except for picking turnips, taters, beans, and 'tree nuts' that Globalists say are so essential to our economy that we must import the rest of the world's indigent labor to pick them.

Globalists are also prone to objecting that "tariffs are taxes on consumers." Of course, this is not at all true. The Wall Street Journal reports that tariffs are paid by Chinese Manufacturers and American importers:

Apparel Companies Fear Tariffs Could Squash Profit

By Esther Fung and Inti Pacheco Updated Aug. 22, 2019

About 40% of all clothing and 70% of shoes sold in U.S. are made in China

Macy's says it will work with its Chinese partners to absorb the extra costs associated with the tariffs.

Most apparel companies are expected to absorb the cost increase themselves or negotiate ways to cut expenses with their Chinese manufacturers to avoid antagonizing customers with higher prices. "We learned from that experience that the customer had very little appetite for those cost increases," CEO Jeffrey Gennette said during the company's earnings call last week. Instead, he said, Macy's would work with its Chinese partners to absorb the extra costs.

So what if American consumers did pay them? Why should Chinese companies extract profits tax-free from USA? Tariffs re taxes paid in lieu of the taxes that foreign producers (including foreign subsidiaries of U.S. companies) do not pay for the privilege of importing product into the USA and extracting profits from our economy by selling it here.

Let's ask why should a company that invests in the USA, hires workers in the USA, pays invoices to suppliers in the USA, and pays taxes to our state, local, and federal governments compete on equal terms with foreign companies that don't do any of those things? This would not matter if our trade were balanced and our companies could profit by producing in the USA and selling in other countries. Nor would it matter if we had a VAT tax like all other countries do, to capture tax revenues at point of sale. But trade isn't balanced, and we don't have a VAT. So why should foreign companies (including foreign subsidiaries of U.S. companies) be allowed to strip-mine the USA of profits without contributing anything to our country?

At a local level, no mayor or city council is going to let a flea market come into town and start under-selling the local merchants. The local merchants pay property taxes to fund the police and firefighters that protect everyone in town. They hire the locals as employees and pay them with money that usually stays in town, and is either saved in a local bank, invested in local real estate, or spent buying goods and services from local businesses. Storefront owners should not have to compete with a flea market that operates in a shabby tent; that doesn't pay property taxes; that doesn't hire locals to peddle its wares, and perhaps obtains its merchandise in dubious ways.

Were such a flea market allowed to operate, the legitimate businesses would fold up, and the place would become a shacktown of boarded up store fronts, chronic unemployment, underfunded public services and despair. People would support themselves with public welfare, or with crime, which would proliferate due to lack of police protection. Even the flea market would move on to another town to suck dry after destroying the town.

Nor is the United States obligated to become the world's flea market for peddling cheap product of dubious origin --- including product pirated from our companies --- sold in our country by foreign companies that do not invest in the USA, hire our workers, or pay our vendors, or pay taxes to our government. That is the necessary and common-sense reason for imposing tariffs to balance the trade by shifting production back to the USA, while collecting equivalent tax revenues on foreign product as we collect on product produced domestically.

The Border Adjustment VAT

A VAT is not quite a tariff, because it applies to products of domestic production as well as imports. However, it can be engineered to tax imports more heavily, since imported products do not add value to the U.S. economy or pay taxes to our governments when they are produced.

Let's consider how to apply a VAT by analyzing the ways that a product can be produced or sold:

1. A product may be produced in the USA and sold in the USA.
2. A product may be imported into the USA and sold in the USA.
3. A product may be produced in the USA and sold in another country.
4. An American-owned company may establish a foreign subsidiary to produce products for sale in the foreign country's market.

The only scenario that is objectionable is #2, and only then in certain circumstances. One circumstance would be if an American company fires its American workers and then moves their work overseas to a cheap labor country to produce product that is imported into the United States. That is a pure destruction of American wealth in the worst possible way, by beating American workers out of their jobs to produce product that is sold in the United States. Another objectionable circumstance would be importing products that we used to make in the United States from other countries, such as China, Japan, and the European Union that do not buy reciprocally from us.

We have given the world's nations decades to voluntarily balance their trade with us. We have given our American companies almost as much time to live up to their promises to use trade as a means of creating jobs in the United States by exporting to other countries instead of destroying jobs in the United States by importing from other countries. Since these promises haven't been kept, we should begin balancing the trade with tariffs.

One way to balance the trade would be to impose a tariff proportional to each country's trade surplus with us. China runs a 300% trade surplus with us. They sell us $4 for every $1 they buy. We could tariff them 300% to equalize the trade. For Japan, the tariff would be 100%, for Mexico 30%, and for Canada zero, since our trade with Canada is closely enough balanced as to make no difference. As the trade deficits declined, the tariffs would decline with them. The other countries could decide whether to manage their trade with us by purchasing more of what we produce or having the trade deficit eliminated by tariffs.

But perhaps we should first try implementing House Ways and Means Chairman Kevin Brady's proposed Border Adjustment VAT of 20% * (USA Revenues - USA cost inputs). It has four scenarios, that coincide with each of the four trade scenarios:

- Let's say a product is produced in the USA with $8,000 of cost inputs and sold for $10,000 in the USA. The BAVAT tax is: ($10,000 - $8,000) * 20% = **$400**.
- A product is imported into the USA and sold for $10,000. The tax is: ($10,000 - zero) * 20% = **$2,000**.
- Product is produced in the USA with $8,000 of cost inputs and exported to another country where it is sold for $10,000. This generates a **REBATE of $1,600** (zero - $8,000) * 20%.
- Product is produced overseas by an American company and sold overseas. No tax event because no USA revenues or cost inputs.

The BAVAT taxes made-in-USA lightly, while imports, which have no USA cost inputs, are taxed at full 20%. Exports receive a rebate because an American company is producing product in the USA and thereby paying wages to Americans and taxes to our governments.

All developed countries except the USA levy a VAT tax, so it is an internationally accepted means to balance trade and bring in venue that reduces government deficits. We need to face the reality that it is not possible to balance either our trade deficit or our federal budget deficit without at VAT. Make it a border adjustment VAT the way Kevin Brady has proposed, and we will begin to balance both. This will reduce the trade deficit while shifting production back to the USA, or imposing taxes on companies that insist on producing overseas and bringing the product into the United States to sell. If the 20% BAVAT does not suffice to balance trade with the most extreme trade deficit creators like China, Japan, the European Union, and Mexico, then we can increase it to 35%, 50%, or 300% with those specific countries until they either decide to buy more from us, or shift production to the USA.

Certain countries, like Canada and Britain (now that it is leaving the European Union) trade fairly with us based on true competitive advantage instead of cheap labor. No American company is going to fire its American employees and move operations to Canada or Britain because it can hire cheaper labor to produce product to import into the United States. The USA could therefore treat Canadian and British (and certain other countries) as if they were equivalent to USA origin, and would therefore be as lightly taxed as American companies are by the BAVAT. It would thus be possible to have a BAVAT and free trade because our partners who trade fairly with us would be treated for BAVAT purposes as if they were part of the United States.

Our chronic trade deficit partners in the European Union, Japan, and South Korea need to understand that they are not being fair in demanding that the United States spend $700 billion on national defense to protect them from perceived "enemies" in Russia and China --- which they trade profitably with ---- while bleeding us dry by inflicting trade deficits on us. Europeans use their trade surplus dollars to lavish their people with government-paid benefits. European kids go to college for free, while American kids get saddled with lifetimes of debt. The Europeans and Japanese expect our kids not only to be taxed their entire lives to defend Europe and Japan, but to die for Europe and Japan if Russia or China attacks them. And there is no reason at all to let any products of Russian and Chinese origin into the USA duty free.

Free Trade Mavens will pretend that the Border Adjustment VAT will bring an end to the civilized world, but let us ask a few questions:

#1 We have had a 25% tariff on imported pickup trucks since 1963 (Mexico and Canada were exempted in 1994 with NAFTA, but the tariff remains in effect for trucks produced in all other nations). Not a single American I have ever heard of even knows about the 25% tariff, let alone complains about it. We produce 8 times as many pickup trucks in the USA now as we did in 1963, even while our production of passenger cars has declined due to imports. Millions of Americans buy American-made pickup trucks. So obviously they can afford them and believe them to be of high quality. The tariff has not discouraged sales of pickup trucks but has multiplied them by 8x and kept production in the USA, thereby adding value to our workers and our economy.

#2 China has had a 25% tariff on ALL imports of American-made motor vehicles, and Germany imposes a 10% to 22% tariff on our vehicles. Those tariffs haven't done anything to dampen the growth of their economies. In fact, China is growing twice as fast as we are, and they are the world's premier trade predator.

Nor does a Border Adjustment VAT "punish" foreign companies that decide to produce in the USA. For example, South Korea's Hyundai has invested billions in its USA auto plant, at Montgomery, Alabama. Their direct and indirect payroll is perhaps around $250,000,000 a year, a considerable boost to the economy. They contract with many small businesses to provide services to their factory. Their employees, their vendors, and the company itself pay taxes to fund our government's civil and military commitments. Why should Hyundai have to complete with another foreign company that doesn't produce in the USA? The Border Adjustment Tax is just as fair to foreign companies as it is to American companies.

We should remember that our trade deficits and budget deficits are not sustainable. They will break the back of the United States by putting us in more debt than we will ever be able today. We must either raise taxes to 50% or more of our incomes, which will depress our standard of living by taxing our people to pay interest on debt owned by foreigners; or, we will have to print paper money to cover the debt, which will make us look like a banana republic. Once we devalue our currency, we will no longer be able to purchase foreign-made products. Nor will we be able to make them at home since we will have lost the knowledge of how to do so. We will become like David Ricardo's Portugal, a nation of barefoot grape pickers and goat herders. We are already straining to pay $21 trillion of debt and are adding nearly $1 trillion more to the trade deficit and budget deficit every year. Has there ever been an individual, corporation, or nation that prospered by drowning itself in debt?

USMCA: The Advent of Managed Trade?

President Trump has completed a renegotiation of NAFTA, that he believes will reduce our trade imbalance with Mexico and with China, since China uses Mexico as a backdoor to pump product into the United States.

Our original trade treaty with Canada was the Auto Pact, which created a common market in autos and autos parts, provided that 90% of manufacturing value was allocated to the USA and 10% to Canada, which is the proportion of sales and profits between the two countries. NAFTA replaced the Auto Pact with an anything-goes free trade agreement that resulted in Mexico producing 25% of North American autos, while being only 4% of the consumer market.

USCMA raises the requirement of NAFTA content from 62.5% to 75% on products to qualify them for tariff-free entry into any of the three countries. It requires North American steel to be used in auto manufacturing. The 75% North American content requirement is intended to screen out European and Asian product from infiltrating into NAFTA countries duty free. It focuses the treaty on being what it should be: a *North American* trading block.

It mandates a minimum wage of $16 / hour on 40% of Mexico's auto production, to limit the amount of work that can be done at Mexico's cheap labor rates. Mexico is a tiny 4% of North America's auto market, but a large exporter of cars to the USA and Canada, contrary to NAFTA promoters' promise that the USA and Canada would export cars to Mexico.

The treaty is designed to be more like the European Union's trading group, which creates a continental group of trading partners that do business on favorable terms with each other, while imposing a common barrier on imports from "non-market" countries such as China.

USMCA contrasts sharply with the now-defunct Trans-Pacific Partnership (TPP) that would have superseded NAFTA if it had been approved. TPP would have lowered the duty-free content requirement from 62.5% to 45%, thereby allowing Chinese-sourced product of up to 55% content to enter the USA, Canada, and Mexico duty free. Early results show that the new USMCA content rules are inducing manufacturers to relocate their global supply chains to North America, including the USA:

https://www.wsj.com/articles/auto-makers-consider-shifting-more-manufacturing-to-north-america-1538737201?mod=hp_lead_pos2

Foreign car makers are considering moving more manufacturing to North America from their overseas plants following the recent U.S. trade deal with Canada and Mexico.

Within days of the U.S. and Canada reaching a pact to replace the roughly 25-year-old North American Free Trade Agreement, executives at several foreign car makers said they are considering changes to their supply chains that would shift more auto-parts manufacturing work to the U.S., Canada, and Mexico.

"We will allocate more U.S. production for the U.S. market," BMW AG CEO Harald Krüger told reporters at the Paris Motor Show this week. He said that the German car maker already sources many parts in the region, but the new trade pact will accelerate a shift in investment.

Part IV. Immigration

Immigration brings, or should bring, talented and productive people to the USA. It saves the lives of some who would otherwise perish in the world's most oppressive countries. There is also the sense that in taking in others, we are validating ourselves. It is uplifting to see how the United States has created a Constitution and a society that can take in people from the farthest corners of the earth and make them Americans. Our founding principles, and the welcoming traditions of our people, inspire optimism that the peoples of the world can live in harmony under our government. The names of those who have come from distant lands to better themselves, and who have bettered our entire country, are endless.

There is the feeling that the United States cannot be a great nation without also being a welcoming nation.

We do not want to be like the old man or woman who creates a beautiful garden and then yells at the children who come to enjoy it, because they might step on a tulip. Immigration connects us with the rest of the world and furthers the outreach of our ideas of liberty and tolerance that would never happen if we lived in cultural and ethnic isolation.

"I always consider the settlement of America with reverence and wonder, as the opening of a grand scene, and design in Providence, for the illumination of the ignorant and the emancipation of the slavish part of Mankind all over the earth," wrote John Adams in 1765, eleven years before we declared our independence from the British Empire. Even in those days there was a sense that America was connected by immigration to all peoples of the earth.

Thousands of heartwarming stories show how immigration knits Americans and foreign-born peoples together into a society superior to what either group could attain without the other. A close friend, who is a landlord, told such a story. One of his Mexican tenants was behind on his rent. My friend told him not to worry about it, just pay it when he could. "Gracias, Senior!" said the Mexican. "This would never happen in Mexico."

The Mexican paid the rent a couple weeks later. A few weeks after that, the sewer main into the apartment building broke. The Mexican tenant came home from work and saw his landlord breaking his back putting in a new sewer line. The Mexican rounded up his Mexican friends to help the neighbor fix the sewer main. Mexicans appreciate being treated with respect by Americans, which is often more than they'd receive from their own countrymen in class-conscious Mexico. Work is about more than money. The United States prospers as a society that values work and humanity.

I am no stranger to immigration. My college roommates were Ecuadorian, German, and Syrian. My first employer after graduating from university in the 1970s was an Eastern European entrepreneur who came to the USA after fleeing communism. He built a world-renowned engineering company. My wife and adopted son were born in Colombia. My business partners have been English and Canadians.

So, let the immigrants come, but in the right numbers, and for the right reasons.

The controversy about immigration is derived from the institutionalized dishonesty by proponents of massive immigration. They are pedantic in insisting that they know with absolute certainty that there are precisely 11 million "undocumented workers" in the United States (a number they have insisted has not changed in 30 years); that immigrants (including Illegals) work harder, pay more taxes, and commit less crime than Americans; and that anyway, more Illegals are leaving the United States than are coming in.

Immigration activists sue in federal court to block questions on the census asking people if they are here legally. So how can they know so certainly who is here illegally? What are they afraid of? Of course, they are afraid of being exposed as propagandists who falsify data about immigration to further their ideological interests (of obtaining more illegal voters from those on the Left) and economic interests (replacing American workers with cheap foreigners from immigration activists on the Right).

Immigration activists "fly off the handle" whenever anybody reports the obvious, which is that unskilled Illegals pay next to nothing in taxes; that they rarely if ever return to their home countries; that tens of thousands are apprehended crossing a porous border every month; that once here they consume hundreds of billions of Welfare State dollars and commit crimes out of proportion to their numbers.

Immigration activists are also dishonest in saying that the United States ruined the world with our "imperialist" policies and therefore the world's poor people are deserving of having a home here. The world's developing countries are poor because they multiplied their population by 4x during the last 60 years and don't have land or resources to provide them with a standard of living we consider adequate.

Let's consider the kind of immigration we should desire:

First, there should be a quota. Even a country as vast and wealthy as the United States cannot take in unlimited numbers of people. We cannot provide jobs for millions of people all at once, nor is it fair to the people who already live here to unbalance the job market by letting in excessive numbers of unemployed immigrants. It is perhaps no coincidence that the two greatest economic collapses of the last hundred years --- 1929 and 2008 --- began during times when immigration was highest. Excessive immigration distorts the economy into an exaggerated boom-and-bust cycle that comes crashing down with financial ruin, unemployment, and mountains of debt that never gets repaid.

There is also a possibility that excessive immigration in too short a time distorts our politics. Richard Taylor, son of President Zachary Taylor, and a Civil War general and historian claimed that:

The vast immigration that poured into the country between the years 1840 and 1860 had a very important influence in directing the events of the latter year. The numbers were too great to be absorbed and assimilated by the native population. States in the West were controlled by German and Scandinavian voters, while the Irish took possession of the seaboard towns. Although the balance of party strength was not much affected by these naturalized voters, the modes of political thought were seriously disturbed, and a tendency was manifested to transfer exciting topics from the domain of argument to that of violence.

Taylor, Richard. Destruction and Reconstruction: Personal Experiences of the Late War (p. 9). Kindle Edition.

It is interesting that the Germans, Scandinavians, and Irish immigrants that Richard Taylor saw as an inflammatory element in 1840 to 1860 are now regarded as part of the core of our American ethnicity. So are Chinese, Japanese, Indians, Vietnamese, and other Asians. Perhaps soon Hispanics, Caribbean Africans, Middle Easterners, and other groups newly arrived in the United States will become core American ethnicities as well.

However, excessive immigration in too short a time might destabilize the politics of a country, especially if the existing citizens consider it chaotic and uncontrolled. The

191

European Union has lost Britain and may lose other member nations because the Globalists who run the E.U. have preferred excessive and chaotic immigration in defiance of the wishes of the people they governed. Politics in the USA is inflamed and made more divisive by excessive and chaotic immigration across borders intentionally left open and uncontrolled by our Globalists.

In addition to the difficulty of assimilating large immigrant populations into the national culture, there is the feeling that they expand the labor supply, making it hard for citizens to find work at the wages they were accustomed to before immigration. Is it coincidental that our standards of living stagnate, and political and economic crises erupt during periods of heavy immigration?

Our legal immigration quota of 675,000 a year seems satisfactory. Every decade it adds a population equivalent to metro Chicago, San Francisco, Houston, Dallas, Washington, or Philly. We don't seem to have any trouble adding enough jobs to support that many people without increasing unemployment and depressing wages for the American citizens. It is also necessary to vet immigrants to make sure that either they have families here who can tide them over until they get on their feet and become self-supporting, or that they are extraordinarily well accomplished in their homelands and are of good character, so there will be little doubt that they will contribute to our society.

So why is there so much controversy and political division over immigration? It is because much of it is now being done for the wrong reasons:

1. Open borders to encourage illegal immigration. Republicans want the cheap labor. Democrats want the votes.

2. Sanctuary cities to prevent Illegals from being deported.

3. Drivers licenses, admission to universities, and normalized legal, banking, and government services to legitimize the presence of Illegals.

4. No verification of Illegals for employment.

5. Illegals entitled to receive government-subsidized welfare, healthcare, housing, and education.

6. No prosecution of Illegals for violating laws that American citizens must comply with.

Politicians in both parties obfuscate their pro-illegal immigration positions by saying "We believe in border security." But of course, it is impossible to believe in border security while at the same time establishing sanctuary cities, providing legal documents to legitimize the presence of Illegals on American soil, and providing government-paid benefits for Illegals who ignore the law, that American citizens who abide by the law are not entitled to.

Democrats oppose border security, including reasonable measures like a physical wall, because they desire to change the voting demographics to favor their candidates. When Democrats say: "We oppose building a wall because it will not keep out Illegals," what they mean is, "We oppose the wall because it *will* keep out Illegals." There is no reason to parse their arguments any further than that.

Republican corporation people favor illegal immigration because it is a cheap labor spigot. They desire to bring people into the country illegally, work them cheap, under onerous conditions that no American would accept and that often violate worker health and safety laws, fail to pay their taxes and insurance, and then dump them off on the public to support when they become too old or ill to work. When Republicans say, "We oppose the wall because of eminent domain" (or other such vapid nonsense) they are really communicating: "We oppose the wall because it will restrict our access to cheap illegal labor." There's no reason to parse their arguments any more deeply than that.

Politicians in both parties seek to obscure their motives by inventing the following propaganda:

- We don't want to build a wall because {it's a waste of money, it won't work}
- We don't want to build a wall because it won't stop people from flying into the country and overstaying their visas.
- We don't want to build a wall because we should be putting pressure on employers not to hire Illegals.

The honest translation of this propaganda is: "We don't want to build a wall because we favor illegal immigration." The honest, straightforward way to control immigration is to secure the border with a barrier sufficient to discourage illegal crossing. Then admit 675,000 legally according to quota every year. People who oppose that honest, sensible approach oppose it for one reason only: because they desire illegal immigration.

There is also the issue of "refugees" who show up unannounced at our border claiming to be victims of dubious oppression back in their home countries. The way to deal with "refugees" is to set aside a quota of 50,000 a year, embedded within the existing 675,000, and vet them in their home countries before they show up here unannounced. Again, a simple and straightforward process.

People who oppose this type of controlled admission of "refugees" do so for one reason: because they want people to come into the United States, pretending to be "refugees" and then disappear into the population and stay here illegally. There is no sense in parsing their motives any further than that.

The next controversy occurs when Globalists pretend that immigrants, including Illegals and fake "refugees," are superior to the existing citizenry. According to Globalists, all immigrants, legal and illegal, are combinations of Albert Einstein, Henry Ford, and Mother Theresa. According to Globalists, they are not coming to the USA to better themselves, but to do us the favor of saving us from ourselves. According to Globalists, immigrants never commit any crimes, always start world-beating businesses, and always pay way more in taxes than they receive in social welfare services. According to many left-leaning Globalists, they are especially superior to the old fogies and ignorant backwoods hicks among American citizens who tend to vote conservative. Because of this propaganda, many immigrants become arrogant, and start presenting themselves as being superior to the existing population.

Here is a typical example of excessively pro-immigrant propaganda:

https://www.wsj.com/articles/the-latino-factor-will-save-americas-economy-1535582497

The 'Latino Factor' Will Save America's Economy

By Sol Trujillo Aug. 29, 2018

Baby boomers are aging out of the workforce—but this demographic is younger and growing. The U.S. is running out of workers...Those millions of retiring boomers aren't disappearing. They spent their working years helping build the economy, and they'll rely on Medicare and Social Security as they age out of it.... If Americans are smart enough not to halt our economic progress...First, educate the next generation of American workers, and train them for the digital economy....Second, develop a diverse workforce. Despite the tech community's demand for advanced engineers—and the focus on H1-B visas—America doesn't only need coders.

Note propaganda points:

1. Latinos will "save" the U.S. economy. (How did we ever do so well all these years without them? And why did our economy fall off a cliff in the 2000's after we let so many of them in legally, and illegally?)

2. The U.S. is running out of workers. (What happened to all those robots and automation that the "robot people" keep telling us are doing all the work?)

3. If Americans are "smart enough" we will not "halt economic progress" (Americans who don't want Illegals flooding the country are presumed to be 'not smart').

4. At present, Americans are not very smart because we need to "educate" them to "learn how to code."

5. But not to worry: We can bring Indians in on H1-B visas to do the coding, while we bring Hispanics in here to pick the turnips and scrub the toilets (But how are Hispanics going to fill the Social Security coffers if they're working low-pay jobs that don't even pay enough to fund their own Social Security and Medicare demands when they are old and feeble, which for many, requires them to draw on Social Security Disability and Indigent Medicaid in their 50's?)

Immigrants chosen carefully in the 675,000 quota *should* on average be superior to the existing population in intelligence and ambition, otherwise why would we want them? For example, the population of India is 1.3 billion. If we have a legal quota of 50,000 Indians per year, we should be picking from among the highest achieving .004% of their people. We will then be augmenting our population with people who are far superior to the existing population. And Indians, by the way, are in general polite, hardworking, entrepreneurial, law-abiding, and family valuing. Because of their cultural mix that included British government, they often seem more American than we Americans do. Indians are a happy, optimistic people, who do well in business and the professions. They are in general the kind of immigrants we desire. The controversy only arises when they are over-concentrated in the IT sector and brought in for the specific reason of removing Americans from employment.

Many immigrants are extraordinary only in their mediocrity. For every immigrant who founds a high value business that grows to employ many American citizens, there are many who operate low-value businesses like fast food joints and cleaning companies. There is nothing at all wrong with these businesses at the bottom of the economic food chain if they are operated legally, but often they are not. Being married into an immigrant family, plus being a business consultant, I know how these businesses operate. Immigrant-owned businesses rarely abide by wage and hour laws. They typically hire Illegals, pay them off the books, and dump them on the taxpaying public when they are injured on the job and show up at hospital emergency rooms as indigent patients.

There is also a question about whether immigrants collectively add any meaningful value to the USA. George Borjas, a Cuban immigrant who became an economist, makes the point in his book *We Wanted Workers* that immigrants, by expanding the labor supply beyond demand, merely redistribute wealth from wage earners to employers:

https://www.amazon.com/Wanted-Workers-Unraveling-Immigration-Narrative/dp/0393249018/

In the long term, the estimates of the fiscal impact [of immigration] are far too dependent on arbitrary assumptions to make them a reliable basis for any kind of cost-benefit calculation. The most credible evidence, therefore, suggests that it is not far-fetched to conclude that immigration is a net economic wash.

After all is said and done, immigration turns out to be just another government redistribution program. *Immigrant participation in the workforce redistributes wealth from those who compete with immigrants to those who use immigrants…And this lesson sheds a lot of light on which groups are on which side of the immigration wars.*

Borjas, George J.. We Wanted Workers: Unraveling the Immigration Narrative (Kindle Locations 2709-2714). W. W. Norton & Company. Kindle Edition.

My experience is that many, if not most, immigrant-run small businesses involve some degree of fraud. When I met my immigrant wife, she was a prosecution witness for an immigrant-owned business that defrauded the federal government of student grants, defrauded its American vendors by refusing to pay their invoices, and cheated my wife and other employees by failing to withhold their payroll taxes. This was a for-profit "business school" honored by immigrant politicians in Chicago. In fact, the owner was a crook who had already been jailed once and was headed to jail again after he was convicted of defrauding the government.

There is also the cost inflicted on legitimate American businesses. How is an honest American business owner going to compete with immigrant businesses that break our laws by failing to pay their obligations for workers' compensation, unemployment insurance, wage and hour laws, worker safety, and so on? American businesses owners who abide by the law can't compete with immigrant businesses whose owners don't abide by the law. The honest American businesses fold, while the slimy immigrant business owners do shoddy work illegally, then disappear when they inflict damages on the public and are sued for restitution.

Nor do immigrant businesses create all that many jobs for American citizens. Immigrant-owned businesses pack their workplaces with other immigrants, legal and illegal. Most Chinese, Russian, Indian, and Eastern European business owners pack them with immigrants from their home countries on H1-B visas. If they're software developers, they may farm out the work to people they know in their home countries where people work cheap. They are taking work away from American-owned software companies and their employees. Immigration on balance probably destroys more employment opportunities for American citizens than it creates. It makes it easy for companies to lay off their higher-paid American employees and replace them with cheaper foreigners. It is one of the reasons why Americans have not made the economic progress they expected in the last few decades.

Immigration may diminish our productivity. Companies don't invest in machinery that improves the productivity of their employees until their labor costs escalate. It's only when investing in automation becomes less expensive than hiring labor that companies invest in labor-saving machinery. Immigrants, by expanding the labor supply, keep labor costs low, and thereby encourage companies to avoid improving their productivity. In that regard immigration makes us less competitive globally than are immigration-averse countries like Japan, China, and South Korea.

There is also the cost inflicted on Americans by overpopulating the country and pushing up the cost of housing in cities that immigrants crowd into. The USA could absorb all comers up until about 1890 when the frontier reached the Pacific and the free lands given away to homesteaders came to an end. We required immigrants for even a couple of decades as we built an urban / industrial economy. We do not need to increase the population for the mere sake of population growth today when our farmland is occupied, and our factories have been relocated to the very countries that immigrants are coming to the USA to get away from.

There is no reason to believe that we are stronger merely because we have more people. We entered World War II with 132,000,000 people, just 40% of what we have now. Our soldiers fought gigantic air, land, and sea battles against the Germans, Italians, and Japanese, while the home front produced enough equipment to supply our armies abundantly, and about 50% of the British / Canadian forces, and 20% of the Soviet Union's war effort. We have 325,000,000 people today. Are we as strong a nation as we were in World War II? Could we produce hundreds of warships, thousands of cargo ships, and hundreds of thousands of motor vehicles and aircraft? Could we win a multifront war if we had to?

Yet another difficulty with excessive immigration is when it is done for political reasons because the Globalists do not like the way that the population of existing citizens vote. This is the explicit policy of the Globalists who run the European Union and Canada. Canada's premier Justin Trudeau articulated it clearly:

https://www.theguardian.com/world/2017/jan/04/the-canada-experiment-is-this-the-worlds-first-postnational-country

The Canada experiment: is this the world's first 'post-national' country?

*...Canadians, by and large, are also philosophically predisposed to an openness that others find bewildering, even reckless. The prime minister, **Justin Trudeau**, articulated this when he told the New York Times Magazine that Canada could be the "first post-national state". He added: "There is no core identity, no mainstream in Canada."*

At least Canada's Prime Minister was up front about why he desires so much immigration. He doesn't so much want to improve Canada as to make a new country that is a microcosm of the world. Canada is historically a fragile country with relatively few people on a large land mass, with many internal divisions. It cannot be foretold whether massive immigration will remake it into a strongly unified, prosperous "post-national" country, or fragment it back into the independent sovereign units from which it emerged in the late 1800's.

There is also the problem of rampant immigration fraud in Canada, as there is in every country where immigration is touted by Globalists as a means of diluting, and ultimately replacing, the legacy population:

http://www.cbc.ca/news/canada/british-columbia/xun-sunny-want-release-fines-immigration-1.4727253

Biggest immigration fraudster in Canadian history left $900K fine unpaid

National Parole Board decision says Xun (Sunny) Wang had to be released one-third through his 7-year sentence

Posted: Jun 29, 2018 1:00

The man imprisoned for committing the biggest immigration scam in Canadian history was released on early parole even though he had not paid more than $900,000 in fines and "minimized his criminal behaviour," according to a November 2017 Parole Board of Canada decision obtained by CBC News.

Wang, 49, was convicted of bringing more than 1,000 people illegally into Canada by falsifying passport entries, faking job offers and supplying them with bogus Canadian home addresses, to thwart immigration requirements.

Get caught bringing in "more than 1,000 people illegally into Canada" and you serve 2.3 years in prison, then get out of jail and start bringing them in again. Immigration fraud is ubiquitous in countries controlled by Globalists.

How much money did the Canadian immigrant smuggler make on each Illegal he infiltrated into Canada? There is an entire cottage industry in the USA and Canada of immigration smugglers and immigration lawyers and immigration document forgers who profit by throwing sand in the gears of legal immigration. We have them in the USA, such as this supposed "non-profit" group that pays its organizers millions of dollars to shelter Illegals:

http://www.foxnews.com/us/2018/06/29/nonprofit-operator-shelters-for-immigrant-kids-facing-more-questions.html

More questions are being raised about a nonprofit group at the center of the national debate about shelters for migrant children [children of Illegals], including charges that the

organization and individual family members who run it are profiteering from a crisis that's costing taxpayers hundreds of millions of dollars a year. Among the more pressing questions is how the Austin, Texas-based nonprofit, Southwest Key, went from a $31-million-a-year government contractor in 2008 to a $458 million one in 2018. Critics and immigration activists are also asking how Juan Sanchez, the CEO, can justify not just a $1.5 million salary for himself, but another $280,000 for his wife, Jennifer, as well as a high-ranking position for yet another family member.

There is also delusional thinking among our Open Borders Libertarians.

Libertarian: "Immigration does NOT = naturalization. Only citizens can vote, but all immigrants pay taxes...."

My Response: "Yes it most certainly is naturalization! Illegals get amnestied. They have "anchor babies." They are represented in Congress. **California has four more congresspersons and electoral votes than it is entitled to because Illegals are counted in the census.** *California is registering Illegals to vote in local elections. It won't be long until they vote in national elections, if they are not already voting in national elections illegally at this moment.*

"And if you think all, or even most, immigrants pay taxes, you are ignorant of the immigrant community. Much of the immigrant community, especially the community of Illegals, dedicated to evading wage and hour laws and not paying taxes. I met my immigrant wife while she was testifying against her immigrant employer in a federal prosecution of immigrant tax fraud. Many immigrants, especially the Illegals, generate negative net value for the USA."

Let's especially note the point that even if Illegals do not vote as individuals, they are represented in Congress, and inflate the representation of "sanctuary" states and cities that harbor them.

There is nothing "racist" about wanting to limit immigration. So long as immigrants arrive in controlled numbers, diversity of immigration is desirable. I have read George Washington's diary. He was once asked by the manager of his Mount Vernon plantation if he only wanted to hire "American Christians" to build some ships to move his goods down the Potomac. He replied: "I don't care if the workers are atheists or Mohammedans, so long as they know how to build ships." But he did not need a hundred million "Mohammedans" to build his ships, nor did he insist on bringing in "Mohammedans" to diversify his labor force. He wanted shipbuilders, without caring about anything other than whether they knew how to build ships.

Likewise, the United States does not need the diversity lottery or the encouragement of Muslims to come here as make-believe fake refugees to diversify our population. If Muslims want to come here as part of the 675,000 legal quota, then let them in after careful vetting and waiting years in queue just like all other immigrant countries. But don't go opening our doors to millions of unvetted fake "refugees" just because they are Muslims --- or because they are citizens of any country that is said to be in distress. A quota allocated from the 675,000 legal immigrants each year is way more than enough to accommodate the handful of "refugees" who are really in danger because they helped the United States in an overseas conflict against factions of their fellow countrymen and are in mortal peril if we do not take them in.

As to bogus immigration by H1-B visas, the companies who sponsor them should pay for the privilege of using foreigners to put Americans out of work. There are a very few instances when H1-B visas are necessary, such as when a company wants to bring a foreign citizen into the USA to serve here in an executive position, or when the foreign citizen has expertise that cannot be found in the USA. In a country of 325,000,000, it is extremely rare that companies will not be able to find Americans with the expertise they need.

The same big tech companies that routinely beat their American citizens out of their jobs, are the very same companies that request 250,000 H1-B visas each year to replace them with lower-paid foreigners. I have seen a well-regarded American IT manager with 25 years' stellar experience at the company be booted out of her job and replaced by a young Indian in his 20's. The American woman did not become expendable until she hired in an Indian. A year later the Indian had her job.

The Phony "Labor Shortage"

Employers who want to replace their American employees with low-paid foreigners often pretend that they are unable to find American workers to fill the job openings. These are the very same American employers who routinely dis-employ their American workers in tidal waves of {layoffs, downsizings, outsourcings, offshoring's work force reductions, involuntary retirements}, and then program their computer systems to discriminate against rehiring them. They are particularly insistent that there is a shortage of job applicants with "STEM" degrees in Science, Technology, Engineering, and Math.

In truth, hundreds of thousands of Americans are graduated with these degrees every year. Our companies don't want them because their pay will eat into corporation profits. They'd rather hire foreign workers on the cheap. The following article in the *Los Angeles Times* tells the story of H1-B visa abuse I have seen dozens of times:

http://www.latimes.com/business/hiltzik/la-fi-mh-the-scandal-of-engineering-visas-20160226-column.html

A phony STEM shortage and the scandal of engineering visas -- how American jobs get outsourced

By MICHAEL HILTZIK   FEB 26, 2016

Leo Perrero had worked for the Walt Disney Co. in Orlando for more than 10 years, helping to run the point-of-sale systems at Walt Disney World and its other local parks, until late 2014. That's when he learned that his job, like 300 others, was going to be turned over to a foreign worker within 90 days, during which time he was expected to train his replacement.

"My co-workers and I felt extremely betrayed by Disney," he told a Senate subcommittee Thursday. "They were going to simply cast us aside for their financial benefit.... I followed my dream of having a career in technology to have my very same desk, chair and computer all taken over by a foreign worker who was just flown into America weeks before."

A year ago, the wholesale firing of IT teams at Disney, Southern California Edison, and other tech-dependent companies and their replacement by offshore workers with so-

called H-1B visas caused a national scandal. _We exposed this loophole_ at the time, and followed up by showing how _Congress connived_ in the visa subterfuge.

"There were more than 230,000 H-1B applications in the first week for just 85,000 spots in 2015," laments the Partnership for a New American Economy, an industry group that lists Disney CEO Robert Iger among its co-chairs. "We should have enough temporary H-1B visas and permanent employment-based green cards to meet the talent needs of our companies and our economies." (_A measure introduced in 2015_ by Sen. Orrin Hatch (R-Utah) and others would raise the cap to as many as 195,000 visa holders.)

Despite claims that H-1B visa holders have advanced educations, most hired by the Indian outsourcing firms hold bachelor degrees or less. (EPI / Ron Hira)

Yet, as was documented in testimony by immigration experts Ron Hira of Howard University and Hal Salzman of Rutgers, most of the H-1B visas aren't being used to hire people with specialized skills. "The vast majority of H-1Bs who are coming in have no more than ordinary IT skills," Hira testified.

About half of all H-1B visas end up in the hands of outsourcing firms that use them to import workers, mostly from India, to replace Americans in middle-level IT jobs. The firms include Tata and Infosys, both of which helped Southern California Edison in its program to shed 500 domestic IT workers and replace them with foreign labor.

These workers aren't uniquely skilled engineering grand masters, but are rank-and-file IT employees, often with bachelor's degrees and supplementary on-the-job training. But their salaries often come to $100,000 or more, leaving them vulnerable to imports of lower-cost workers.

In fiscal 2015, Hira testified, 41% of the jobs approved by the government for H-1B visas were at the lowest skill levels for the jobs, which applies to "beginning level employees who have only a basic understanding of the occupation [and] perform routine tasks," such as those done under "internships." Those workers typically are paid 40% below the average wage. Even better, from the employer's standpoint, is that the workers know that their visas are tied to their employment, which makes them especially submissive employees.

How does that conform to the claim that H-1Bs are all about hiring the best and the brightest employees available globally?

Evidence is ample that the very claim of a STEM shortage in the U.S. is phony. Salzman noted that "overall, our colleges and universities graduate <u>twice the number of STEM graduates</u> as find a job each year." The mismatch is especially stark in the biomedical field. There, <u>according to a 2014 paper</u> by experts from UC San Francisco, Harvard and Princeton, "the training pipeline produces more scientists than relevant positions in academia, government, and the private sector are capable of absorbing."

As a result, "a growing number of PhDs are in jobs that do not take advantage of the taxpayers' investment in their lengthy education." As <u>we reported last year</u>, the same high-tech corporations that poormouth their ability to find skilled workers simultaneously lay them off by the thousands.

High-tech firms in the U.S. cut nearly 80,000 employees last year, according to the job placement firm Challenger, Gray & Christmas. That included 47,000 announced layoffs from Hewlett-Packard, Intel, Unisys, and Microsoft. (The former CEO of the latter, Steve Ballmer, is also a co-chair of the Partnership for a New American Economy.)

Companies go to extraordinary lengths to exclude Americans from employment opportunities, such as only offering contract work at low pay that will attract foreigners or saying that "we only hire locals" unless they are Indians on H1-B visas from 12,000 miles away. There's now an F1 Visa to replace American airline pilots with Indians. Airline executives pretend to believe that there aren't any Americans who want to become commercial airline pilots, that only Indians can be trained to fly planes!

https://flyhaa.com/student-resources/international-students/f1-visa/

F-1 Visa

Airman's Proficiency Center (APC) is a division of Hillsboro Aero Academy and is accredited by the Accrediting Commission of Career Schools and Colleges (ACCSC). APC is approved to offer the F-1 Visa for international students interested in training full-time at APC.

The F-1 Visa program is designed for professional pilot training, either airplane or helicopter, from zero hours to initial flight instructor rating. The F-1 Visa is issued for 24 months for both the professional pilot airplane and helicopter programs and may be extended if the training is not completed. Students on the F-1 Visa may take vacation only during published school vacation periods.

Ninety (90) days prior to completion of CPT, the student may apply for Optional Practical Training (OPT). Once the Employment Authorization Document (EAD) has been received, the OPT period is 12 additional months, and the student may apply for work as a commercial pilot in the United States.

The vested interests promoting these fraudulent H1-B and F1 visas, are for-profit schools, immigration lawyers, and companies looking to replace their American workers with cheap labor. The H1-B program needs to be made costly to reflect the true costs of replacing American citizens with foreigners here on false pretenses. H1-B and F-1 visas should be sold at auction for bids beginning at $100,000 a year. Auction off 10,000 at a minimum bid of $100,000. If employers are so all-fired desperate to hire these people, then they will not mind paying $100,000 or better --- but only if the people are as valuable as the employers claim they are.

And what about the labor shortage in general? Are we really "short six million workers?" As we have seen, as recently as 2017 American companies were bragging about how they don't need to employ people:

https://www.wsj.com/articles/the-end-of-employees-1486050443

The End of Employees

Updated Feb. 2, 2017 12:41

Never before have American companies tried so hard to employ so few people. The outsourcing wave that moved apparel-making jobs to China and call-center operations to India is now just as likely to happen inside companies across the U.S. and in almost every industry.

American companies desire a "gig" economy of low-paid, part-time contract workers who are paid only for working peak demand periods, and then are dismissed the instant demand slackens. Employment statistics purporting to show "full employment" are therefore misleading. Yes, people are working jobs, but a lot of those are intermittent part-time jobs that have no benefits other than an hourly minimum wage. Many are "jobs of last resort" like being paid a commission for collecting credit card debt or selling on commission for fly-by-night companies.

An unemployment rate of 3.6% two generations ago, meant that 96.4% of the labor force had full-time work that would last until retirement at 65. An unemployment rate of 3.6% today means that 96.4% of the workforce has any job, including working part-time, or "employment of last resort" gigs such as tearing up their cars as Uber free-lancers, and that these jobs will last only until the next layoff. The jobs may be there, temporarily, but the quality and stability of the work has diminished due to overloading the labor force with too many immigrants, legal and illegal, relative to the demand for work.

Also bear in mind that many so-called "job openings" are counted dozens of times when they show up in different Internet search engines. Many "job openings" that are advertised turn out to be by "resume farmers" who are building mailing lists of people to sell to recruiting agencies. And many "job openings" aren't filled because employers won't pay the market rate for wages. As we have seen, businesspeople believe in a free market for everything they want to sell, but rarely for what they buy. According to them, labor is always too expensive; the free market never supplies people who will work as cheap as employers want to pay.

The economy *is* recovering briskly now that President Trump has cracked down on the employment of Illegals, and has imposed tariffs, companies are suddenly able to fill their open positions with Americans. However, there is still a ways to go, in improving the quality of jobs

https://www.wsj.com/livecoverage/july-2018-jobs-report-analysis?mod=article_inline?mod=hp_lead_pos1

U.S. Economy Added 157,000 Jobs in July

Last Updated Aug 3, 2018

The professional and business services sector added 51,000 jobs in July, bringing its total over the last 12 months to 518,000 jobs. ***More than half of last month's gains came in temporary help services.***

That means part-time, minimum wage jobs with no security. Employers are only just now beginning to loosen up on their over-rigorous jobs screening:

Employers Eager to Hire Try a New Policy: 'No Experience Necessary'

Inexperienced job applicants face better odds in the labor market as more companies drop work-history and degree requirements

By Kelsey Gee July 29, 2018 7:00 a.m. ET

Americans looking to land a first job or break into a dream career face their best odds of success in years.

Employers say they are abandoning preferences for college degrees and specific skill sets to speed-up hiring and broaden the pool of job candidates. Many companies added requirements to job postings after the recession, when millions were out of work and human-resource departments were stacked with resumes.... Long work-history requirements have also relaxed: Only 23% of entry-level jobs now ask applicants for three or more years of experience.

The last sentence says it all:

Only 23% of entry-level jobs now ask applicants for three or more years of experience.

Why would an employer require years of experience for an "entry level job?" in the first place? In a recessionary economy, like we had from 2008 to 2016, they were getting 2,000 applications for each job opening. Since it is impossible to look at 2,000 resumes, they were using excessive credentialization to screen out 99% of the job applicants before they start examining them in detail. Now perhaps, they are only getting 20 applicants for each position, and they don't need to whittle them down by excessive screening.

We should bear in mind that when company managements pretend that "we can't find qualified people who will work force us" that what they really mean is, "We can't find Americans who want to work for us, because of our low pay, lack of job security, and poor hiring methods." Company managements who claim they can't find workers are banging the doors for more immigration of low-paid foreigners to beat the Americans they already have on their payroll out of their jobs.

However, in 2019, it does seem that there is hope for company managements finally beginning to understand this:

https://www.wsj.com/articles/a-kitchenaid-recipe-for-a-tight-job-market-11550840415?mod=hp_lead_pos5

KitchenAid's Key Ingredient: Investing in Workers. 'It's Not a Dead-End Job Anymore.'

Companies discover investment in workers as a way to keep churn low

Updated Feb. 22, 2019

Jennifer Hanna would be a dream hire for the many companies wrestling with talent shortages these days. Having worked in factories since 1991, she is responsible for more than 1,000 people building KitchenAid stand mixers that sit on countertops around the world.

Ms. Hanna, though, has worked for KitchenAid's owner Whirlpool Corp. since she was a high-school graduate figuring how to pay for college. It would be hard to lure her away.

The appliance giant helped pay her way through community college and Ohio's University of Findlay, then handed her increasing responsibility, encouraged her pursuit of an M.B.A. and put her on KitchenAid's senior leadership team.

As the U.S. labor market continues to tighten, companies are reaping decades of underinvestment in their workers. Blame it on a wave of skilled baby boomers retiring or colleges teaching the wrong things or a lack of loyalty among younger workers. The harder it gets to find the next generation of Jenni Hannas, the bigger the headaches get in the human-resources department.

Bright Horizons recently polled 22,000 people about the effectiveness of training programs and the data indicates they improve attraction and retention. Nearly 80% said the aid made them more likely to stay with the organization and 60% were offered a promotion within two years of graduation.

The following exchange on a blog tells the story from the viewpoint of Americans who know what is going on:

STEM is like everything else. When you value it, you get people trained to do it. When you tell the people that are already doing it that they have no value and boot them out the door, then of course people are not going to want to work for your companies. The more foreigners we let our companies bring in here, the more they are going to pretend to be "short" of American STEM people, even while laying off the ones they already have.

I can absolutely, unequivocally certify that this is correct. I work in the [technology] industry; I know what is going on. The US high tech industry is lowering the wages by flooding the market with foreigners. Even if they pay them equivalent salaries, the H1's work 80 hours a week (unpaid), thus lowering the wages. Does not bode well for American citizens and home-grown technology. Lot of these graduates will suck this country dry and then take all their skills back after destroying American Engineering.

There are many qualified American kids who cannot get accepted into STEM programs in college as so many spots are taken by foreign students (who happen to pay double the tuition). Herein lies the problem. Then we hear that there aren't enough American STEM graduates!

Business should also remember that you can't talk about how wonderful the free market is when you want to avoid government regulation, and then pretend that the free market doesn't work when you want to hire somebody for less than market wages. The labor market, like all markets, is always in balance between supply and demand. If you need to hire to fill positions, then increase the pay until people migrate to your business from other companies. The inefficient companies that can't afford to pay market wages will go out of business, and the more efficient companies will acquire their customers as well as their employees. That is how the market is supposed to work.

If employers can't obtain people to work for them at market wages, then the market is telling them that they are not producing goods and services of value that consumers are willing to pay for. If they were producing goods and services of market value, consumers would pay enough for them to hire the people they need to do the work. Again, this how markets are supposed to work. No business has any special right to bring in foreigners to work for below-market wages.

Immigration and the free market

Conservatives and Libertarians talk about free markets, but they never seem to believe that free markets apply to wages. If there really were a "labor shortage" in any part of our economy, free market theory says that wages will be increased until they are sufficiently high to attract new workers to that market. Or the work will be automated. Or, if the work has marginal economic value and can't be done profitably with higher labor costs, the businesses that employ these workers will fold and the workers will move on to higher-paying jobs with more efficient employers who are able to work them more profitably. No economic law mandates that every business that depends on cheap labor deserves to survive. When poorly run businesses close, their owners become employees of other companies and expand the labor supply.

However, Conservatives and Libertarians have been taken in by the notion that the labor market should not be a free market, and that the cost of labor should devolve down to the lowest common denominator for everybody's job except theirs. If there aren't enough people who want to sling burgers or dig turnips for minimum wage, or to program computers for less money than Americans can afford to work for, then open the borders to foreigners who will come in and beat the Americans out of their jobs.

A common refrain of the cheap-labor people is: "We need to attract workers as the current population ages." The problems with this

1. It really means "We need to attract younger foreigners who work cheap (and often off the books) so we can beat Americans in their 40's and 50's out of their jobs." Granted, there are some jobs like picking turnips that Americans won't do for any amount of money. These are the jobs that *should* go overseas. We should be importing turnips from Guatemala where the cheap labor already is, instead of bringing in Guatemalans to pick turnips here.
2. It delays automation. Robots and automation are expensive. They require large capital expenses up front, followed by a return on investment that takes years. Companies will not invest in robots and automation so long as low-paid foreigners are being imported into the country. **Automation does not lead to wage increases. Wage increases lead to automation.**

3. It delays the process of natural reproduction of the existing population. Responsible middle-class people are not having as many kids because wages are not high enough to support raising them. Bringing in foreigners depresses wages and slows population growth.

4. Many immigrants are not young. On average, they are seven years older than the legacy population of American citizens. *As Table 3.4 shows, the gender mix of natives and immigrants is essentially the same.... but immigrants are 7 years older. The popular perception that immigration is composed mainly of young men is simply incorrect. Borjas, George J.. We Wanted Workers: Unraveling the Immigration Narrative (Kindle Locations 798-800). W. W. Norton & Company. Kindle Edition.* Immigrants bring in their elderly parents and enroll them in Medicaid to pay their healthcare expenses. Even young immigrants will one day be old. They, too, will be treated with Medicare and Medicaid at public expense, while having paid next to nothing in payroll taxes to support these programs.

Only when labor really becomes scarce due to high demand for workers, are companies forced to automate and streamline their procedures to accomplish more with less labor. Low-value companies that can only compete with cheap labor will fold up and go away, because they are not adding value to the economy that customers are willing to pay for. As a blogger familiar with agriculture put it:

We are in a remarkable era: There is now a machine available to pick almost every fruit and vegetable. However, farm and orchard owners are loathe to increase their capital investment, which would reduce short-term profit. What is absurd in this reality is that the total cost of labor is becoming ever-more expensive due to the rising costs of medical treatment, education, and social-welfare coverage (SSDI etc.) [of immigrant labor]. The reality is that the general state and federal budgets are being loaded up for future disaster, while the current illusory profits go in the pocket of those that still focus on the use of cheap immigrant labor. We are selling out our future by accepting a delayed burden we will not be able to afford.

There is no guarantee in a free market that companies can hire labor as cheap as they would like. They must pay the going market rate to get the people they need or make do without them when other employers raise wages to attract qualified people in a competitive market.

Cheering Illegals

Globalists claim they are not for illegal immigration, but of course they are. The fact that they favor sanctuary cities to shield Illegals from deportation and oppose a border wall to prevent them from entering the country, proves they want Illegals to live and work in the USA. Sanctuary cities and sanctuary states like California have passed laws forbidding law enforcement from notifying Customs and Immigration when criminal Illegals are released from prison, giving proof that Globalists want all Illegals, including criminals, to have a safe harbor here. At least seven reasons motivate people to favor illegal immigration.

1. They believe social justice requires improving the lives of poor foreigners by letting them into the United States.
2. They are opposed to President Trump and are for illegal immigration because he's against it.
3. They are business owners without ethics who refuse to comply with employment law. They want cheap labor without incurring expenses to hire it legally. This includes the Republican-leaning Chamber of Commerce and other big business interests.
4. They are politicians paid by big business to do its bidding, or a big-business media enterprise funded by big business advertising.
5. They want more liberal and Democratic voters.
6. They believe that the U.S. has a demographic shortfall and don't care who fills it.
7. They want the United States to look more like "the rest of the world" and therefore increase its racial diversity.

Liberal-leaning Democrats are inclined to favor illegal immigration for #1, #2, #5, and #7. They became especially interested in #5 when they lost the 2016 election, like the 2000 election, by a small number of votes in a few critical states. They are still angry over those losses. Their interest is in tilting the votes their way by bringing Illegals into those states and training them to vote Democrat.

Republicans who cater to big business interests favor Illegals for reasons #3, #4 and #6.

I am often asked to "show proof" that any reputable person or mainstream constituency of the Republican or Democratic Party favors illegal immigration, so that is where I will start:

https://www.wsj.com/articles/one-more-immigration-try-1525993394

One More Immigration Try

By **The Editorial Board** *May 10, 2018*

House Judiciary Chairman Bob Goodlatte has introduced legislation to legalize Dreamers. But the bill is riddled with poison pills including **an e-Verify mandate** *for employers, self-deportation of undocumented farm workers and stringent limits on family-based immigration. This would effectively force Republicans to choose between legalizing Dreamers and selling out employers.*

https://www.wsj.com/articles/exporting-jobs-instead-of-food-1526600254

Exporting Jobs Instead of Food - The U.S. farm labor shortage is driving production overseas.

By **The Editorial Board** *May 17, 2018*

…. immigration restrictionists are detached from the reality of the American farm economy and a worker shortage that's driving food production overseas.

House Judiciary Chairman Bob Goodlatte is whipping votes for a bill that would limit farm worker visas to 410,000 annually, which would include the existing immigrant workforce. This isn't nearly enough. Worse, **falsely documented workers** *[Illegals who steal Americans' social security cards] would be required to come out of the shadows and return to their home countries before they can be readmitted.*

In these two articles we have the Editorial Board of the nation's most respected business publication calling e-Verify a "poison pill" and complaining that "falsely documented workers" who steal American citizens social security cards should be allowed to stay in the country without fear of prosecution.

Next comes the plethora of "sob stories" alleging that Illegals are virtuosos of hard work and morality, whose merits earn them the right to stay in the USA:

Fiestas and Apple Orchards: Small-Town Life Before Trump - My corner of Pennsylvania was thriving again—until immigration agents began carting people away.

By Crispin Sartwell June 9, 2017 York Springs, Pa.

President Trump has had a difficult time getting much of his agenda off the ground. But one thing I've already seen change under his administration: Immigration law is being enforced more aggressively. Out in rural Pennsylvania, in a county Donald Trump carried with 66% of the vote, this is already having a devastating effect on the economy and culture.

Welcoming the Hard-Working Stranger

When I met Angel, he was in urgent need of an immigration lawyer. Now I'm hoping he votes GOP.

By Lou Weiss Aug. 6, 2013

One of the consequences of building a house on a former slag dump in Pittsburgh is that we have a lot of weeds. Not just any old weeds, but Japanese knotweed and other highly invasive and fast-growing monsters.

While the house was still under construction, our efforts to rid the yard of these pests led us to draft several local teenagers, family members and friends to do the pulling. But even at $15 an hour, they were not that great. Some accidentally pulled good growth, some never showed, and some of the teenagers weeded under the influence of another weed. Finally, a friend recommended a young man named Angel—and that he was.

Initially we didn't ask Angel where he and his associates [other illegal friends and relatives] were from—we followed the don't ask, don't tell rule. But when my wife started cooking the occasional dinner for his team—after they said an extensive grace—he started telling. OK, maybe we did a little asking. It turned out that Angel is Honduran—and he was in urgent need of an immigration lawyer, which he now has.

215

Some questions are in order. First, do the hirers of Illegals ever consider the costs they are imposing on the rest of us, in exchange for fulfilling their selfish goal of obtaining cheap labor?

Do they care that the rest of us must bear the cost of medical care for the Illegals when they injure themselves on the job, as they surely will, and show up at the hospital as indigent patients? Do the Pennsylvania apple farmer and the Pittsburgh slag heap homesteader care that if one of their workers breaks an arm or a leg on the job, that the public is going to be billed the $30,000 cost of the operation? Do they care about who is going to pay for the Illegals indigent old age when they get too old to work, or are crippled by an accident?

If the apple farmer in Pennsylvania (who is a college professor, not a full-time farmer) can't afford to hire labor legally, then why is he in business? Apples are grown in many countries that already have cheap labor, including some in Latin America that are sending their people in the USA to pick apples illegally. If he can't make money legally, why not close his hobby business and concentrate on being a professor, and we can buy our apples from Mexico, Central America, Argentina, and Chile. After all, isn't that what free trade is supposed to be about? Or maybe a fulltime farmer will invest in machinery to pick apples with less labor. Why should honest American apple growers who hire labor legally compete with a farmer who hires Illegals?

The slag heap homesteader hired Illegals because he thinks the local kids weren't any good at the work, but he must be aware that there are hundreds of licensed landscapers and home builders in a big city like Pittsburg --- American business owners who pay their employee's taxes, workers comp, and insurance as required by law. Is he proud of putting these honest American businesses and their employees out of work? Is he proud of giving business to employers of Illegals who don't have any of the overhead of legal businesses, and who expect to freeload off the public in their indigent old age or incapacitation by injury? Do these hirers of Illegals care that they are committing tax fraud by paying their Illegals in cash off the books? Would they be proud to do business with other companies run by people like themselves?

Now that we've seen how special interest groups on the right and left cheer for illegal immigration, we can understand the motivation behind their propaganda against securing our border. They claim:

1. "The Wall won't work. If it's a 20-foot-high wall, Illegals will climb it with 21-foot ladders."
2. It's too expensive.
3. Drones and electronic sensors are better than a wall.
4. It can't be built because of property rights.
5. It won't work because Illegals will arrive here on airplanes.

Globalists invent that propaganda because they favor Illegal immigration and know that the wall will diminish it. They don't care about the expense of the wall. They are always claiming that we can't deport Illegals "because that would be too expensive." It's a thousand times less expensive to build a wall to keep Illegals out of here than to get them out after they become entrenched in the sanctuary city scofflaw ecosystem. The judicial processes of deporting an Illegal out of the United States are so expensive and time-consuming, that it is not possible to deport most of them, which is exactly what the cheerleaders for Illegals want. The wall will pay for itself by keeping the Illegals out of here:

https://www.forbes.com/sites/theapothecary/2018/02/26/how-american-citizens-finance-health-care-for-undocumented-immigrants/#5e192c4812c4

How American Citizens Finance $18.5 Billion In Health Care for Unauthorized Immigrants

...rough estimates suggest that the nation's 3.9 million uninsured immigrants who are unauthorized likely receive about $4.6 billion in health services paid for by federal taxes, $2.8 billion in health services financed by state and local taxpayers, another $3.0 bankrolled through "cost-shifting" i.e., higher payments by insured patients to cover hospital uncompensated care losses, and roughly $1.5 billion in physician charity care.

All told, Americans cross-subsidize health care for unauthorized immigrants to the tune of $18.5 billion a year.

Then figure the cost of incarcerating Illegals who commit crimes, of educating their children in public schools, paying for their indigent old age, and so on.

Illegals Cheerleaders pretend to favor "drones and electronic devices" only because they know Illegals will ignore drones and walk right over ground-based electronic sensors without missing a step. If they have any value, they will steal them and sell them. They are pretending to believe that real border barriers can't be built because private property owners don't want it, and will presumably sue in court to block it:

https://www.wsj.com/articles/trump-cant-build-a-border-wall-without-the-real-estate-1487290376

Trump Can't Build a Border Wall Without the Real Estate

The president's plan would require massive, not to mention expensive, use of eminent domain

By Evan Siegfried Feb. 16, 2017

President Trump stands behind his campaign promise to build a wall along the entire U.S.-Mexican border. On the campaign trail, he insisted he could get the job done for no more than $10 billion because he is the master of completing construction projects quickly and under budget. This past weekend the president took to Twitter to lash out at reports that the true cost of the border wall would be well north of $10 billion.

The critics are almost certainly correct. Mr. Trump fails to take into account the major hurdle the wall faces: eminent domain.

To build the wall, the U.S. would need to own all 1,954 miles of the border. Most of this land is now private property—especially in Texas, where the U.S. government owns only 100 miles of the 1,254-mile border. To acquire the rest of the land it would need, Washington would need to employ eminent domain, the authority under the Fifth Amendment to seize private property for public use upon payment of "just compensation."

What utter rubbish. First, the wall has already been built on the most populous parts of the border, for example, around big cities like San Diego and El Paso:

http://a.scpr.org/i/2b0f59407340746bab53ffca040168f3/59637-full.jpg

So of course, it can be built. And property owners favor it, because it keeps Illegals from trespassing on their property, and often vandalizing and burglarizing it. Furthermore, the United States already owns 60-foot easements along every inch of the USA / Canada border, and most of the USA / Mexico borders. Our federal government has absolute sovereignty over what can and can't be built on the easement:

http://wildernesswatch.org/pdf/Wilderness_Watch_Northern_Border_Paper.pdf

Early 20th Century Border Easements. Two different U.S. presidents early in the 20th century took actions to withdraw U.S. land right on the international borders with Mexico and Canada in order to facilitate the federal government's ability to control the nation's borders.

• Border with Mexico. In 1907, President Theodore Roosevelt withdrew a strip of land 60 feet wide along the Mexican land border with California, Arizona, and New Mexico from "entry, settlement or other form of appropriation under the public land laws and set apart as a reservation...." Roosevelt's proclamation also withdrew the 60- foot strip "from the operation of public land laws...." This action is now referred to as the "Roosevelt Reservation."

• Border with Canada. Similarly, President Taft withdrew 60 feet along the Canadian border in 1912 "from entry, settlement, or other form of appropriation and disposition under the public-land laws and set apart as a public reservation" in order that "the customs and immigration laws of the United States can be better enforced.

The president can decree an easement along the border wherever he / she decides it is needed and can request that Congress authorize whatever funds are needed to build structures to prevent illegal immigration. Cheerleaders for Illegals lie and obfuscate about that because they want Illegals to come in across open borders. These are the same people who promote sanctuary cities to protect Illegals once they get here.

Illegals Cheerleaders are also pretending to believe that we shouldn't build a wall because they say it doesn't stop foreigners from coming here on airplanes and then either refusing to show up at their asylum hearings, or, if they have visas, or to go home when they overstay their legal visas. "We can't build a wall because people overstay their visas" is like saying that a person who has a heart attack and cancer should not be treated for one disease because he or she has the other. Build the wall **and** deny entry to dubious asylum seekers (which is almost all of them) and deport people who overstay their visas.

The anti-wall propaganda is invented to protect Illegals and employers of Illegals from prosecution. The only thing the Establishment Democrats and Republicans are ever "bipartisan" on is keeping our border open to illegal immigration:

https://www.washingtonpost.com/politics/whats-in-the-1169-page-border-security-bill-to-avert-a-government-shutdown/2019/02/14/fb422a96-3068-11e9-8781-763619f12cb4_story.html?noredirect=on&utm_term=.fa23b205c352

Trump didn't get any of the $5.7 billion he demanded for a concrete or steel wall. The $1.375 billion is enough for 55 miles for ***"pedestrian fencing"*** *in Texas's Rio Grande Valley, but that money is subject to numerous restrictions. The barriers can only use existing designs and are banned in five ecologically or historically sensitive areas, including the National Butterfly Center, which had sued the federal government to stop construction of the wall and other use of its land along the border. In addition, the Department of Homeland Security must consult with local officials before embarking on construction.*

Republican and Democratic party leaders need to understand that they are playing with fire by promoting illegal immigration. Democrats cherish Illegals because they want to amnesty them in as citizens and herd them into the voting booths as another allegedly aggrieved minority voting bloc.

And even if Illegals do not vote directly, they are counted in the Census and their numbers used to inflate the number of Democratic-voting congressional districts and electoral votes.

It's also worth mentioning the propaganda about e-Verify, the proposal to require employers to vet the legal status of the people they hire via a database of people whose social security numbers qualify them to work in the United States. It is not at all a bad idea at face value, but it is also used as a propaganda ruse to block border enforcement: "We don't need to build a wall, because we can pass laws requiring e-Verify to make sure Illegals can't be employed."

The most common reasons I've heard immigration activists claim that immigration can be controlled by enforcing sanctions on employers who don't verify the legal status of their employees is:

1. Immigration activists are trying to absolve Illegals from culpability for sneaking across the border, by blaming the employers for hiring them after they sneak across.

2. They are trying to perpetuate and maximize illegal immigration by pretending to believe that it can be reduced by means other than barricading the border, when they know perfectly well that the only way to prevent illegal immigration is to keep the Illegals from getting in here by putting up a wall, which they never want to allow constructed.

3. They don't care whether people employ illegals. They will be the first to file suit to block e-Verify if it is ever enacted. They are only pretending to care about employment of Illegals because they think that will obfuscate the question and take the heat off Illegals, so more can come in.

In most big cities, at least 1/3rd of the employers hire Illegals. I know this because my immigrant relatives (who are here legally) work for those employers. We're not going to fine 50,000 businesses in the city of Los Angeles or 5,000 in Orlando, or 10,000 in Chicago, or hundreds of thousands in other cities that employ Illegals.

Even in the unlikely event that e-Verify laws are passed, employers of Illegals will not use it. They don't care about violating all other employment laws and committing employment fraud and tax fraud against the U.S. government, so why would they care about complying with e-Verify? Aside from that, e-Verify is easily defeated by immigrants who steal other people's social security numbers:

http://www.foxnews.com/us/2018/08/22/mollie-tibbetts-murder-suspect-illegal-immigrant-cristhian-rivera-allegedly-passed-e-verify-system.html

Mollie Tibbetts murder suspect, illegal immigrant Cristhian Rivera, allegedly passed E-Verify system

The Mexican national accused of murdering college student Mollie Tibbetts in Iowa last month lived in the United States illegally for several years -- but was reportedly still able to pass a government system designed to weed out illegal immigrants from obtaining American jobs.

Cristhian Rivera, 24, was arrested and charged with first-degree murder Tuesday after the body of Tibbetts, a 20-year-old University of Iowa student, was discovered in a cornfield about 12 miles southeast of Brooklyn, where she was last seen running. Police said Rivera was in the country illegally and an immigration detainer was placed on him after his arrest.

Rivera's employer, Yarrabee Farms, confirmed Tuesday that Rivera worked at the farm for four years and said Rivera passed the federal E-Verify check, which is intended to maintain a database of I-9 forms and tax records of employees across the country.

Employers of Illegals are rarely prosecuted, because there are thousands and tens of thousands of them in every sizeable city. They will hire attorneys to jam the courts with complaints about lack of due process, and the judges will dismiss the charges, because there is no way to bring millions of business owners to trial, let alone incarcerate those who thumb their noses at the law.

We rarely prosecute Illegals for crimes like hit-and-run driving that citizens would be prosecuted for. Sanctuary cities do not permit criminals here illegally to be deported by ICE when released from prison. So, we are just kidding ourselves if we think that employers of Illegals will ever be held accountable. Employers of Illegals vote, and no politician is going to risk losing their votes by advocating for prosecution of employers of Illegals. The only way to stop the hiring of Illegals is to build a wall to keep them out and deport them instantly when they are discovered to have arrived in the country through other subterfuges.

What other laws shall we break?

In the previous section we saw cheerleading for "falsely documented workers" who work illegally by stealing social security numbers from American citizens. If well-to-do businesspeople won't respect the law, why should ordinary people? If the wealthy and privileged are above the law, then why isn't everybody else? Are we allowed to burglarize those people's homes or rob them on the street?

The ultimate fallback of illegal immigrant cheerleaders is to claim that "no harm is done in breaking the immigration laws because Illegals do jobs Americans won't do." No responsible parent or supervisor would accept that sort of excuse from a child or subordinate who violated a law, house rule, or company policy. It is stupid to tell people that they are the judges of what laws they decide they want to break.

And how do we know that Americans *won't* do these jobs? Maybe Americans aren't doing them because Illegals have undercut the wages to the point where Americans can't afford to do them. Americans won't start cleaning companies, landscaping companies, and other businesses that require hands-on labor if employers of Illegals have beaten the wages down to the point where American companies that operate legally can't compete. Some of my family's neighbors, acquaintances, and relatives do housekeeping in hotels, change bedpans in nursing homes, and clean rental properties in places where immigrants are scarce. Americans do these jobs when wages are not undercut by Illegals.

Whenever a cheerleader for Illegals says, "We must have Illegals because Americans won't do those jobs," we must remember that Americans aren't doing most of them *because* Illegals and employers of illegals have been invited into this country to displace Americans from jobs.

More than wages are being undercut. Cheerleaders for Illegals want us to believe that Illegals are paying a full share of income and Social Security taxes that they will never benefit from! Why would any employer of Illegals withhold taxes for people they know are working illegally? My wife was a witness in a federal prosecution of an employer of Illegals who never withheld taxes for any of the dozens of Illegals on his payroll. Why *would* an employer of Illegals pay unemployment taxes or abide by the wage and hour laws? Why would they pay unemployment insurance and workers' comp? They don't pay taxes and don't abide by wage and hour laws, thereby making it difficult for honest employers to stay in business.

Now, it is no doubt true that Americans would not do **some** jobs that Illegals are put in harness to do. Americans would not stand out in the hot sun and pick turnips or tomatoes all day. These are precisely the low-value jobs that should be done overseas where labor is cheap. But these are the jobs that Globalists insist on keeping in the USA by importing Illegals! If Guatemalans are the only human beings on Planet Earth who will pick turnips, then they should be picking them in Guatemala, and we should be importing them from there.

If the USA was the only place in the world that grew turnips, it would still be possible to automate the process. Turnips would be grown indoors hydroponically and harvested without labor in the fields. In that regard, illegal immigration diminishes productivity advancements.

It is a myth that increasing productivity raises wages. Productivity increases diminish wages by putting people out of work. The only way wages rise is when labor becomes scarce. When wages rise, employers start investing in automation. Rising wages increase automation. Automation does not increase wages.

There is no reason --- other than for the convenience of low-value, low-wage, dishonest employers --- why Illegals need to be working in the U.S. Making excuses to break whatever laws inconvenience us teaches that anybody can break any law that inconveniences them. If employers of Illegals don't pay taxes, why should any American citizen? Let's all band together and refuse to pay our taxes. If it's OK for some to break the law, why not for all? Where does the cheating stop? This is one of many reasons why laws must be respected As Abraham Lincoln said:

"Let reverence for the laws, be breathed by every American mother, to the lisping babe, that prattles on her lap - let it be taught in schools, in seminaries, and in colleges; let it be written in spelling books, and in Almanacs; let it be preached from the pulpit, proclaimed in legislative halls, and enforced in courts of justice...let every man remember that to violate the law, is to trample on the blood of his father, and to tear the charter of his own, and his children's liberty."

Yet, advocacy for breaking the immigration laws are published in many Liberal and big business publications:

https://www.wsj.com/articles/immigration-and-an-ohio-town-1534793111

Immigration and an Ohio Town What happens after an ICE raid?

By James Freeman

Aug. 20, 2018

Today this column is fortunate to share the following dispatch from reader Richard Buta:

My hometown of Salem, Ohio was recently in the news and not in a pleasing way. In June, U.S. Immigration and Customs Enforcement teams arrested almost 150 Latin American meat-packing plant workers, men and women, mostly Guatemalans, for alleged immigration-related offenses. Fortunately, some have since been released, including those who had legitimate documentation but just didn't have it on them at the time of the raid. Yet the community remains on edge.

As I learned over the past several years, the Guatemalan employees had earned a reputation for reliability and hard work.

But what about the illegal Guatemalan, who killed an NFL player in Indianapolis while intoxicated:

https://www.denverpost.com/2018/02/07/man-charged-in-edwin-jackson-fatal-crash/

Guatemalan man charged in drunken-driving crash that killed Indianapolis Colts player

Manuel Orrego-Savala was deported in 2007 and 2009, and was again living illegally in the U.S. at the time of the crash

INDIANAPOLIS — Prosecutors on Wednesday charged an immigrant illegally living in the U.S. in a drunken-driving crash that killed Indianapolis Colts linebacker Edwin Jackson and his Uber driver

And we have just seen an Illegal arrested in the murder of Mollie Tibbetts.

225

So how do we reconcile the virtues of Illegals who are tolerably honest vs. the crimes of Illegals who are rapists and assassins? We *can't* reconcile it. The correct approach is to obey the law and keep the Illegals out.

Once we establish the principle that our immigration laws will not be enforced, we commit ourselves to accepting unlimited numbers of Illegals. A pro-Illegals candidate in New York City has defeated one of the top Democratic Congressmen in a primary election. She campaigned on a pledge to end border enforcement. Predictably, other Democrats are now *championing an end to all border enforcement:*

https://www.breitbart.com/big-government/2018/07/17/alexandria-ocasio-cortez-occupy-all-ice-offices-borders-u-s-airports-occupy-all-of-it/

Alexandria Ocasio-Cortez: Occupy All ICE Offices, Borders, U.S. Airports, 'Occupy All of It'

Socialist Democrat candidate for Congress Alexandria Ocasio-Cortez in New York's 14th District is calling on left wing and open borders activists to "occupy" all United States airports, all borders in the U.S., and every office of the Immigration and Customs Enforcement (ICE) agency.

http://www.foxnews.com/politics/2018/06/29/abolish-ice-goes-mainstream-as-gillibrand-de-blasio-back-calls.html

'Abolish ICE' goes mainstream as [New York Senator] Gillibrand, [New York City Mayor] de Blasio back calls

"I believe that [Immigration and Customs Enforcement] has become a deportation force ... and that's why I believe you should get rid of it, start over, reimagine it and build something that actually works," Gillibrand said in a CNN interview Thursday night. Gillibrand's endorsement is notable as she's the first sitting senator to back the 'abolish ICE' push -- and is considered a potential 2020 presidential contender.

"We should abolish ICE," [New York City Mayor] de Blasio said Friday morning on WNYC radio.

Violations of one law lead to violations of other laws. Now we have Illegals trying to crash the border in "caravans" numbering in the thousands. We have respiratory ailments from Central America infecting our population and overloading the hospitals with indigent immigrants as well as Americans. We have dubious voting patterns in immigrant-heavy states with large numbers of people whose legal status and residencies can't be verified.

The escalation of law-breaking continues until society breaks down and authoritarian government is imposed upon the people. The best policy in immigration, as in all other walks of life, is to obey the law.

Part V. "...and whither we are tending"

As we contemplate Mr. Lincoln's question of "Where we are, and whither we are tending," let us be guided by the best of our American traditions. Our first tradition is being the beacon of freedom, peace, and prosperity.

"I always consider the settlement of America with reverence and wonder, as the opening of a grand scene, and design in Providence, for the illumination of the ignorant and the emancipation of the slavish part of Mankind all over the earth," wrote John Adams in 1765,

That is what motivated our people to get out from under the British Empire, and it is what must motivate us to get out from under the globalist empire. Part of the "emancipation of the slavish part of Mankind" involves immigration. We cannot be a great nation without being a welcoming nation. But let us take care to make it lawful immigration. Respect for the law must be paramount, as Abraham Lincoln reminded us:

"Let reverence for the laws, be breathed by every American mother, to the lisping babe, that prattles on her lap - let it be taught in schools, in seminaries, and in colleges; let it be written in spelling books, and in Almanacs; let it be preached from the pulpit, proclaimed in legislative halls, and enforced in courts of justice...let every man remember that to violate the law, is to trample on the blood of his father, and to tear the charter of his own, and his children's liberty."

Immigration must be lawful.

As we consider reforming our foreign trade to make it better serve our interests, let us remember our tradition that manufacturing is a pillar of our strength as an economy and nation:

Hamilton's Report on Manufacturers, December 5, 1791

The expediency of encouraging manufactures in the United States...appears at this time to be pretty generally admitted. The employment of machinery forms an item of great importance in the general mass of national industry...if it is the interest of the United States to open every possible avenue to emigration from abroad, it affords a weighty argument for the encouragement of manufactures; There seems to be a moral certainty that the trade of a country which is both manufacturing and agricultural will be more lucrative and

228

prosperous than that of a country which is, merely agricultural. . . . Not only the wealth, but the independence and security of a country, appear to be materially connected with the prosperity of manufactures. Every nation, with a view to those great objects, ought to endeavor to possess within itself all the essentials of national supply. These comprise the means of subsistence, habitation, clothing, and defense. . ..

Let us remember Secretary of State Seward's advice to:

"Open up a highway from New York to San Francisco. Put your domain under cultivation and your ten thousand wheels of manufacture in motion. Multiply your ships and send them forth to the East (Japan, China, and India). The nation that draws the most materials and provisions from the earth, and fabricates the most, and sells the most of production and fabrics to foreign nations, must be, and will be, the great power of the earth."

Let us remember that most productions of the world are in surplus and that every other country sees the United States as their flea market to dump their surplus and keep their economies strong and growing, while making our economy weak and stagnant.

Let us remember that free trade that is used to beat Americans out of their jobs and depress their wages runs counter to Adam Smith's philosophy that:

No society can surely be flourishing and happy, of which the far greater part of the members are poor and miserable. It is but equity, besides, that they who feed, clothe, and lodge the whole body of the people, should have such a share of the produce of their own labour as to be themselves tolerably well fed, clothed, and lodged.

The wages of labour are the encouragement of industry, which, like every other human quality, improves in proportion to the encouragement it receives. A plentiful subsistence increases the bodily strength of the labourer, and the comfortable hope of bettering his condition, and of ending his days, perhaps, in ease and plenty, animates him to exert that strength to the utmost.

Where wages are high, accordingly, we shall always find the workmen more active, diligent, and expeditious, than where they are low;

Let us remember that the most ardent advocate for free trade in the 19th Century was Karl Marx, because he believed that it impoverished workers and made them desperate for revolution:

*But, generally speaking, **the Protective system** in these days **is conservative,** while the **Free Trade system works destructively.** It breaks up old nationalities and carries antagonism of proletariat and bourgeoisie to the uttermost point. In a word, **the Free Trade system hastens the Social Revolution.** In this revolutionary sense alone, gentlemen, I am in favor of **Free Trade.***

Contrary to Globalists' hysteria, we do not have to accept massive trade deficits as a cross we have to bear to be accepted by the world's political and business community. No other country tolerates massive trade deficits, and neither should we. Let us remember Al Gore's promise in the original NAFTA treaty that:

"NAFTA will...greatly accelerate [our trade with Mexico]; we will have a larger trade surplus with Mexico than with any country in the entire world."

Since that promise was not kept, there is no reason to maintain the treaties on which the promise was based.

Let us remember that there is no reason why domestic product that is produced in the USA and pays taxes in the USA should have to compete with foreign product that is imported into the USA, sold at a profit that is removed overseas, and avoids paying taxes in the USA.

We need to impose Kevin Brady's Border Adjustment VAT of 20% * (USA revenues – USA cost inputs), which has four scenarios:

1. Let's say a product is produced in the USA with $8,000 of cost inputs and sold for $10,000 in the USA. The BAVAT tax is: ($10,000 - $8,000) * 20% = **$400**.
2. A product is imported into the USA, either from a foreign-owned company or the subsidiary of an American-owned company and sold for $10,000. The tax is: ($10,000 - zero) * 20% = **$2,000**.
3. Product is produced in the USA with $8,000 of cost inputs and exported to another country where it is sold for $10,000. This generates a **REBATE of $1,600** (zero - $8,000) * 20%.
4. Product is produced overseas by an American company and sold overseas. No tax event because no USA revenues or cost inputs.

This will reduce the trade deficit while shifting production back to the USA, or imposing taxes on companies that insist on producing overseas. If trade deficits with certain countries persist, then the 20% BAVAT can be increased to 35%, 50%, or 300% with those countries until they either decide to buy more from us or shift production to the USA. Those few countries that do trade fairly with us can be treated as if they were part of the United States for trade purposes and therefore allowed to deduct their cost inputs to lower their VAT.

We need to withdraw from NAFTA and negotiate trade directly with Canada and Mexico as separate nations. Canada may qualify as a free trade equivalent of a United States territory. Their businesses would be subject to the same reduced BAVAT as American companies. Mexico cannot be treated as a USA equivalent territory because it has a cheap labor economy that is used to lure jobs out of the United States.

Another option for trade with Canada would be to restore the ***proportional trade treaty*** we had with Canada prior to NAFTA known as The Auto Pact. The pact allowed for tariff-free trade in motor vehicles, provided that 90% of value was added in the USA, and 10% in Canada, which was, and still is, the ratio of auto sales and profits in the two countries. That worked fine. Then we had to go and sign on to NAFTA, a non-proportional trade pact that included Mexico. It was well-intentioned but worked opposite from what was promised. Instead of the USA and Canada working together to export cars, Mexico became the platform to export cars to the USA and Canada.

We should revoke NAFTA-WITH-MEXICO, since the treaty was sold on a pack of lies, then restore the proportional 90% / 10% auto common market with Canada.

We need to withdraw from the World Trade Organization and the General Agreement on Tariffs and Taxes, because these organizations are subverted to open our borders to other countries imports, while allowing them to keep our products out.

Let us remember President Cleveland's words that big business, and especially their current incarnation as multinational corporations, have interests that do not coincide with ours:

Corporations, which should be carefully restrained creatures of the law and the servants of the people, are fast becoming the people's masters.

231

The existing situation stifles all patriotic love of country, and substitutes in its place selfish greed and grasping avarice.

Communism is a hateful thing and a menace to peace and organized government; but the communism of combined wealth and capital, the outgrowth of overweening cupidity and selfishness, which insidiously undermines the justice and integrity of free institutions, is no less dangerous than the communism of oppressed poverty and toil, which, exasperated by injustice and discontent, attacks with wild disorder the citadel of rule.

Multinational corporations are wrapping their arms around internationalist organizations like the European Union, NAFTA, the World Trade Organization, and the World Court to defeat the sovereign will of the people. They seek to extract profits by producing goods and services in low-wage countries, selling them at inflated price lists in the developed world, and laundering the money through tax havens.

The internationalist system created by the big government / big business elitists cannot endure. It depends upon issuing mountains of unpayable debt in the developed countries to cover the shortfall of employment that is transferred to low-wage countries. If the Globalists are not defeated, their mountain of unpayable debt will bring down the governments of the developed world and impoverish the prosperous consuming middle classes. When their purchasing power is destroyed the companies and banks will fail, as in 2008, and this time there will be no more trillions of government-issued debts to bail them out. The world will descend into chaos and anarchy. As is usually the case in chaotic, hopeless times, wars of vast destructiveness will flare across the world, as rival powers seek supremacy.

Let us remember first and foremost that Globalism is no friend of Conservatives and Libertarians. It seeks to destroy the wealth and political power of the middle class and transfer it to self-dealing Globalists in big business, international banking, and supra-national bureaucracies. It is against every founding principle of the United States that Conservatives and Libertarians hold dear.

The New Center for the New Century

Sometime around 2010 we began to realize that the so-called "centrist" candidates promoted by the major parties' establishments no longer carried the aura of charisma and authority that they had in the 1990's. The Establishment's preferred candidates fell flat. The Republican rank-and-file rallied behind Donald Trump. Ms. Clinton's grip on the Democratic Party was sufficiently overpowering to enable her to prevail in her party's nomination, but Bernie Sanders, a Socialist, ginned up the most enthusiasm.

In 2016 we rejected the old self-aggrandizing center of both parties' establishments. Now we are looking to build a new center that represents "we the people." We are going to have to do this ourselves, by supporting candidates who are not prisoners of Establishment propaganda and Establishment money. I don't know if the Populist Right can ever make common cause with self-styled "Progressive" Liberals, but we *can* ally with *Libertarian Liberals*. These are socially liberal people who own small businesses that they feel are threatened by combinations of big business and big government manipulated by Globalists. I reviewed Ralph Nader's (Nader was one of the fathers of the anti-corporation, consumer rights movement in the 1960's) book *Unstoppable: The Left-Right Alliance to Dismantle the Corporate State:*

https://www.amazon.com/Unstoppable-Emerging-Left-Right-Dismantle-Corporate/dp/156858525X/

Mr. Nader has written this book to convince Libertarian Conservatives and Liberal Progressives that the time has come for to unite in a party dedicated to replacing the two major parties that he believes have been suborned by corporations to act exclusively in their interests.

Being conservative, I've always thought of Mr. Nader as being "over the top'" in of excoriating our big business corporations. However, he's always seemed personable on TV appearances, so I believe that his yearning for reform is based on a sincere desire for social justice and not on the negative trait of hating businesspeople merely because they accumulate wealth.

It also can't be denied that things have changed in a big way since the economic crash of 2008. It now looks like Mr. Nader was not so much a fanatic as a man ahead of his time. We've learned that depressing the wages of the working middle class by excessive job elimination via globalization does not prosper the country. In times like these, desperate people start thinking about founding new political parties that will return the government to the business of representing the interests of the people. We've had Populist movements in the past, and their result has been to push both major parties back towards the interests of the people.

Mr. Nader makes the case that when corporations become excessively powerful, they become detrimental to the people's interests:

Corporatism or "corporate statism," as Grover Norquist [a California Libertarian fighting for tax reductions] calls it, is first and foremost a doctrine of corporate supremacy.

Large corporations usually push, with whatever political, technological, economic, marketing, and cultural tools are required, the frontiers of domination in all directions...However you might describe them, it is hard to deny that their DNA commands them to control, undermine, or eliminate any force, tradition, or institution that impedes their expansion of sales, profits, and executive compensation.

That is what is meant by corporate statism. And as it gets stronger, it delivers a weaker economy for a majority of Americans, a weaker democratic society, and record riches for the few. Key to understanding corporate behavior is the recognition that, while its propagandists trumpet the irreconcilable differences between Right and Left, corporations are remarkably flexible in relation to these divisions. What is behind this plasticity is a laser-like focus on expansion, profits, and bonuses.

I reviewed populist conservative Laura Ingraham's book ***Billionaire at the Barricades: The Populist Revolution from Reagan to Trump*** which makes many of the same points:

https://www.amazon.com/Billionaire-Barricades-Populist-Revolution-Reagan/dp/1250150647/

Conservatism and populism overlap in their opposition to "big things" --- big government, big international organizations, big media, big business cronyism. These distant, uncaring entities rob people of decision making and ignore their interests.

Conservative populists tend to support a policy of economic nationalism --- people-centered economic policies that put the nation and its workers first.... They also believe high taxes are bad because they sap workers' wages and economic freedom. Similarly, they are against huge trade deals and international organizations like the World Trade Organization because they take power out of the hands of voters and give it to a far-away and often hostile global elite.

Trump won because his message of economic nationalism and a less interventionist foreign policy reflects the will of the people. He won because he vowed to put America first again. He won because both parties had gotten fat off the status quo, while many in the middle were being squeezed.... He won because Americans had had it --- with Washington's failed promises, with political correctness, with open borders, and with career politicians, consultants, pollsters, and pundits.

The elites had been blindsided before ---by Reagan's 1980 election. Many in the party dismissed him as well. He was just an actor. He was "too divisive."

Ms. Ingraham explains how Reagan and Trump identify with working middle class Americans:

Reagan. "Our nation's capital has become the seat of a 'buddy' system that functions for its own benefit—increasingly insensitive to the needs of the American worker who supports it with his taxes."

Trump: "My dad, Fred Trump, was the smartest and hardest working man I ever knew. I wonder sometimes what he'd say if he were here to see this and to see me tonight. It's because of him that I learned from my youngest age to respect the dignity of work and the dignity of working people. He was a guy most comfortable in the company of bricklayers and carpenters and electricians and I have a lot of that in me also. I love those people."

Reagan's transformative presidency inspired a new generation of young conservatives (like me)—and Trump's, if successful, can do the same. But it won't be easy. We know what doesn't work: global trade deals that enrich other countries at the expense of our own workers; lax immigration policies that compromise the nation's security, health care system, schools, and jobs; a tax and regulatory regime that stifles economic growth and competitiveness and strangles innovation; and an imprudent interventionist foreign policy that costs us trillions of dollars and thousands of American lives. For decades, a bipartisan Establishment blindly embraced these ruinous policies. The resulting economic and personal pain, felt across the vast American landscape, has fueled the rise of populism and its stalwarts—from Goldwater to Reagan, Buchanan to Trump.

Let's remember that we founded our nation to get out from under a global empire. Our mission today is to roll back the excesses of globalism, to avoid living in an empire where big government and big corporations conspire to hog the world's wealth and opportunity exclusively for themselves, while dribbling the crumbs out to us; where speech is regulated to allow only sentiments favorable to Globalists; and where the sovereignty of the people residing in nations is handed off to globalist crony capitalists operating in supra-national organization beyond the law. Let us restore the United States to its original destiny as the light that leads the world toward liberty and prosperity, rather than continue to allow our Globalist elitists to diminish us to serve their ends. As Franklin Roosevelt said just before becoming president:

Say that civilization is a tree which, as it grows, continually produces rot and dead wood. The Radical says: Cut it down. The Conservative says: Don't touch it. The Liberal compromises: Let's prune, so that we lose neither the old trunk nor the new branches.

This country needs, and unless I mistake its temper demands bold, persistent experimentation. It is common sense to take a method and try it. If it fails, admit it frankly and try another. But above all try something. The millions who are in want will not stand by silently forever while the things to satisfy their needs are within easy reach. The election will bring about not just a victory for my political party, but a revolution---the right kind, the only kind of revolution this nation can stand for---a revolution at the ballot box.

Franklin Roosevelt, 1932

Let build the new center for the new century here in the United States. Let us dedicate ourselves to supporting candidates who represent our interests as Americans. Let us reject the candidates of all parties who owe their allegiance to *"the communism of combined wealth and capital, the outgrowth of overweening cupidity and selfishness, which insidiously undermines the justice and integrity of free institutions.*"

The Pocket Guide to Refuting Globalist Propaganda

Here is a quick guide to refuting the primary Globalist propaganda talking points:

Globalist: "Free trade is the keystone of prosperity!"

Response: "Then why did the economy fall off a cliff in 2000 and 2008, *after* we signed all those free trade treaties? Why was our economy growing at 3.6% per year before free trade with Mexico and China, and 2.10% per year after?"

Globalist: "We have to import manufactured products from China and Mexico, because Americans can't afford to buy products made with American labor."

Response: "Didn't you just tell us that all work in manufacturing is nowadays done by robots? Do robots in China and Mexico work cheaper than robots in the USA? And how did we afford to buy products made with American labor *before* we started trading with Mexico and China?"

Globalist: "Trade deficits are signs of healthy prosperity. It's like you having a personal 'trade deficit' with the grocery store."

Response: "The trade deficit is like mortgaging a paid-off house to generate cash to pay your bills. Sooner or later, you're going to lose the house and your ability to pay your grocery bills."

Globalist: "We have trade deficits because Americans consume more than we make. Trade deficits can only be resolved with an increase in savings, meaning US consumers need to change their behaviors.

Response #1: "We consume more than we make because what we used to make has been offshored to other countries. We're going into debt buying from other countries that don't buy from us. Going into debt is nothing to brag about."

Response #2: "This would be like if someone steals your car, and the police tell you it's your fault because you consume too much. You should have put all your money in the bank instead of the buying the car, and then nobody would have stolen it."

Globalist: "If trade deficits are a problem, then why do we have full employment?"

Response: "Because millions of folks who had well-paying jobs lost them to Mexico and China, can no longer make ends make on minimum wage part-time jobs. They have left the labor force and are no longer seeking work. They are living from early Social Security, disability, and government welfare. Many others are employed at part-time or temporary jobs. These 'jobs of last resort' are counted as full employment, but people want higher quality jobs like we used to have when most products we bought were made here."

Globalist: "You have no right to restrict my ability to buy what I want by imposing tariffs on imports!"

Response: "Do you think you should be permitted to buy stolen merchandize that was burglarized from your neighbor's home?"

Globalist: "Tariffs are taxes imposed on consumers."

Response: "Tariffs are imposed because foreign producers that don't pay taxes to American governments, *don't* invest in producing in the USA, *don't* pay wages to American workers, and *don't* pay American suppliers. Do you think an American-based company that *does* pay taxes to American governments, *does* invest in producing in the USA, *does* pay wages to American workers, and *does* pay American suppliers, should have to compete on equal terms with a foreign-sourced supplier who doesn't pay taxes to the United States?"

Globalist: "Smoot-Hawley tariffs wrecked the economy in 1929."

Response#1: "Then what wrecked the economy in 2008 when we had free trade?"

Response #2: "No informed person believes that Smoot-Hawley tariffs of 1930 travelled back in time and wrecked the economy in 1929. Many factors, including financial fraud and excessive immigration caused the economy to fail, the same reasons that caused it to fail again in 2008."

Globalist: "Industry is like agriculture. It doesn't employ many people, so we don't need to worry about losing it."

Response: "If agriculture doesn't employ many people, then why do you insist that food can't be produced in the United States unless we keep the borders open for tens of millions of Mexicans and Central Americans to come in here to pick them turnips and hoe them taters? If industry doesn't employ many people, then why are you so hot to move millions of American jobs to cheap-labor countries?"

Globalist: "I don't want tariffs because they cause farmers to lose business to Mexico and China."

Response: "You never cared about farmers before. Now, you're Mr. Greenjeans' best friend? Why didn't you care about the millions of industrial workers who lost their jobs to Mexico and China? Tell the farmers the same thing you told the industrial workers who lost their jobs: learn a new career or die. At least the industrial workers were making products that were sold in the USA."

Globalist: "I'm a free trader. I believe that if anything can be imported more cheaply from overseas, then we should import it."

Response: "Then why do you insist on protecting American agriculture by opening our borders to millions of foreign fruit pickers? Why don't we import ag products from other countries, if it's not economical to grow them here? Why do you want to protect two-cent turnips and taters, remove the manufacture of high-value products out of the country?"

Globalist: "You want to protect obsolete industry with tariffs! That makes you a Luddite!"

Response: "You're the one who wants American companies to move overseas to harness cheap labor in Mexico and China, instead of investing in the USA to modernize their factories with robots and automation. You want to protect agriculture, which is ten thousand years older than industry, with immigration of millions of illiterate fruit pickers. *You're* the 'Luddite' on both counts!"

Globalist: "You remind me of those buggy-whip manufacturers who complained that Henry Ford obsoleted their businesses when he started making cars. Don't you know that new industries always replace old industries?"

Response #1: "Did Henry Ford create those new automotive jobs in China and Mexico, or in Detroit?"

Response #2: "Then why did the economy fall off a cliff and go into the Great Recession as soon as we signed all those trade deals that moved American jobs overseas?"

Globalist: "Free trade and immigration brings fresh blood into the country."

Response: "It's great to have a blood transfusion of the right blood type when you need one. It's not so good to pump blood of the wrong type into your body when you don't need it, or to open up all your veins and bleed out in a blood bath."

Immigration:

Globalist: **"We must have massive immigration to get people in here to do all the jobs that Americans won't do."**

Response: "What happened to all the robots and automation you keep talking about?"

Globalist: **"A wall won't keep the Illegals out."**

Response: "Do *you* have walls around *your* property to keep out people who don't belong trespassing on it?"

Globalist: **"What about the foreigners who arrive at airports and overstay their visas?"**

Response: "You never cared about foreigners who overstay their visas before, so why are you pretending to care about them now? The solution is to build the wall and deport foreigners who overstay their visas."

Globalist: **"We have to open the borders to foreigners because Americans are too {lazy, stupid, mal-educated, overpaid} to know how to work."**

Response: "Does that include *you?*"

About the Author

"Understanding history is a key to understanding the present and extrapolating the future."

- Alan Sewell

I've devoted my life to analyzing historical and current events and applying their historical lessons to today's business and economic issues.

Although every day is a new day, the new days are layered on top of repeating cycles of history as old as Mankind. The more we understand the cycles of history, the more complete will be our understanding of the present.

My writing is focused on American History. I've been commended for "interpreting the American experience" into five other critical watershed periods when political and economic crises were resolved to advance the country into the next era of its history:

FRAGMENTATION - FEDERALISM - UNION (1783 - 1815)

SECESSION - WAR - NATIONALISM (1861 - 1868)

WEALTH - DEPRESSION - EXPANSION (1890-1900)

WEALTH - DEPRESSION - LIBERALISM (1925-1933)

CHAOS - HUMILIATION - CONSERVATISM (1968-1981)

GLOBALISM --- GREAT RECESSION ---- {POPULISM or PROGRESSIVISM} (2008-?)

My most recently revised book *The Diary of American Exceptionalism* covers these crises that lurched us out of the old rutted political and economic ideologies and embarked us on new paths. It is written in diary format to reveal the thoughts of our leaders during their most discouraging moments.

https://www.amazon.com/Diary-American-Exceptionalism-Alan-Sewell-ebook/dp/B01H2HGCNC/

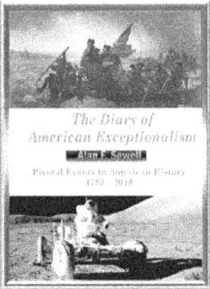

Please address feedback to alsnewideas@gmail.com

http://www.amazon.com/Alan-Sewell/e/B00557PQDY